THIS
BOOK
BELONGS TO

Neal Mulholland
31 Ophir Gdns

Belfast
BT15 5EP

Paper
Doors

Paper Doors

Japan from Scratch

ANGUS WAYCOTT

ANDRE DEUTSCH

First published in Great Britain
in 1994 by André Deutsch Limited
106 Great Russell Street, London WC1B 3LJ

ISBN 0233 988 866

Printed in Great Britain by
St Edmundsbury Press, Bury St Edmunds, Suffolk

Contents

1 | View from a Bathtub

THE BATH was where everything came most sharply into focus. Not that there was anything especially revelatory about the bathroom itself. From floor level up to waist height, its walls were covered with plain white tiles, and above that were painted with a thin coat of yellow emulsion stained by long-established patches of damp that loomed through the steam like the outlines of unknown islands and undiscovered continents. The floor was a random mosaic of black and white pebbles set in concrete and then covered with a smooth, clear glaze. It had a built-in slope, so that any spilled water would run down to a drainhole in one corner. The drainhole was supposed to be covered by a grille, but it was missing.

But the bath itself was different from what we were used to, and seemed exotic. It was rectangular, about five feet square and two feet deep: half of this depth was sunk into the floor and the other half was defined by a low wall which we could sit on, or drape an arm over while lying in the water, or use as a shelf for shampoo, facecloths and so on. Originally designed for two adults, the bath was just about big enough for all four of us to use at the same time.

The children flopped from one side to the other like dolphins – you couldn't call it swimming – or else concentrated on organising boat races between the two halves of a blue plastic soap dish. My wife lay back and relaxed, looking pretty with her eyes shut and her long black hair casually pinned up. And I . . . I waited. Waited for the moment when they would all climb out to get dry and dressed, leaving me the whole bath to myself. Then one of the children would bring me a little flagon of warm *sake* and an eggcup-sized cup and put them on the low wall beside me. If it was the right time in the evening, I could slide open the wooden-slatted window and then lie back in the water, sipping the *sake* and looking at the moon shining in the black sky beyond the leaves of a small maple tree that grew outside, next to the house. It was the best time of the day to remember, to think, to make plans.

*

At one of the souvenir shops in Moscow Airport, the girls discovered *matryoshka*, those wooden dolls you can pull apart to find another, smaller one inside, then another inside that. I bought them one each to play with in the restaurant while we waited for our lunch to arrive. Eventually it came, each institutional white china plate bearing a few beets, a lump of leathery grey meat and some cold potatoes. We ordered orange juice, but it never materialised.

The Indians who had shared our flight from London settled down patiently among their piles of luggage to wait for their connection to Delhi. They were still sitting there, grizzled grandfathers in burgundy turbans and corpulent matrons in flowing saris, gesturing languidly at each other with bangled wrists, when we filed out of the terminal in the middle of the afternoon and returned to the aircraft that was to take us on to Tokyo. There was more room to spread out now, as several of the worn, shabby seats were empty. I recalled my first Aeroflot trip, back in Brezhnev's time, when grim-faced overweight stewardesses served slabs of cheese with dark Russian bread and waddled up and down the gangway with an open bottle of red wine in each hand, filling and refilling the passengers' glasses as they went. Now the company was trying to present a new, modern image. There was still no on-board movie, but there were vodka-tonics in clear plastic cups and meals served on cream-coloured plastic trays with little moulded compartments. A young Japanese couple across the aisle from us poked dubiously at the food with their disposable forks and then laid them aside, settling down to sleep with their heads leaning uncomfortably together.

From the window I looked down at Russia spread out below us, its endless expanses of forest bisected by a wide, slow-flowing river that slid sinuously across the landscape like a huge silver snake. Far behind us and receding rapidly lay England and our previous life – a life laboriously dismantled, packed in cardboard boxes, stored in attics, loaned to friends, assigned to agents of uncertain reliability. Ahead lay Japan, where we planned to live for a year, perhaps more. For Reiko, my wife, it was the first opportunity for ten years to visit friends and family in her homeland. For our daughters, aged eight and six, it was an adventure into the unknown, where they would meet new relatives, go to a new school, learn a new language. And for me . . .

Well yes, why exactly was I going to Japan? For the benefit of the children, of course, so that they would be able to grow up knowing and taking pride in both the countries in their background. Everyone I told this to found it an excellent answer. 'How I envy them,' they would say. 'And you too, of course. How brave of you to just give everything up and go. And what a wonderful time you'll all have.' Of course it was the truth, what I said, but it wasn't the whole truth. I was more than ready to go back myself.

I thought back to my first visit, 15 years before. Arriving with nothing, finding a room in a cheap section of north Tokyo, exploring its dingy alleys, idling in tiny parks up against the tram tracks, puzzling over the strange street signs and incomprehensible language, ordering simple meals by pointing at what some other customer was eating. Walking every night to the public baths and sharing the tub with the fishmonger, the tobacconist and the cross-eyed postman who weaved around the neighbourhood all day on his ancient bicycle. Travelling round the country, climbing mountains, staying in temples, sleeping on beaches. Finding out what foreigners could do for a living, getting hired as an English conversation teacher, working regularly, being paid a salary large enough to live on for the first time in my life. And later, becoming a freelance writer, mostly in advertising, doing promotional video scripts, brochures, instruction manuals and executives' speeches. For the last ten years in England I had been doing similar work in a dogged effort to keep my small publishing company afloat. At the same time, the government was busy trying to reinvigorate the national economy by making it as difficult as possible for people who wanted work to get any. By the look of the economy, the strategy wasn't very successful. And I was tired of fighting it. An encore in Japan looked like a good bet; the country beckoned to us, dangling its world-famous wealth of golden opportunities before our eyes.

Reiko's sister and her husband met us at Narita Airport and led us to their car, which was parked in the bright October sunshine outside the terminal building. We stacked our luggage into the boot. Even though we had only one suitcase each, it was still too much to allow the lid to close, so we tied it awkwardly down with string. The security guards at the airport gate studied the knots with dubious expressions before waving us through.

There wasn't much to be seen from the highway to Yokohama except for brief glimpses across the fields to where the occasional red maple or flaring yellow gingko showed that Japan's famous autumn colours were beginning to appear in the hills. We stopped to get a drink at a rest area where the service was all automatic: there were no attendants, only a long bank of tall machines dispensing different kinds of coffee, tea, soup, cola, lemonade and canned drinks with unfamiliar names like Pocari Sweat and Yodel Soda (Gives You A Clean And Fresh Taste No Matter Where You May Try It). Back in the car the children fell soundly asleep, exhausted by the long journey. I kept nodding off myself, but as we passed over Tokyo's complex network of elevated highways I woke up and looked out again on the huge, featureless jumble of concrete buildings topped with garish corporate symbols, the grubby, pocket-sized patches of waste ground, the cars jammed grimly together in the narrow streets. In the windless air, a brown haze of pollution hung over the city like vapourised gravy magically risen from the urban stew.

I thought I had forgotten what Hiroshi and Yoko's house was like, but as soon as we pulled up outside I saw that nothing had changed since I last saw it. Single-storied, clad in cheap tin sheeting painted to resemble timber and set close to an open field where cabbages were growing in long, neat rows, it stood well away from its neighbours and had a small yard where Hiroshi grew kiwi fruit and raised gnarled *bonsai* in shallow ceramic pots. Two trees were hung with shiny orange persimmons: they were ripe, and he picked a few for us to eat. In the kitchen, Yoko welcomed our children to Japan with the gift of two large stuffed toys, rabbits dressed as little girls, each with its own miniature wicker chair. These went down well, but even better entertainment value was provided by Ryu-kun, the family mynah bird, which perched on a bar inside his little bamboo cage, listening intently to the humans talking with his head on one side and occasionally crying out his name in a shrill, piercing voice.

A proper welcome starts with food, and Yoko quickly got to work on serving us a lunch of grilled salmon, white rice, pickles (shredded cabbage, tiny salted plums and slices of yellow radish) and whole ginger roots, the stem of the plant still attached, which we ate raw with a smear of rich, savoury *miso* paste. The persimmons from the garden were peeled, pitted, cut into quarters and placed decoratively in a bowl in the middle of the table. Hiroshi, who had gone out early that morning to Yokohama docks with his rod and tackle, took a couple of fish from a blue plastic bucket, quickly filleted them on a thick wooden chopping board and served up the diced scraps of soft raw flesh with soy sauce and hot green mustard. The memory of Aeroflot's hard, dry pastries, tackled in stupefied silence only a few hours before, flickered briefly in my mind and disappeared.

Afterwards we sat at the table sipping mild, aromatic green tea and hearing about our new home. Daunted by the prospect (to say nothing of the cost) of putting up at a hotel and trailing around real estate agencies in search of a house, we had called ahead and asked Yoko to look for something on our behalf. Ever energetic and resourceful, she had scoured several districts of Yokohama before finding something she thought would suit us. The rent was below average, she said, and there was plenty of room. 'The area is residential,' she said. 'They're putting up a lot of new houses around there. It's convenient, I must say . . . although it's a bit of a walk to the nearest station.' As the one who would be walking to the station most often, I was anxious to know just how far she meant. But I didn't ask. There would be plenty of time to find out. 'You can move in this afternoon,' Yoko continued, 'and tomorrow I'll come round and we'll all go to see the agent together.' The fact that we had immediate access meant that she had already paid the necessary money: she looked relieved when Reiko quickly assured her that we had brought sufficient funds to reimburse her.

In bright sunshine, and with a warm breeze wafting through the car windows, we drove over to see the house. It stood near the bottom of a steep hill that descended into a narrow valley, close to the ever-shifting border between the concrete megalopolis and the cabbage fields, market gardens and patches of scrubby woodland which would be the developers' next target. Most of the other houses on the hill looked new or at least clean, well cared-for by loving owners who probably spent their evenings tapping the buttons of their calculators and gloating over the recent crazy spiral in local property prices. Common architectural features included shady verandas, panelled mahogany front doors with heavy brass fittings and off-road parking in the form of small rectangles of concrete covered by car ports with pink plastic roofs. Most had gardens, half-shielded from the road by thick shrubbery – camellia bushes, clumps of bamboo, orange trees hung with fruit. The place that Yoko had picked out for us, with economy in mind, made quite a contrast. It looked more like a shack than a house. Old and weatherbeaten, it stood perched on thin, badly-cracked concrete foundations and was clad with narrow planks of cedar whose brown paint was peeling off in several places. There was a dent in the front door, as if it had been struck with a blunt instrument.

The ground floor was divided into an entrance hall, a kitchen, the white-tiled bathroom with the maple tree outside the window and two small-to-medium rooms whose floors were made of new, green-tinted *tatami* mats edged with braid. Upstairs there was a narrow landing and two large rooms with wooden floors. This design was the brainchild of the original owners, a couple of retired schoolteachers who had lived downstairs and used the upstairs rooms to run a private cram school for local children. But they were long gone, and the present owner was a young man who lived elsewhere in the city and obviously had better things to do than turn up to meet his new tenants. Not that we needed him to help us find our way around. The back room had floor-to-ceiling French windows fitted with opaque glass, which we opened to find a token garden – a strip of concrete and a flowerbed – underneath a sagging iron balcony whose steel supports were eaten away by rust. I took a long, hard look at the door lintels, which were at just about the same level as my nose: I would have to develop the habit of stooping every time I passed through, or suffer painful consequences.

As we had expected, the house was quite empty – there was no furniture, no kitchenware, no hot water heater, in fact no heating of any kind, no letterbox, not even an official address, since for a long time there had been no occupant to register the house as a permanent residence. For the last few years it had been rented out in a succession of very short leases to newcomers to the area who had camped out in it for the last month or two while construction of their own new homes was being completed. The shelves were all bare and the light fittings all tilted at crazy angles, their ancient cables matted with grease and fluff. There was a lot to be done to make the place habitable, but nothing that couldn't be achieved with soap and water and a few basic tools. We carried our suitcases from the car, plus a few basic essentials we had borrowed from Yoko, and moved in.

The next morning we went around to introduce ourselves to the house agent and sign the contract. This involved a ritual exchange of bows and courteous remarks, exclamations of interest in the children, who were then shunted into a corner to entertain themselves with another songbird in a cage, several cups of green tea and some lengthy explanations of various clauses in the agreement. The agent was a middle-aged woman with thin, sharp features, black-rimmed spectacles and a rather severe business suit that made her look like a headmistress: she spoke politely enough but had a look in her eye as though she might easily make me go and stand with my face to the wall if I didn't do as I was told. Having listened to a long and well-rehearsed lecture on the rights and responsibilities of both parties to the contract – we would have to pay to replace the *tatami* mats and the paper doors when we eventually vacated the premises – we finally got on to the subject of the money.

By Japan's standards, it was an average deal: one month's rent in advance, the same again as a returnable deposit and the same again for the 'key money' or 'thank you money'. Like tipping slow waiters in other countries, the precise purpose of this disbursement is preferably not discussed. It doesn't buy anything tangible, but you have to pay it anyway. Essentially, it amounts to a gesture of goodwill and appreciation to the landlord for his kindness in giving the tenant somewhere to live free from the threat of eviction until the next rent review in two years' time. The custom is not an old one: it first took root after World War II, when large numbers of people from the countryside moved to the cities to find work and quickly found out that finding somewhere to live was a lot easier if they made a cash payment – that is to say if they made some appropriate gesture of respect – to a prospective landlord.

In most countries, the procedure is known as extortion and is banned by law. In Japan it is regarded as a mechanism for establishing harmonious relations between landlord and tenant and the law has nothing to do with it. So like everyone else we had no choice – we paid up. In addition, we had 10 days of the current month still to go, which meant an additional third of a month's rent. The final bill gouged a large chunk from the savings we had brought with us – a painful expenditure but not unanticipated, and still leaving us a sufficient margin to buy the basic items we needed to survive until I found work and my earnings started to roll in.

Stopping off at a nearby post office for directions, we next paid a visit to the local secondhand shop, where we picked up a two-burner gas cooker, a gas water heater, a washing machine, a fridge and a table. Yoko claimed to know someone who was moving out of another house in a few days, from whom we would be able to obtain two sofa beds, a book case and several other items. I went out in the afternoon to buy some new light fittings from a small electrical shop nearby, which led to a long explanatory conversation with the proprietor and his wife: they knew our house and seemed quietly amazed that anyone had actually had the courage to move into it. That evening they called round in their little white Honda pick-up with a paraffin heater and a television set, which they sold us for next to nothing. Every gap in our inventory, it seemed, was being filled as soon as we noticed it.

Our first regular visitor was a homeless black and white cat, which delighted the children by turning up every morning at breakfast time, prowling around in the flower bed and miaowing for something to eat. They named him Patch, and started to make a pet of him. But to the scars Patch had earned in half a lifetime of street warfare was added an unusually mangy, grubby appearance, which got him barred from entering the house. In fact, with a piece of dirty string tied round his middle he would have been perfectly cast as a feline baglady. Still, Patch was not the kind of cat that sits back and waits for good things to arrive by themselves. He knew that this is a tough world, and that you have to get out there and prove yourself. Determined to gain entry by winning my wife's affection, he crowned his efforts one afternoon with the gift of a well mangled rat, turning her tentative distrust into something more akin to implacable loathing.

We had better luck with our next door neighbours, whose

house was much newer than ours but not much bigger – very cramped, it seemed to me, for all the people who lived in it. In addition to Mr Higashitani, a salaryman in his late forties who set off for the station every morning at 7 and didn't return until about 11 at night, there was his wife, two grand-parents, the husband's retarded brother, two teenage sons and a nine-year-old daughter called Sumiko. Apart from courteous greetings exchanged in the street with any member of the family who happened along, most of our contact was through Sumiko, who boldly used to invite herself round after school to play with our daughters. She would bang briskly on the door, step inside without waiting for it to be answered, and while taking her shoes off in the hallway would call out *'Ojama shimasu!'*, one of the standard phrases used in this situation, which literally means something like 'I'm going to be a nuisance!' She was never anything of the kind, but we soon got used to hearing this announcement at all hours, together with its past tense equivalent at the end of her visit, *'Ojama shimashita!'* or 'The nuisance is now over!' The lack of a common language was a bit of a barrier to communication, but much less than I had expected: the children would make sketches together, look at photographs and act out their wants and preferences. Sumiko would also bring her friends around to inspect the foreigners and they too would kindly warn us that they were going to be a nuisance before coming in and giving absolutely no trouble at all. Before long our daughters began to acquire non-verbal skills such as *origami*, the art of making birds and other objects out of folded paper, or else would disappear for long periods to go on picnics in the park.

The park was about five minutes' walk away, occupying two or three acres at the top of the hill. There was a large grassy area suitable for informal games, a fenced-off baseball field, and two almost derelict tennis courts. Neither of the courts had any lines marked on their bare-earth playing surface, but one had a torn, ragged net strung between two rusty supports. At the far end there was a thin, weedy hedge and beyond that a dusty square where a group of old age pensioners gathered every day to play an informal, simplified version of croquet called 'gateball.' Elsewhere in the park was an infants' playground with swings, a sandpit and several jungle animals moulded in concrete, a rectangular building for the practice of *karate* and other indoor sports, and a swimming pool. The best feature was the network of paths which linked these facilities together: they were lined on each side by mature cherry trees, which promised a fine display of blossoms in the spring.

Getting to the nearest shopping centre involved walking up the hill from the house, along the edge of a large vegetable field, cutting across the park and then going down the other side of the hill to the main road, a two-lane highway which must have started life as a cart-track for local farmers. Since then it had grown a lot in importance but not much in size, becoming a busy bus and truck route that was permanently clogged with traffic. Many of the houses close to this road were elderly wooden shacks erected during the poverty-stricken postwar years, when building styles were limited by considerations of economy and utilitarianism. Wretched though they looked from the outside, they made perfectly tolerable dwellings once you adapted yourself to the lack of space, as I knew from having lived in a couple of them myself during my previous stay in Japan. But the road's role as the principal artery of communication with everywhere else had also made it a focus of local commerce, so that the old houses which fronted onto it were now being demolished one after another and replaced by new buildings made of concrete.

Exploring the adjacent side streets, we found a hardware store, a chemist, a haberdasher, a fishmonger, a pickle dealer and a *tofu* maker, two chemists, two stationers and two doctors' clinics, three beer-and-*sake* shops and a bakery which sold excellent bread but only on Thursday mornings. Two of the booze shops had tiny wooden bars tucked away in their dim interiors, where local men would drop by for a few glasses of cheap *sake* at the end of their day's work. There was also a supermarket called A-COOP (pronounced 'A-COP') with a large tarmac yard at the front where a fat man with glasses and hardly any teeth sold portions of grilled chicken on sticks from a little stall permanently shrouded in billowing clouds of blue smoke. Two or three times a week this yard was transformed into a small open-air market – sometimes on a household theme, with bolts of cloth, socks (three pairs to a pack), clothes pegs, pot scourers and other kitchen items, all extremely cheap, and sometimes exclusively for foodstuffs like fish, fruit, locally-grown vegetables, home-made pickles and sauces, and utensils such as plates, bowls, teacups, chopsticks and saucepans. Here, for a small sum, we picked up a small, shallow plate with a surface of rough grooves on which to grate fresh ginger, and a set of different-sized bamboo draining baskets.

None of these competitors seemed to diminish A-COOP's business, although it was difficult at first to see how they could all make a satisfactory living out of the local housewives who were the only customers. One explanation was the remarkable diversity of products available within any given category: in addition to potatoes, carrots and other familiar standbys, A-COOP's vegetable section offered walnuts, chrysanthemum leaves, eleven varieties of mushrooms, snow peas, watercress, red and white radishes, Chinese cabbage, fresh and dried ginger, red onions, pumpkin, lotus root and mountain potato, the last-named being a knobbly, irregularly shaped tuber with a hairy skin which is difficult to cultivate successfully and is therefore still mostly collected in the wild. Even there it is not easy to find unless the searcher recognises the thin stalk that grows from the root and trails, often for several yards, over other nearby vegetation. Following this stalk back to where it emerges from the ground discloses the location of the precious and fragile root, which is usually two or three feet below ground level and has to be carefully dug out with a spade-like instrument whose blade is only about three inches wide. Cooking is not required: mountain potato is peeled, finely grated, beaten with a raw egg to a mucus-like consistency and then eaten – or rather slurped – with plain cooked rice.

Vegetables, of course, only accounted for a small part of what A-COOP had to offer. There was also a large fish section selling several kinds of roe, whole bream and goldeneye, crab legs, octopus tentacles, eel, crayfish, squid, oysters and scallops. Some of the produce was prepared in advance, filleted, dried and (sometimes) sprinkled with sesame seeds, or in the case of *sashimi*, fish eaten raw, carefully cut into bite-sized pieces and artistically arranged in polystyrene trays, each with its own individual packets of green horseradish mustard and soy sauce.

If the theme of the fish section was diversity, the meat section next to it was based entirely on the idea of convenience in preparation. The quality gave no grounds for complaint, but the comparatively feeble range of choice underscored the tradition of Japan as a country of fish eaters who used grills and frying pans, but not ovens. There was plenty of chicken, either in the form of whole boned breasts or else of any other cut ready-diced for use in casseroles or *yakitori*, little kebabs served on bamboo skewers. Apart from that, in descending order of taste and value, there was plenty of minced beef, some sad little steaks bearing the teeth-marks of an automatic tenderising machine, slices of pork (no chops) and packets of imported streaky bacon, drenched in preserving chemicals and hardly fit to eat. Lamb was conspicuous by its total absence: specialist butchers' shops sometimes stocked it, but most people disliked its distinctive taste and smell.

Besides vegetables, fish and meat, A-COOP sold a bewildering choice of sauces and condiments, dried beans and seeds, packets of make-it-yourself cakes and cookies, including a series of home baking products generically titled 'Mrs Bread', and a range of canned, ready-to-microwave meals such as borscht, beef stew or rolled cabbage which were sold under the admirably straightforward label 'My Dinner.' A-COOP's Achilles heel was the dairy section, where a depressingly bland selection of cheeses touched bottom with an industrial-quality product called 'pizza cheese', which was sold ready-grated in large, family-size plastic bags. But in a country with relatively little dairy farming and so many other good things to eat, the local absence of good cheese hardly seemed to matter.

The distance from home to the shops was about a mile, with a steep hill in between, so toting the bags demanded more effort than we would have chosen to expend. A car would have been no help, since there was nowhere to park it, but we noticed that many of our fellow-shoppers used

50cc scooters instead. Meanwhile the nearest train station was two miles away: we had already discovered that it took half an hour to get there on foot, and almost as long by bus, since the main road was nearly always choked with traffic. Some sort of two-wheeled transportation, if we could find it, was beginning to look like a good idea. But there was no big hurry. It was one of those ideas we could consider and talk over at our leisure – for instance, while taking a bath.

2 | Horses of Instruction

THE WORK involved in settling into a new home generates a momentum of its own, and we soon found the energy to start exploring further afield. One destination that looked promising was the string of seaside resorts along a shore line known as the Shonan Coast, about 20 minutes away by train. The area's popularity was not due to any particular natural beauty but to its proximity to Tokyo and Yokohama: a few years before, it had been the focus of one of Japan's many leisure 'booms', which multiplied property prices and blocked the shoreline road with smart cars whose owners had taken up the fashionable pastime of 'cruising', in imitation of how smart young Californians supposedly spent their time. But by the time we arrived, the boom was over and the Shonan Coast – a name which evokes much the same sense of promise and excitement as 'The English Riviera' – had returned to its normal state, which was that of a slightly tatty collection of overgrown villages catering to urban weekenders in the form of families, fishermen, yacht-owners and hordes of young windsurfers whose wetsuits were decorated with fluorescent pink or yellow flashes.

The first place we tried was Enoshima, which we reached by changing trains at a main line station and taking a rattling old three-car tram which wound its way slowly through a maze of back streets on a narrow, single-gauge track. At every third stop or so, there was an extra loop of track where the tram would wait briefly to allow another to pass in the opposite direction. Getting on and off the tram required a lot of strenuous pushing, since all of its cars were jammed with passengers and their luggage – old couples out for a trip to a nearby temple, their lunch tied up in neatly-knotted cloths, schoolgirls toting the day's essentials in tiny rucksacks printed with cartoon characters, and resigned-looking Mums and Dads taking small children laden with buckets, balls and long-handled fishing nets to play for a few hours on the beach.

Enoshima was bright and gaudy and cheerful and tacky, its streets lined with hamburger stands (one with the unappetising name of 'Mossburger'), ice cream stalls and several souvenir shops selling plastic jewellery, chinaware, objects made of shells glued together, colourful dolls roughly carved from coconut shells and many kinds of hats with slogans printed on them. Some also did a brisk trade in bags of assorted shells and the preserved corpses of creatures taken from the sea for no other purpose than to be sold as ornaments: imaginatively repainted bass and trout mounted in expensive glass cases, racks of stuffed hawksbill turtles whose brilliantly varnished shells gleamed brightly enough to help customers forget that the trade in this dying species is banned under international agreement, and entire shoals of dried porcupine fish hanging from the ceiling on strings like prickle-covered balls and staring into space above the customers' heads with sightless plastic eyes.

The seafront consisted of two long, sandy beaches separated from each other by a causeway with a road on top of it which linked the mainland to an island about 300 yards offshore. We decided to go across and explore. The island was a large chunk of rock with steep cliffs that fell steeply away to a narrow, rocky shore on all sides: after being funnelled along another street crowded with identical souvenir shops, visitors could climb up and around it by following a network of narrow footpaths and long flights of stone steps. The top turned out to be a flat plateau where dozens of tourists were patiently queueing to go up a tall, white-painted observation tower while others wandered along still more footpaths that wound here and there among still more souvenir shops, stalls selling grilled corn and a few small restaurants. We decided to have lunch in one of these restaurants and were shown to a table on a narrow concrete balcony with nothing underneath it but a sheer drop of 150 feet to the rocks at the sea edge. Fried noodles with vegetables and a couple of bottles of beer were quickly brought and we began to eat while looking happily across at the symmetrical white cone of Mt Fuji glistening in the sunshine on the other side of the bay – the same white cone and the same bay as in Hokusai's famous picture, but this time featuring a sea of glassy smoothness instead of angry waves curling over tiny fishing boats with menacing claws of foam. Instead, drama arrived in a different form. No sooner had we got stuck into the food than we were spotted by a large and fierce-looking bird of prey, one of the sea-kites which scavenge in large numbers all along the Shonan Coast, wheeling slowly in the sky and then swooping abruptly down to snatch a choice morsel from the generous quantities of refuse left lying around on the beaches. Following what was no doubt a well-practised manoeuvre, this feathered son of a bitch soared high into the air (in my mind's eye I could see its hooked beak twisted into a grim smile), zoomed dramatically out to sea, made a tight wheeling turn and then roared towards us, performing a series of low passes over the table like a jet fighter. While the children cowered in terror, I tried to affect an air of casual amusement, especially for the benefit of the old bat who ran the place and whom I could hear quietly cackling in the background. 'Do come back and eat with us again soon,' she croaked with a sly smile when I went to the cash desk to pay the bill.

Outside the restaurant, a flight of concrete steps led to the rocky shore below, so we clambered down and spent an hour jumping over narrow inlets where the seaweed swirled this way and that as the water rose and fell with each succeeding wave, and peering into clear pools where crimson

anemones waved their thin tentacles and tiny, almost trans-
parent fish darted in and out from behind the stones and
rock ledges. Several people were fishing, with impressive
success, casting their lines again and again from low ledges
of rock where the incoming waves broke with a quiet hiss
and sloshed softly around their ankles. The atmosphere was
slow, calm, benign, as peaceful and unhurried as Sunday
afternoon: only the rough, pitted surface of the rocks and
their fractured appearance reminded us how savagely the
sea batters this coastline when the wind is high, and what
the consequences can be for those who venture too close.
Only about a week before there had been a newspaper report
about three schoolboys who had drowned in this very place.
Two had been carried up the coast by the tides while the third
had been found right here, head down in the water, his left leg
broken and the ankle stuck fast in a crack in the rock.

*

As far as installing the children in school was concerned,
our plan had been to play it by ear. In other words, we
didn't have a plan. But rather than sling them straight in
from the beginning, we had decided that it would be best
to give them as much time as they needed to adjust to the
new and unfamiliar environment in which they now found
themselves. Learning the language, of course, had started as
soon as we arrived: every mealtime found us huddled round
our low table building up vocabulary and practising useful
phrases such as 'this is an apple', 'this fish is delicious' and
'thank you for having me.' But this was no substitute for real
contact with real people, and about three weeks after our
arrival, it was the children themselves who announced that
they were getting bored and wanted to go to school. Sending
them to one of Yokohama's 'international' schools, where the
curriculum is based on English or American standards, was
not really a practical option – partly because of the distance
(they would have had to commute for an hour and half each
way) and partly because of the cost, which is comparable to

the fees at an expensive private school in England. Nevertheless, in order to feel that I had at least checked out the possibilities, I went to visit one. The building and facilities were unremarkable, but it was a big surprise to discover that well over half the children were the sons and daughters of wealthy Japanese, who were paying premium rates (more than foreign parents) for their offspring to enjoy the assumed benefit of associating with *gaijin* during their schooldays and perhaps eventually going on to an American or European university. When I gently brought up the fact that I might have difficulty with the fees, it was strongly hinted that in my particular case it might be possible to arrange a reduction. This was all couched in very diplomatic terms but I was left with the clear impression that the school was keen to take on more white faces. Failing that, half-white faces would do. It didn't take much reflection to persuade us that we would do better to choose schooling closer to home.

We had already paid a visit to the ward office, or headquarters of the local authority, to register our presence in the district and obtain identity cards for the family's foreign contingent, so we went round again to ask for the name of the nearest local school to which the children were entitled to go. The ward office was a smooth, disciplined machine for processing all kinds of official municipal business. It was where people went to register the ownership of their cars, apply for health insurance, pay rent for city housing, obtain revenue stamps to stick on application forms, seek trading permits and sign up for social benefits. But it wasn't like similar places in other countries. There were no queues of disgruntled people waiting in a litter of cigarette butts for their turn to do battle with some dim, uncooperative clerk. There were no vandalised benches with filthy lumps of foam rubber poking out through knife-slashes in their vinyl covers. There was no atmosphere of dirt and depression, no sense of people wearily defending hopeless causes. Immigration offices in Japan are like that, not ward offices. This one looked more like a hospital than a nest of bureaucrats. It was painted cream and the different sections at its long counters were designated by neat signboards slung from the ceiling and divided from each other by white gauze partitions in moveable aluminium frames. Counter clerks handed out forms and received them when completed with a bow and a few polite words. Other staff in identical beige jackets worked away at a line of identical computers. The place hummed with calm, controlled efficiency.

The clerk at the 'Education' section produced a detailed map of the area and spread it on the counter. Once he had located our house, he quickly identified our catchment area and the school to which we should apply. It was called 'Matsugaoka Sho-gakko', or 'Pine Hill Primary School.' We called it up on the spot and fixed an appointment to meet the headmistress on the following Saturday afternoon.

Pine Hill Primary School was indeed built on the side of a hill, but any trees, pines or otherwise, that had formerly grown on its slopes had long been cut down to make way for a new estate of suburban commuters' homes. The school itself was a large, three-storey cube of concrete fronting onto a playground of bare earth and surrounded by a low hedge beneath which a few sparrows darted here and there pecking nervously at the dusty ground.

Inside, the school building was cavernous and still, like a museum after hours. The pupils had already left for what remained of the weekend. Leaving our shoes in the main doorway, we helped ourselves to plastic slip-on sandals from a large rack and made our way in silence along a wide corridor. Children's paintings were pinned to the walls, along with examples of satisfactorily completed homework assignments, sports team lists and hand-written admonitions about the proper place to leave wet umbrellas.

Up ahead, a door with a frosted glass window swung open and a thin, balding man wearing dungarees emerged with a cigarette in his hand. I took him for a janitor, but he came quickly forward with a look of solicitous enquiry on his face and introduced himself as the deputy head.

'And you must be . . . Waycott-san?'

We bowed in assent. The deputy head gave a broad smile and launched into a speech of welcome.

'And these are your daughters? My, they're beautiful, aren't

they? Hello, there! And hello to you too! Welcome to Matsugaoka Primary School! This is quite an event for us, you
know – we've never had any foreigners in the school before.
Plenty to learn, plenty . . . for all of us, don't you think? What
an opportunity! Everyone here's looking forward to it. I'm
sure you are too. So you've just moved in to the area? From
America? Oh no, England, that's right. England . . . must be
a wonderful country – all that history! And now you've come
to live in Japan.' He shook his head in wonder, as if he could
hardly believe that anyone would voluntarily do such a thing.
'Well, well, come along. Hattori-kocho is expecting you. She's
waiting in her office. It's this way, just around the corner.'

He led us to the end of a line of lockers and then along
another corridor to a door with 'Kocho' (Principal) on it in
black lettering. He gave it a quick couple of taps, then opened
it and ushered us into an empty room.

'Oh, she's not here. That's odd. I thought . . . oh well,
never mind. She'll be with you in a moment. Just make
yourselves comfortable. Would you like some tea? I'll have
someone bring it along.'

Smiling warmly and bowing, he backed out of the door
and shut it behind him. The Principal's office had a large
window looking out onto the playground and an impressive
wooden desk with lots of small drawers and pigeon-holes, but
was otherwise furnished in a graveyard style that made me
think of the mid 1950's, when my own schooldays had begun.
There were two armchairs upholstered in moth-eaten brown
leather and a long, low table whose plate-glass top rested on an
oversize doily in white crochet. A glass fronted cabinet against
one wall held a few bulging files and some dusty objects that
could have been souvenirs from an archaeological field trip.
From a hook on the opposite wall hung a dull, characterless
landscape that looked as though it was painted on the afternoon of a particularly sad funeral, in the days before colour
was invented. Even though corporal punishment has been
abolished in Japanese schools, I found myself instinctively
looking round for the cupboard where instruments of cor-
rection might be stored.

After a few moments, Principal Hattori joined us, followed

at once by a woman carrying three china cups of green tea on wooden saucers, which she placed on the table in front of us. After the introductions were completed, the interview proceeded in friendly but formal fashion, so I sat quietly while Reiko spoke on our behalf. Principal Hattori, however, did most of the talking, only occasionally bestowing a cool, slightly bemused glance in my direction as if she were wondering what manner of creature I might be. She was dressed in dowdy tweeds which complemented her ample figure and owl-like face, whose best feature was a pair of dark eyes that twinkled softly behind her standard-issue tortoiseshell-rimmed spectacles.

What lay ahead of us – all of us, she took pains to stress – was an adventure that Might Not Be Easy: in all the years of Pine Hill Primary School's existence, no foreigner had ever previously crossed the threshold and who could say what the effect of this intrusion into Japan's famous and much-beloved homogeneity might be? There was no question of our application being rejected, but it was clear that the situation contained an element of unpredictability, than which nothing generates more anxiety in the Japanese mind. But Principal Hattori looked like a lady with a long history of rising to challenges, and she would deal with this one as she had dealt with all others in the past. We would unite to tackle any problems, she told us, by Doing Our Best: this would achieve the end we all desired, or at least as close an approximation to it as any of us had a right to expect.

One such problem was that we had arrived when the school year was already more than half over, and since every stage of every year's academic curriculum was precisely defined, little or no flexibility could be shown to accommodate the difficulties which the newcomers would inevitably face. They would just have to catch up as best they could. Principal Hattori made no secret of her belief that education operated on two different, though complementary, levels. One was conventional – a cooperative venture involving the school and the parents, designed to fill the children with a blend of factual information and moral principles by which they could be prepared for adulthood. The other, expressed in vague, allusive terms, amounted to the infliction of a stern social discipline designated to inculcate the vital spirit of group cooperation treasured by Japanese educators and regrettably misinterpreted by some foreigners as supine conformity and surrender to a lifetime of exploitation.

To achieve these important goals, Principal Hattori repeated, and to overcome any instances of culture clash which might arise, we were to invoke the magic power of *gaman*, or endurance, which is the main contribution made by each pupil to his or her own education. Confronted by any difficulty, discouraged by any problem, fearful of any failure, the child should rely on the spirit of *gaman* to win through to success. Everyone is endowed by nature with a well of *gaman*, and one of the main responsibilities of a teacher is to give each individual child ample opportunities to practise lowering the bucket and drawing up the tenacity required to solve mathematical problems, the strength to accept censure, the determination to keep running for the team in spite of cramp and even the fortitude to carry on functioning when the classroom heating breaks down. The imperative form, *gambatte kudasai*, is one of the commonest expressions heard at all levels of Japanese society, and it was with these words that Principal Hattori smilingly ushered us out of the door. The children were to start the following Monday. Having understood practically nothing of what had been said, they were eagerly looking forward to it. I took this as a sign that their *gaman* levels were up to par.

3 | Change Here for Tokyo

Ａs the days began to slip by, we found our expenses mounting at an alarming rate. All we had to live on was the savings we had brought with us, and these were beginning to look dangerously inadequate. It was time to look for a job. Still, that wouldn't present much of a problem. After all, as I frequently reminded myself, I had lived in Tokyo before and anyway was an old hand at finding work. Mr Experience. True, it might take a few months to track down the ideal situation, but getting enough bread and butter stuff in the meantime, to provide that basic income, would be easy.

I soon had occasion to revise that opinion. It wasn't easy. Tokyo had changed. The last time around, there had been far fewer foreign residents, and those were spoiled for choice when it came to employment. It was not at all unusual to be approached on the train or in the street by total strangers who wanted to be taught English conversation. Advertising copywriters, as I came to find out, had it even better: they were as rare as rubies, and in an economy that was almost entirely geared for exports, had practically been able to name their own price. Lucrative commissions succeeded each other with bewildering rapidity. They came from agencies that were regular employers and from agencies that one had never heard of. They came from translation houses and film production companies. They came from other copywriters who were too overloaded to accept everything they were offered. They came directly from clients. Sometimes it seemed that they came through the window by themselves, even in the middle of the night.

Fifteen years on, the atmosphere was very different. For a start there were Westerners everywhere, on every street, at every train station, in every coffee shop. Half of them, I quickly began to feel, were working as copywriters. The other half were going around saying they were copywriters, causing wild variations in work quality and dragging pay scales down. Meanwhile, political pressure from abroad about Japan's famous trade surplus had brought about a reduction of emphasis on exports and a frenzied stimulation of the domestic market instead. Japanese consumers had money in their pockets and it was boom time for anyone in the business of helping them spend it. Local ad agencies had mushroomed, their domestic interests overtaking and sometimes eclipsing their own international divisions, some of which were split off and then resurrected as separate organisations that drew from the growing pool of underworked freelancers to serve their short, specialised list of clients. In some cases, they didn't have any direct clients at all, but obtained their work from the big-name agencies, which knew exactly how little to pay without inducing bankruptcy. The big agencies still had in-house positions for foreign writers, but now considered it amateurish to hire off the street: the new trend was to employ foreign headhunters to recruit native talent in London, New York, Los Angeles and Sydney.

In short, competition had become fiercer, work generally more scarce and pay lower. The gravy train days were all over. As my job search progressed, I began to feel more and more like a redundant species of dinosaur, woken from centuries of hibernation to find that all my fellow copywritosauruses had died out and been replaced by a new, more efficient breed of young, lean, hungry business school graduates with sharper teeth, quicker brains and miraculously adaptable limbs that could perform complicated tasks on computers as easily as I had once been able to stretch out my neck and munch lush green assignments from the tops of long-extinct trees.

I decided on a two-prong offensive, one in which I would apply for advertised positions and the other consisting of good old-fashioned footslogging. The first would get things up and running, but the second would ultimately prove more effective since the key to success in Japan is getting to know people and building up a network of personal contacts. But the place to start was the small ads, and that meant consulting the *Japan Times*.

There are four English-language daily papers published in Japan, of which the *Japan Times* has the biggest circulation. Like its rivals, it offers a mix of national and regional Japanese news, edited Reuter and AP wire reports from abroad, sport, business and finance, arts and reviews. It also carries various locally-produced columns that have gone on for years and years and even more years, and – its most valuable feature – a large section of classified ads.

Searching the classifieds for a job is as daunting and discouraging a business in Tokyo as anywhere else, but the different approaches of companies from different countries provide an entertaining diversity to be enjoyed along the way. British employers are instantly recognisable by their long-winded, overblown style.

'... *requires full-time assistant to provide secretarial support to staff members in the Technical Section.*'

The Technical Section needs a secretary.

'*Flexibility and willingness to adapt to changing demands are very important.*'

You'll do whatever you're told.

American companies prefer to focus on a mutual exchange of some highly desirable abstraction, such as excellence:

'*The ideal candidate will be self-motivated and possess excellent communication skills. He/she should have an excellent record in sales. Excellent salary/benefits package.*'

Then there are the ads expressed in code:

'Fast-growing international PR firm ... great chance to grow with an exciting company.'
This means that if they don't get a couple of good new accounts in the near future, they'll be going out of business. I was almost more tempted by this: *'Lingerie sales representative required. Set your own hours. Enthusiastic foreigner welcome.'* But I didn't call. Somehow it's easier to keep your enthusiasm for lingerie if you don't depend on it for a living.

Instead I had a go at the fast-growing international PR firm, but another applicant had got there first. Fortunately, the boss knew of something else going and gave me a number to call. 'It's only short-term, as far as I know,' he said, 'but at least it's something.'

The job he recommended turned out to be still available: it was just for a week, helping to finish off a long-standing project being undertaken for the Ministry of International Trade and Industry. A small army of foreigners (hourly-paid, which caused them to drop out rapidly as they found other, more substantial employment) had been hired to proofread and amend the entries in a massive computerised dictionary that was to be used for machine translation. The idea was that in the future people would be able to key in a text in either Japanese or English and then the computer would spew out an equivalent version in the other language, which could then be rewritten into acceptable prose by a native speaker.

The company which had secured this contract was one of Tokyo's many translation houses, staffed mostly by young women (called 'co-ordinators') whose job was to visit potential client companies, solicit documents requiring translation, quote a price, commission a translator, find a rewriter to brush up the English and then return the completed work to the client. The girls were all on commission, which meant that they worked harder, under more pressure and for better pay than salaried people. They were also uniformly gorgeous, which was clearly an important qualification. Apart from the fact that they didn't change their clothes in the office, it was a bit like being closeted in a dressing room full of models at a fashion show. The lowly foreign proofreaders were self-evidently too short of money to merit much attention from this intriguing sales force, but benefitted anyway from their inspiring display of short hemlines, gold jewellery, vermilion fingernails, beautiful shoes, silk scarves and fluffy boas. All day long they would swoop in and out of the corporate nest like exotic tropical birds, depositing their latest acquisitions into the gaping beaks of the translators and then making a few quick phone calls before fluttering off to canvass some other part of the jungle.

I was teamed up with a Japanese lady translator called Yuriko. From nine o'clock each morning we sat together at a desk enclosed by partitions, and worked our way slowly through the entries in our assigned section of the dictionary. If I found something that looked or sounded bizarre, I would ask her to explain exactly what the Japanese version meant, and would then try to reduce what she said to a brief and comprehensible English equivalent. The boredom of the exercise was relieved by its unpredictability, since dictionaries are not compiled by subject but simply by the alphabetical order of words; we might therefore spend three quarters of an hour wrestling with some subject neither of us knew the first thing about, such as the names of the parts in some electronic machine and then turn a page and alight quite suddenly on something more promising like 'vaginal secretion' or 'seductive glance'. On the last morning I was there we had to spend quite a bit of time sorting out the exact meaning of two different entries, both translated as 'love technique': it finally transpired that one of them was sort of airy-fairy and diffi-cult to pin down, basically signifying 'courtship technique', while the other was hard-nosed nuts and bolts stuff – 'sexual technique.' At first Yuriko acted a bit embarrassed, but after a while she gave every appearance of enjoying herself as much as I was. It was a good game – peering down into the steaming cauldron of human sex with notebooks in our hands, like a couple of scientists. And then we would turn the page once more, hoping to encounter something with the same level of interest, and find ourself confronted by 'hydrochloric acid' or 'inter-continental ballistic missile'.

For most of the week I went for lunch with Yuriko and half a dozen other translators and writers to a little Indian restaurant close to the office, but on this final day the long morning we spent bringing the love technique problem to a conclusion found us still at work after everyone else had gone out, so we took a late lunch together at another place down the street. Doubtless because of the mood created by the morning's labours, Yuriko was in the mood to talk further, and her story emerged in a drama-filled hour over a bowl of noodles. She had only recently moved back to live in Japan herself, and this was her first job for many years. Her family in Osaka didn't even know she had returned, and she had no intention of telling them until she had got back into the swing of things and saved enough money to secure her independence. Curious as I had been from the start to know why this attractive, forty-ish woman who dressed in well-tailored suits should be working in a hack job for low pay, I had been careful not to ask any questions and had gleaned no more until now than that she had spent several years in Boston, which accounted for her excellent English ability.

'My father owned a chemical company until he retired a few years ago,' she said, 'so I was brought up in a comfortable home and went to an exclusive private school. At university I studied Japanese literature, but it never interested me. I never had a job, either. My parents gave me an apartment of my own and an allowance, so I couldn't see any point in trying to make a career. What I enjoyed mostly was going out with friends, shopping, playing tennis . . . just passing the time. I went to Europe a couple of times and stayed a few months: I liked it, but I was bored because I didn't really manage to meet anyone, make any friends. And I couldn't speak any foreign language then – not more than a few words, anyway.'

'Didn't your parents put pressure on you to get married?' I asked.

'Of course they did,' she answered. 'They kept fixing up *omiai* meetings with likely young men introduced by my father's colleagues or by friends of the family. But I didn't want to marry any of them. I never wanted to marry a Japanese man. They're all slaves to their companies. Their idea of family life is the wife staying at home. Like my brother. "I wouldn't marry a woman who worked in the same company as me," he told me once. I asked him why not and he said that if she worked in the same company, she would be able to find out how much his salary was. Then it would be difficult for him to put a little money on the side for "play." "I pity the woman who marries you," I told him. "Look at you! You're planning to deceive her before you've even met her!" You see, that's the way Japanese men think. Well, not all of them, perhaps. You hear about some that are not so selfish. But I never met any eligible ones like that.

'One day my father was invited to a reception in a big hotel near the docks in Kobe. Some new ship was being launched . . . a lot of important local businessmen were asked along as guests. He took me with him, and that's where I met Alan.'

Alan, it seemed, had stepped straight from the pages of a romantic novel. He was tall, courteous, charming, wealthy and a lawyer to boot. They had fallen for each other on the spot. When he went back to America, the letters flew back and forth. Yuriko signed up at an English conversation school and began studying round the clock. An American son-in-law was not exactly the stuff of the parents' dreams, but at least he was respectable and had good prospects. Matters took their ordained course.

'Right after we were married, Alan was made a judge and we moved from his apartment to a big house in an exclusive area of Boston. He was incredibly generous – almost every day he brought me something, a necklace, clothes, flowers, tickets to go somewhere. Several times we went on cruises in the Caribbean, always first class, and whenever we went abroad we stayed in the best hotels and were driven about by chauffeurs. He took me to all the places I had heard about – Milan, London, Madrid, Vienna.'

It sounded good, but her wistful expression suggested a crisis around the corner. 'And how about life in Boston in between times?' I asked. 'What did you do while he was working? Play tennis? Go shopping with friends?'

'No,' she said, looking past my shoulder into the distance. 'That was the problem. Alan was very jealous. He made a scene if he thought anyone else was paying attention to me.'

'Even women?'

'Yes, even women. He didn't want me to have any friends. He just wanted me to be at home, waiting for him. He had the idea that all Japanese women were like that anyway, and that's what he wanted for himself – a sort of doll that he could show off in public but never share with anyone else. For instance, he wouldn't let me have a car.'

'No car? In America? How were you supposed to get around? I mean, you must have had to go to the shops sometimes – for groceries, things like that.'

'We had a servant for that, an old Mexican woman. She was the only friend I had, although she obviously didn't think much of either of us. She always left the house as soon as she could, never stayed to sit around and chat. I didn't blame her. She had a family of her own to take care of.'

'And you never had any children?'

'No. We couldn't. I mean . . . it was impossible.'

'Oh, I see.'

'No, it wasn't that. I mean, not because there was anything wrong, physically wrong. It was just that . . . we never made love.'

'Never?' I tried to keep the incredulity out of my voice. 'You mean, you . . . sort of gave it up after a while?'

'No, it never started. Alan didn't want it. He didn't like that kind of sex.'

It was impossible not to ask. 'What kind did he like?'

She took a fresh package of cigarettes out of her handbag and looked down at it while slowly stripping off the cellophane. 'He liked . . . you know. Oral.'

'Oh.' There didn't seem much to say. I tried a little levity. 'Well, that's better than nothing.'

She raised her eyes from the cigarettes and looked me in the eye. 'It was only for him,' she said. 'Never for me.'

He probably didn't like that either, but I didn't want to know. 'Every day, right after he came back from work,' Yuriko went on in an even tone. 'Same time, same place, same way every time. No talking. And that's all. Apart from that he refused to discuss the subject in any way. It was like a box, locked up and never opened. Naturally I soon realised the way things were. It was incredibly shocking and shameful to me. Not that, I don't mean, not doing it. That was just boring. But realising that I had been brought up to think of myself as someone special, someone privileged, someone who could do better than marrying an ordinary selfish Japanese man. Yet this man, the first man I had ever fallen in love with, had married me simply to perform a task that any streetwalker could have done for him, probably better than I could.'

I couldn't think of anything to say. In my mind's eye I saw a Boston courtroom and a succession of troubled people appearing in the dock and having their lives changed by the decisions of a man who was probably only half listening to them, probably just counting the minutes until he could go home and be sucked off by his toy wife from Japan.

'How long did you stay with him?'

'Twelve years. Ridiculous, isn't it, to have stayed so long? But I was too ashamed to tell anyone, too shy to ask for help. I couldn't get away. He kept our passports in his safe, and would never allow me to have more than a few dollars. "Anything you want, I'll get it for you," he'd say. "Anything, all you have to do is ask and it's yours. But I'm not letting you go." In the end I got him to let me attend a sewing class – it took months to persuade him. I made friends with one of the other women there and sometimes asked her round to the house for coffee. Alan was suspicious at first, but Edith, this woman, was much older than either of us and I think he thought that there was no chance of her getting me into bad company. That was the excuse he always gave for not letting me go anywhere without him, that I might get into "bad company".

'Finally this woman helped me get away – she arranged for me to stay at the house of a friend of hers in another part of the city. I went to the consulate and told them I had lost my passport. They gave me another. My friend sold some of my jewellery for me so I had money to live. I stayed in Boston for about six months, hardly ever going out, while Alan looked for me. Once I got in touch with him and met him at a restaurant in the city. He wept and sobbed and begged me to go back home with him. He promised he'd change, it would all be different. It was strange, listening to him, as though it was all happening to two other people. I didn't feel anything for him at all, no pity, no dislike, nothing. I just got up from the table and left him there. Finally I ran out of money, so I decided to come back here. When I've got back on my feet I'll go back to Osaka and live there. I hate Tokyo, the people are so snobbish and unfriendly. But I don't want to go home broke. My parents don't know anything about what happened, and they aren't going to like it. My father will take the Japanese attitude – it's the wife's fault. If the marriage doesn't work out it's because the wife hasn't learned to behave as she should, hasn't learned how to please her husband. So I won't stay with them. And I'll need money to find a place of my own to live.'

'What will you do for a job?' I asked.

'I don't know – probably work as a cabaret hostess. All you have to do is dress well and spend the evenings sitting with rich men and listening to them talk about how successful they are. I know how to do that. I had a lot of practice when I was with Alan.' She looked at her watch. 'We should go back now. Thank you for listening to me. Sometimes it's good to talk about yourself to someone you don't know and will never see again.'

4 | Mouthing Off

THE DICTIONARY JOB paid in cash at the end of the week, but as soon as it was over I was back on the street again pounding on doors. First I visited all the big-name agencies, more with the intention of making my name known around town than in any expectation of being hired. Curious creative directors, unused to giving up their time to interview unsolicited applicants, nevertheless received me courteously in comfortable offices decorated with framed advertising awards and luxuriant plants in elegant ceramic pots, listened to my pitch, glanced politely at my resume and studied the work samples in my portfolio, some of which they would have photocopied for future reference. Then they would turn to informal conversation, asking a number of seemingly irrelevant questions which were designed to find out what they really wanted to know: could I speak Japanese and, most important of all, what kind of person was I? It was to my advantage that I had plenty of experience in advertising, but by and large they took that for granted. Without it, I would hardly be likely to be approaching them at all. Much more interesting to them was the discovery that my wife was Japanese and that my children attended an ordinary Japanese school. These facts indicated an attitude to Japan, a degree of commitment, that won instant approval. The conclusion of these chats, however, was always the same: they all regretted that no vacancy was currently available but assured me that they would keep my name on file and give me a call if any suitable opportunity to make use of my services arose. There was no particular reason why they should do so, and I didn't think they would. But they might.

This kind of head-on approach is sometimes a complete waste of time, as I found at an agency which kindly arranged an appointment for me to meet their president in person: after listening to me in polite silence for half an hour, the great man gently broke the news that he couldn't help me because his company never did any work in English. But failure in the intended direction can also open up new and unsuspected avenues of possibilities, an instance of which occurred the very next day. In this case the creative director I had come to see had been obliged to go out shortly before I arrived, and since there was no-one else in the department who felt inclined to talk to a total stranger they had never heard of, it had been decided to shunt me along to the translation department, where there were at least a few people who spoke English.

The translation department employed four women who sat in front of their computer terminals in a small dingy room rendering various texts from Japanese into bad English, after which they were rewritten by a young American who worked part-time, four afternoons a week. As it happened, the American was not there that day and a crisis had arisen. Someone had written a report for one of the agency's foreign clients, describing the advertising being done on their behalf in Japanese and accounting in detail for the expenditure incurred along the way. This report was already late, and ought to be dispatched at once. Would I be willing to sit down right now and rewrite it?

An hour later the job was complete and the translation department was bubbling with appreciation. The supervisor, Miss Kato, now had another urgent job for me, and asked if I did any narrating. Unsure what she meant, I said yes, plenty. She showed me a short script – it was the commentary for a video about car tyres – and proposed that I should accompany her down to the agency's own sound studio, which was located in the basement of the same building, and read it into a microphone. The recording took another hour or so to complete, after which we went back up to the translators' room where Kato-san, regretting that she was unable to pay me immediately, wrote down the details of my bank account, which the accounts department would need when the time came. She also promised to get in touch again if she had any more work I could do.

Not only had this visit produced some immediate work, with money to follow, but it also gave me a useful insight into the organisational shambles that tends to surround almost any job undertaken in English by a Japanese company. I had no confidence at all that Kato-san would call me again: she hardly knew me (there had been no time to go through the details of my life, career and future intentions) and had only made use of me because chance had directed me to her door at the right moment. Instead, I resolved to call her – and keep calling until I got a result.

Another bonus from this encounter was that it opened my eyes to the rich reservoir of work available in Tokyo for narrators – being the 'voice' on the many commercial and corporate videos being produced for Japanese companies, as well as on TV commercials, video marketing reports and so on. Hitherto, my only role in advertising had been as a writer, but it was easy to see that the abilities needed by a newcomer to the narrating scene were quite straightforward: a relatively deep voice, clear articulation and the brass nerve to pretend to have had plenty of experience. Feeling that I qualified on all three counts, I returned to the local stationers who had printed my business card, identifying me as a 'writer', and had them print me another one, in a different colour, in which I offered 'narration and script services.' To give it a bit of extra authority, I had the stationer add a trading name in large letters at the top. The name I chose was 'Sounds British', which met the important criterion of being easily comprehensible to prospective recipients of the card. To start the ball rolling, I mailed one to Kato-san.

Not long afterwards, she found a new assignment for me, concerning the production of a TV commercial. In this instance I was not the voice – the client had asked for an American – but was required to be on hand to alter the wording of the script if we found that it did not fit the video. This sounded very strange, and was the first time I found out that instead of writing the script first and then making the film afterwards, the production method in Japan is the other way round. Their way is to shoot all the footage first, edit it, and then write the script last. In the case of English-language productions, the original script is often written in Japanese and then translated and rewritten, usually by people who have not seen the video. This inevitably means that some tortured last-minute changes are necessary at the time of recording, when it is realised that a vital piece of spoken information lasting 12 seconds is too long to fit the eight-second sequence that illustrates it – or, equally common, that a long and supposedly evocative video sequence, included for its aesthetic charm, is not strictly relevant to the production but requires some spoken commentary anyway. Having a writer in the studio ensures that these little problems can be dealt with on the spot.

The narrator was already at the studio when I arrived – a burly, dark-haired American who introduced himself as Duane Gordon. In addition to his crisp white shirt, striped tie, smart blue blazer and well-creased slacks, he wore two chunky gold rings, a gold Rolex watch and lit his Parliament-brand cigarettes with a heavy gold Dunhill lighter. His voice was extraordinarily deep and powerful, like viscous gravel sliding down a steel chute. While we waited for the studio technicians to get everything ready, he sat down beside me and began at once to recount the almost intolerable hardships imposed on his life by the fact that he earned so much money. It was far too much to give a precise figure, but in rough terms he estimated his annual income at rather more than 100 million yen, something close to a million dollars. Naturally he claimed for every deduction he could think of, including a brand new

Lamborghini, but what could you do? On an income like that, the tax people showed no mercy. The way he described their attentions, I could visualise a team of inspectors following him around Tokyo, licking the stubs of their pencils and gloating over the enormous revenue his activities would bring them.

Naturally I didn't believe a word of this grotesque boasting – he had a fine voice, but how could it bring him a million dollars a year? – yet I couldn't help being impressed by the studiedly casual way he managed to portray himself as the hottest property in town, making sure that everyone in the studio got the message. Perhaps he was like those people you sometimes read about who lose everything, buy a Rolls Royce on credit and go around in the last set of smart clothes they possess, pretending to be successful and re-making their fortunes solely by means of the conviction they carry. Whichever way it was, he added the finishing touch when we left the studio by climbing into a burgundy-coloured Lamborghini parked in the street outside, adjusting his Gucci shades and driving away with an ostentatious scream from the tyres. The narration business obviously deserved close study.

With writing work, however, I was at least on familiar territory, and another classified ad from the newspaper led me to a small company with the unlikely name of 'Hi-Life Advertising,' which was looking around for a freelance copywriter. Hi-Life Advertising was located near Ginza, not far from the offices of Dentsu itself, The World's Mightiest Advertising Agency, and had a high turnover of low-level work of which at least half was farmed out to it by its famous neighbour. The owner was a woman, Mrs Ikeda, who reminded me at once of the Philippines' ex-First Lady Imelda Marcos. Mrs Ikeda had the same cream cake features, the same extravagant taste in clothes, wore the same kind of flashy jewellery and gushed with the same excessive and improbable charm.

My application, she explained while stirring two sachets of sugar into her coffee with a slim golden spoon, was extremely fortuitous: it was a rare and extraordinary chance for me, so newly arrived in the country, to be plunged so quickly into the heart of things, in fact into the very nerve-centre of the Tokyo advertising scene, where I could shortly find myself doing vitally important work on some of the most exciting and challenging accounts around. At the same time, by coincidence, Hi-Life Advertising needed to find an immediate replacement for their previous freelance writer, Mr Cathcart, who had not only been brilliantly inventive and skilful with words but also – so rare these days – a real gentleman, smartly dressed at all times, well-mannered and always cooperative. Why, Mrs Ikeda had been able to call on him for help and advice at *any* time, even late at night, if she had something to discuss. Yes, she was going to miss Mr Cathcart. She had really relied on him, and for so long too. What was it now? Nearly ten years? No, he hadn't returned to America. He was dead. Apparently he had had a heart attack at the age of 51 and that was it. Gone forever. Who could she find to replace him? For a moment I thought Mrs Ikeda was going to shed a few tears. She certainly sniffed a bit. But almost at once she felt better and began to speak once more of the bright future awaiting me if Hi-Life Advertising found my abilities up to scratch. Personally I was more concerned to know what kind of pressure Mr Cathcart had been under, and whether it was the demands of Hi-Life Advertising that had sent him to his early grave.

Despite Mrs Ikeda's hype, her company was primarily a production farm doing relatively unimportant jobs subcontracted from bigger agencies which then trebled the price before passing them off to the clients as the work of their own high-priced creative departments. Hi-Life Advertising took on video scripts, product brochures, company chairmen's speeches, exhibition panels, city guides, golf club promotions, corporate slogans, calendar blurbs, press releases, hotel pamphlets – anything and everything that came their way. In addition, through some old family connection, Mrs Ikeda was in cahoots with the president of a cosmetics company through which she also ran a profitable sideline publishing and selling glossy picture books about the natural way to health and beauty.

It soon became clear that what Hi-Life Advertising needed was not a copywriter but a rewriter, since virtually all their work arrived in the form of bad translations from Japanese.

These would then be given to a writer to be recast in comprehensible English. How difficult each job was depended partly on the subject – some were straightforward, while others, particularly the speeches, were pure gobbledegook – and partly on the translator, whose ability might be anywhere on the scale between excellent and hopeless. A good translation of something factual and specific, like a press release about the launch of a new line in outboard motors, might only need a little touching up here and there – sentences changed to include a few verbs instead of the dreary abstract nouns, or the judicious substitution of more interesting adjectives for such frequently-used formulations as 'user-friendly,' 'high-quality' and 'leisure-oriented.' But a badly-translated address to a group of American college students by the personnel manager of a real estate empire, already weak on content and riddled with platitudes in the original, demanded a much more robust approach. Such jobs had to be treated as a baker treats dough: they required prolonged and energetic kneading to remove the nonsense about the bright future awaiting humanity in the 21st century and the company's commitment to the promotion of harmony among all the countries of the world, and then the addition of entirely new ingredients which would give the listeners at least the illusion of having something to chew on.

One day, Mrs Ikeda asked me to rewrite a video script about the construction of a new shopping mall in a Tokyo suburb. The prologue, complete with helpful alternatives provided in places where the translator was unsure of the intended nuance, read as follows:

LIFE ZONE OF BEAUTY AND LOVE
THE OGAWA STATION MALL

The world and the environment changes momentarily through an encounter beyond the race and the culture. Emotion (impression?), development and creation are all born of an encounter.

Encounters of a person and a person, and of a culture and a culture . . .

And new sense of value that is born there.

A stage (arena?) of such better encounters for the life space of people . . .

With all such a wish, a new base (strategic point?) has come into the world.

What all that baloney meant was: 'this new mall is a good place for people to go shopping and meet each other.' But whereas an English scriptwriter is expected to stick rigorously to the point – otherwise the audience will go to sleep on him – his Japanese counterpart likes to paint in broad strokes on a big canvas, preferably of galactic dimensions. This conceptual difference is evident throughout Japanese advertising, where even mundane products like shoe polish or canned coffee are declared to be the fruit of years of careful research by dedicated scientists who only live for the joy of creating new products which will raise the material and spiritual standard of living for every human being on the face of the planet as we move boldly forward to meet the challenges of the 21st century.

An important reason why this unctuous tone is so resistant to change is that there is no word for 'cliche' in Japanese, nor any understanding of what it means. Repetition of the same trite ideas in the same words, over and over again, is not considered boring or irritating or false: on the contrary, it is reassuring. And the more it is repeated, the more reassuring it becomes. This state of compulsory no-think is implanted by Japan's schools, where repetition and rote learning are used to load pupils with packaged reactions and viewpoints, just as a computer is loaded with software. Repetition is good, because its consequences are predictable. Independent thought is not good, because it might lead anywhere. The resulting lack of ability to form an opinion or make a critical judgment is touted as a national benefit, a shared commitment to social harmony, a built-in disinclination to rock the boat. Far from regretting it, many Japanese still regard it as a sign of their country's uniqueness and cultural superiority. Naturally, this view is encouraged by commercial companies, which prefer uncritical customers who can easily be manipulated with simple slogans. The problem comes when they want to use the same approach when advertising in foreign markets. It makes no difference whether the company makes cars, cameras, computers or cosmetics. If the decision about what to say to overseas customers is concocted by Japanese people in Japan, it will always be some version of one of their stock formulas: enriching human life, contributing to the welfare of the global community, building a better future with communications technology, bringing a smile to the faces of children in every corner of the world, and so on.

Even so, some clients can still be made to understand that a foreign audience is likely to perceive such concepts as lies. It's not easy, but it can be done, provided extreme tact is used. But as often as not, the story doesn't end there. The decision to avoid fake, domestic-use concepts may be overruled by someone further up the corporate tree. Or some well-meaning section manager, relying on the English he thinks he remembers learning at school, may insert a few last-minute changes before the text is sent to the printer. Many people wonder why even world-famous Japanese companies go on producing funny-sounding texts which no native speaker could have written. The reason is simple – that's the way they talk to their markets at home. And that's why it's going to continue.

5 | Temple Gates

DURING THE FIRST few weeks, our forays around the immediate neighbourhood had convinced us that everything in it was either a private house, a shop or a vegetable field. There were no places of interest, nor much that could be thought of as typical of traditional Japan. But we persevered with exploring in all directions on foot and thus one day came by chance upon the local Shinto shrine, which was set in a grove of tall old trees on the side of a low hill. At its entrance stood a big stone *torii*, the gateway that symbolizes the division between the sacred and secular worlds, and beyond that a stone-flagged pathway with gravel borders led through a little garden to the steps of the shrine itself. As well as several towering cedars, the garden contained a fine old stone lantern, as massive and roughly cut as a prehistoric dolmen, and several azalea bushes, all enclosed by a low fence of bamboo stems lashed together with rope. There was also a short, rectangular stone obelisk, with the three wise monkeys – See No Evil, Speak No Evil and Hear No Evil – carved in relief on three of its faces. Beside this was an old stone trough into which water trickled steadily from a bamboo pipe set at an angle above it. On the lip of the trough lay six small aluminium ladles with slim wooden handles, with which visitors could help themselves to a mouthful of water (an act of ritual purification) before approaching the shrine. On the other side of the path there was a shallow pool of clear water surrounded by black, deeply-pitted boulders of volcanic rock. On the gravel bottom could be seen dozens of low-denomination coins which worshippers had cast into the water as offerings. The surface of the water was scattered with different coloured leaves which had fallen from the overhanging trees and bushes, and shoals of grey, orange and white carp swam lazily among the clumps of green and tawny yellow weed.

Beyond the pool, the path stopped at the foot of a flight of steps flanked by two more stone lanterns, one on each side. Performing the same gateway function at the top of these steps were two 'lion dogs' sculpted in stone. These ubiquitous shrine guardians are thought to be Taoist in origin and represent the *yin-yang* duality: the mouth of the passive female is closed, that of the active male open. Beside the two dogs stood a pair of ancient gingko trees whose yellow, fan-shaped leaves had mostly fallen from the branches and been blown by the wind into random heaps around a wide, open courtyard. On one side of the courtyard was a simple hut with a banner hung just below the eaves: on it was inscribed 'Boy Scout of Nippon Yokohama District Troop 49 Headquarters.' On the other side was the priest's house and a children's playground, with a swing, a slide and a climbing frame painted in bright colours. For anyone used to the idea of sacred precincts being occupied by a graveyard and requiring visitors to display a stiff, solemn demeanour, the cheerful informality of a Shinto shrine comes as a welcome surprise. Many have children's play equipment set up in their grounds, even in the centres of large cities.

The shrine itself was a compact, solid structure made of cedar weathered to a greyish-brown colour by long exposure to sun and rain. A flight of wooden steps led up to a platform where the double doors were usually firmly closed: bending down to look below the platform, we could see that the building was supported by pillars arranged in a simple

geometrical pattern of verticals and horizontals, with the foot
of each upright set on a small block of black-flecked marble. In
one corner, a few of these marble blocks had been replaced by
more recent concrete ones and some of the timbers had been
renewed as well, presumably because of earthquake damage.
Just below the lip of the roof were two carvings in relief – one
of a dragon with a long, flaming tail coiled around it and the
other of a magic bird that looked like a pheasant, apparently
drifting among clouds. From an iron retaining ring beside these
carvings were suspended a battered sphere of copper about
the size of a melon, containing some stones and gravel, and a
thick, grubby white silken rope hanging down to the level of
the platform, with two foot-long sections bound respectively
with red cloth and a sleeve of faintly tarnished brass. Behind
the rope stood the shrine's *saisen-bako*, a large wooden chest
with slats across the top which allowed coins to be thrown
inside but not retrieved. The manner of prayer was breezy and
upbeat. You began by mounting the steps to the platform and
casting a small coin into the wooden chest, after which you
took hold of the rope and gave it a vigorous shake, which
made the stone-filled sphere at the top sway slightly and emit
a hoarse, sluggish rattle. Then you took a step backwards,
clapped loudly twice, to attract the attention of the deity
within, bowed and silently said whatever you had to say.
That was all.

Half a mile away stood the local Buddhist temple, which
we found more easily since it was close to the shops. The
temple differed from the shrine in a number of ways. It stood
inside a compound surrounded by a thick, cream-painted
wall about two meters high and capped with heavy grey tiles.
Next door was a stone-walled graveyard containing dozens
of closely-packed tombstones, many with vases of flowers
in front of them and special racks to hold long, slim, flat
wooden memorial tablets, each inscribed with the name of a
deceased relative of the family to which that grave belonged.
A few of the tombstones were older and grander than the rest,
gigantic slabs of granite with names of families cut deeply into
their polished surfaces. You entered the compound through
heavy double doors of wood which hung on thick iron hinges

and were kept open during the day by rocks jammed against their foot. Here also, a path made of beige-coloured stone flags led across a gravelled area, past trees and bushes, a tall pagoda-like structure with some symbolic significance and a line of statues, six Jizo (Buddhist deities) wearing gentle, beatific smiles and cherry-red bibs around their necks and clasping strings of tiny stone beads in their neatly-carved fingers. The temple was not only a good deal bigger than the Shinto shrine, but also more elegant and beautiful. A wide flight of steps led up to open doors through which could be seen a large room on whose tatami-mat floor lay a pale blue carpet with fluffy fringes and a pattern picked out in white and green. There was abundant gold leaf, not only on the altar, where it had been used for the statue of a seated Buddha, several candlesticks and two larger-than-life lotus plants, but also in the light fittings, inlay on the furniture and decorations on the huge old wooden beams. There were several low tables, a tray stacked with teacups and a packed bookcase: this was where the priest conducted services and ceremonies and no doubt regaled his flock with improving sermons.

One other feature, outside in the compound, was a massive bell made of bronze, which hung inside its own little open-walled wooden shelter on a high stone platform. Opposite one side of the bell and parallel to the ground, a heavy log of wood was slung from the roof with ropes. By hauling on the ropes, you could swing the log backwards and forwards until it gathered maximum momentum and crashed into the bell with a massive, hollow reverberating boom. The children loved it. And while we were there one day, taking it in turns to beat on the bell and no doubt disturbing everyone for miles around, a man came out of the temple, scurried down the steps and hurried eagerly towards us with a friendly smile of welcome on his face.

His name, he said, was Hasegawa. He was the owner of a fish-processing plant close by, in fact just on the other side of the graveyard. And since he could speak a little English, he had thought . . . that is to say, if we didn't mind . . . that he might come over and make himself known to us.

Mr Hasegawa was a small, slight man with a flat, moon-like face, black-rimmed spectacles and a thin moustache. He had a slight stoop, which made him seem older than the fifty-seven years to which he admitted, and he had an engaging way of opening his eyes wide and smiling broadly in response to any remark at all. In his youth he had spent a year in the USA, attending the University of Kansas, and this experience, whose every detail he had rehearsed over and over again to his acquaintances, had established him as the local expert in the mysterious ways of foreigners. Trying hard not to appear too nosey, he sought a full account of what we were doing in the neighbourhood, how long we had been there, what school the children attended, what I did for a living and exactly where we lived. When I had finished telling him everything, he nodded enthusiastically and said how much he hoped we would be happy living in the area.

'By the way,' he said, 'do you know Hee-ru-ding-u?'

He had already asked if I knew 'go-ru-hing-u', hunching his shoulders over an imaginary putter by way of illustration, so I wondered if this was some other kind of sport.

'No, no, Hee-ru-ding-u. HEE-RU-DING-U. He is American. He lives here.'

This was interesting news. I hadn't seen a single foreigner in the area since the day we moved in.

'No,' I said, 'I don't know him. Does he work around here? Where exactly does he live?'

Mr Hasegawa explained where Hee-ru-ding-u lived, but I didn't know the streets well enough to follow his directions. Apparently Hee-ru-ding-u was a teacher of English conversation. Mr Hasegawa took a crumpled notebook out of his pocket, wrote down his own phone number and that of Hee-ru-ding-u and then tore out the page and handed it to me. Then I had to write my address and phone number for him. 'I call you sometime,' he said, 'and we go out together. And you call Hee-ru-ding-u, too. He is good man. My friend. He be your friend too.'

This seemed worth following up. I had spent so much time slogging round Tokyo that I had done nothing to cultivate social contacts close to home. That evening I telephoned to

Hee-ru-ding-u but he was out. His wife took my number and said he would call back when he got in. It was midnight when the phone rang, but Dennis Fielding – universally known by his unpronounceable surname – was for getting together immediately. I walked up to a corner of the local park, where he picked me up in his car and took me back to his house to drink Scotch. Apparently he had only been in the area a few months himself, and had been teaching at an English conversation school which he had set up with a previous wife, from whom he was now divorced.

Fielding's story was a complicated one, and it took several weeks and a lot of patient jigsaw work to put it together. He was born in Utah and brought up in circumstances of spectacular deprivation – both parents permanently drunk and in and out of trouble with the law over petty crimes. During his schooldays, his mother died and the father married again. Home life then became even worse than before. As soon as he was old enough, Fielding joined the US Navy and sailed away on an aircraft carrier. For a few months he steamed around from one Pacific base to another, and was then sent to do his year in Vietnam. In Saigon, they gave him a desk job, typing out forms, permits, shore leaves and ID cards for other navy personnel.

After his year was up, he did something that I had never heard of any other discharged American serviceman doing: he stayed on to live in Saigon as a civilian. The war was raging around him, but Saigon was cheap and since he had nothing to go home for, he couldn't see any reason to leave. Somewhere along the line he got married to a Vietnamese girl and had a son, but never adapted to the idea of being a husband and a father. Instead he teamed up with a partner who was still in the Navy, and they concocted a plan to fake up some ID cards, get some dud chequebooks and do a little shopping in Japan. They made half a dozen trips, visiting the various US military bases, buying goods with bad cheques and then reselling them to other servicemen in Vietnam. Eventually, they got caught. Fielding was sent to the civilian prison in Saigon, while the authorities tried to figure out whose jurisdiction he came under. Four months later, they came to the conclusion he was America's problem, not theirs. Somehow he persuaded the tribunal not to deport him to California, but to Hawaii, where he served a further brief term in prison. After his release he did what all self-respecting layabouts at the time were doing: he went on welfare. He also began to apply his knowledge of cars (his father was a car body man) to gaining a little extra income, making a few bucks here and there scrapping wrecks and dealing in secondhand tyres, spare carburetors and bent stereos.

What happened next was quite unexpected: a Japanese girl from a very wealthy family fell in love with him. Fielding didn't reciprocate her feelings, but went along with it anyway. Sachiko was pretty, vain and self-centred but she had other qualities that Fielding lacked: she was quick-witted, intelligent, energetic and ambitious. And rich? She was more than rich. Her family absolutely stank with money. The father was a doctor, the mother a property owner and they had only the one child on whom to lavish their generosity. Under the circumstances, it didn't take Fielding long to come to the conclusion that he might have been wrong in his original judgment and that this might very well be True Love after all. He and Sachiko got married. She worked in Hawaii as a tour guide for Japanese visitors and made a small fortune on the side by selling them shell necklaces and other souvenirs at way over the normal price. The pair of them enjoyed playing at being rich in Hawaii, dressing well and driving about in a Cadillac convertible. After a while, the parents gave them money to put down as a deposit on a house. And so life went on – sunshine, seaside, and no tomorrow in sight.

They stayed on Hawaii for seven years, at the end of which time Sachiko was pregnant. This, Fielding admitted, was something of a miracle because his wife was one of those girls who considers herself a born businesswoman, with no interest in having babies and not even very much, except for the initial burst of enthusiasm, in trying. But of course Fielding could overlook that, since there were other girls around to amuse himself with, and also because he himself knew nothing about business and was no good at making money. With any luck, he thought, this problem had been solved: here was a promising chance of being kept for life. But when Sachiko found out she was going to have a baby, she decided to go back to Japan, where she would be closer to her parents' care. So they sold the house and set off. Naturally the parents fixed them up with a nice apartment in an expensive part of Tokyo. Fielding bought a motorbike, played guitar with various friends and drank beer. For appearances' sake, he attended a college course in Japanese and did a little English teaching on the side.

Then Sachiko's father had a bright idea: he would bankroll them to start an English conversation school of their own. Fielding would be the head teacher, while Sachiko would run the show. As it turned out, she did have a good head for business: the school opened branches in half a dozen places and the money was soon rattling in. Their private life, however, was showing serious cracks. Fielding was more and more drunk, more and more unfaithful and less and less inclined to take the school seriously. He was well pleased with his new son, but that wasn't enough to keep him at home. Eventually he and Sachiko got divorced, but without too much rancour, and of course they stayed in touch because of the child. Fielding spent the next year or so drifting around in Tokyo, eventually winding up in the arms of a home-loving, taciturn, rather plain girl called Kiko, who was in every way the opposite of the not-much-lamented Sachiko. Lonely and bored, he was ripe for the drop when Kiko declared everlasting love, adding that she didn't care what he did, even if he had other women or whatever – she just wanted to marry him. It sounded like a good deal, so Fielding accompanied her down to the local ward office and signed up for marriage number three.

Round about the same time, Sachiko opened a new branch of the English-teaching business in Yokohama and offered Fielding the job of being its senior teacher. He and Kiko lived for a while in a room at the school, then found a spacious, inexpensive house nearby and moved in. Kiko then got pregnant.

What happened next was never clearly explained, probably because Fielding never really understood it himself. In essence, Sachiko the Business Genius concocted some new scheme to get even richer than before and to finance it, borrowed a large sum from a loan-sharking company run by gangsters. She guaranteed the loan by faking a document that purported to put her parents' property in Tokyo up as collateral. The scheme collapsed and the gangsters came looking for their money. They then found that the guarantee was a fake and that the parents' property was in any case already mortgaged with a bank and that they therefore had no hope of recovering their loan. Disappointed Japanese gangsters are well known for being difficult to deal with, so Sachiko and her parents took the only course open to them: they hastily gathered up any valuables they could lay their hands on and fled to America. Fielding was left with no job, a pregnant wife whom he was already getting tired of and – for the first time in years – no Sachiko-money to fall back on. From now on he would have to survive by his own efforts. And it was within a few short weeks of these events that Mr Hasegawa, who had been attending Fielding's school to keep his English conversation up to scratch, gave me the phone number of his favourite teacher.

Not that Hasegawa had any real interest in speaking better English. His intention in joining the school had been to cultivate the acquaintance of some English-speaking foreigners with whom he could share his main social activities, which were drinking and karaoke. I had already found out for myself that there were only two types of establishment in the neighbourhood where people could go out at night: karaoke bars and restaurants. Many of the restaurants had karaoke machines too, but Hasegawa mostly stuck to the bars. They were all pretty much the same – small, smoky, dimly-lit places with velvet upholstery, run by more or less voluptuous mama-sans, as motherly as their title implied, assisted by two or three young or not-so-young women in evening gowns who prepared drinks at the bar, flitted around serving snacks, programmed the karaoke machine to play the customers' selections and sang along with them if they liked to be accompanied, or just sat at crowded tables and tried to be interested in conversational gambits they had already heard a thousand times before.

All these bars were either owned or controlled by one or other of the major booze companies, from which all drinks sold on the premises had to be obtained. It was therefore quite normal to enter a bar and find that it was displaying as many as 100 bottles of whisky on its shelves, all of the same brand. These bottles were the property of regular customers, whose names were written on them in felt-tip pen: when those customers dropped by, their drinks would be made from the contents of their own bottles, which would then be replaced on the shelf until their next visit. Thus they could go out drinking and pay only a cover charge for each session until the bottle was empty, at which point they bought another, for about three times the price in the shops. This system, called 'bottle-keep,' was popular with the salarymen who made up the bulk of the bars' clientele because it allowed payment to be deferred, a convenient arrangement for people whose pocket money was doled out at infrequent intervals by their purse-holding, account-keeping wives.

The drawback was that each bar sold only one brand of whisky and one brand of beer, apart from which there might well be little or nothing else available. Furthermore, whisky was served the same way in every place: a tumbler was filled to the brim with seven or eight ice cubes, a little whisky was dribbled in on top, the tumbler was topped up with mineral water and the thin, almost tasteless mixture was vigorously stirred. I never saw it served any other way, and never saw any customer ask for anything different. *Sake* was rarely drunk in karaoke bars, apparently because it would have seemed too unsophisticated for the surroundings. I myself preferred to stick to beer, but if politeness required me to accept whisky, I would always ask for it straight, with no ice. This was so unusual that the news would spread round the bar in an instant: customers would get up from their seats, come over in turn to inspect my glass and exclaim with astonishment. Was that how people in England drank their whisky? Sometimes, I would answer – it depends on their preference. They can drink it any way they like. This was even more remarkable. You mean they don't all drink it the same way?

Hasegawa had a passion for karaoke bars, and was especially pleased when Fielding or I accompanied him because the local scarcity of foreigners inevitably focused an unnatural amount of attention on our table. Hasegawa had local political ambitions – he had stood in the district's mayoral election the previous year and lost, much to the amusement of his friends – but undiscouraged, continued to campaign for some future opportunity by eagerly seeking out any situation that could help to put him in the public spotlight. He had a special fondness for jokes in the form of stories, which are much less common in Japan than repartee and one-liners, and never tired of getting me to repeat one I had told him about a Mercedes and a Mini in dispute over a parking space in London. Spotting its availability, the Mini driver managed to slip in ahead of the slower-manoeuvring Mercedes, and then said cheekily to the latter's driver 'That's what you can do if you have a small, nippy car.' Irritated, the Mercedes driver backed up and then drove hard into the side of the Mini, damaging it severely. 'That's what you can do if you have a big, heavy car,' he said as he drove away.

It wasn't a particularly funny story, but once Hasegawa had 'got' it, he wanted it to be told in every bar, sometimes twice if a new group of friends arrived too late to catch the first performance, or if he decided he could use it as an introductory card to some other circle of people he felt like getting to know. He would rise from his seat like a master of ceremonies, clap his hands for silence and announce 'Joke! Joke!' before stepping back and gesturing to me that I had the stage to deliver my masterpiece. The announcement that a joke was coming up was indispensable, because otherwise the straightfaced delivery of everything up to the punchline would wrongfoot the audience completely, leaving them mentally unprepared for a tale of disaster. The joke was always successful and never had to be replaced with another.

The other important ingredient of trips to these bars was the singing. Customers made their selections from a glossy catalogue in which hundreds of songs were listed, three closely-printed columns to a page, and then handed the bar staff a piece of paper on which they had written the corresponding code number. This went to the bottom of the waiting pile, as the selections were played in the order they were requested. Some of the songs were current or classic pop, but most were either *enka*, a category of emotional ballads whose rendition is an art in itself, or regional folk songs. With singing taught as an academic subject from the very beginning of every school career, and practised both for pleasure and as a bonding agent in every group activity from New Year parties to company bus trips, most Japanese have a prodigious knowledge of folk songs. Each area of the country is known to people elsewhere by two characteristics, its local food and its local songs, and I was constantly impressed by the ease with which obscure towns, distant mountains, regional accents and dialect words, historical references and literary allusions from far away were instantly recognised by people who were not only drunk but rarely left suburban Yokohama.

The songbooks also contained a short section of English and American titles, from which I was repeatedly asked to make a choice. At first I declined, palming my turn off on Fielding, but after a while he succeeded in convincing me that my refusals were causing more than just disappointment. 'You don't want to sing because you're afraid of being embarrassed,' he told me. 'You think you're no good at singing, and you're probably right. But look around you. Everyone else is lousy at singing too.' It wasn't quite true. Several were quite good, or could at least manage to keep time and stay in tune. But many more, equally enthusiastic performers, were dreadful, croaking like frogs, hitting false notes, uttering horrible quavering sounds or just mumbling incoherently into the microphone. 'Don't you see,' he went on, 'that singing – being good at singing – doesn't have anything to do with it. They don't want you to sing because they think you'll be good, and certainly not to embarrass you. They just want you to join in, that's all, to do what everyone else does. I guarantee, if you sing you'll bring the house down, no matter how lousy you are.'

Everything he said was right. I sang. I was lousy. And I brought the house down. A low platform was provided for the singer, who faced out towards the audience. On a stand in front of him, at chest height, was a TV monitor which played a video to accompany each song, displaying the words across the bottom of the screen. To help the singer keep the right place in the song, the words changed colour, one by one, at the moment when they were supposed to be sung. I started off with an easy one, 'Yesterday,' which was accompanied by a video of a stunningly beautiful naked girl undulating around on a bed covered with blue satin sheets. From there I progressed to 'The Green Green Grass Of Home,' illustrated by footage of a crumbling log cabin and cherry trees coming into bud somewhere in rural America. And after a few false starts, I managed to extend my repertoire to include 'Mary Jane,' an extremely simple rock song with an energetic guitar solo in the middle, which featured a misty-eyed girl on a beach, a driftwood fire and various other romantic ingredients. But I couldn't be persuaded to attempt 'Love Letters In The Sand,' nor yet 'The Tennessee Waltz.' Not that they were the worst options. For the ultimate in simplicity in English, 'Happy Birthday To You' was available, while at rock bottom there was 'Chibi Maruko-chan', the theme song of a popular children's cartoon on TV. Young female customers liked singing it in baby voices.

If my performances won loud applause and cries of encouragement between verses, they were nothing compared to Fielding's. As well as previous stage experience, which showed itself in a whole array of theatrical poses and gestures, he had a rich, powerful voice that never strayed out of tune and could also sing several songs in Japanese. Hasegawa showed him off like a performing bear, taking special pleasure in having him sing in front of audiences which had never seen him before. As he walked up to the platform and took the microphone, the voices of people telling each other that a *gaijin* was next up could be heard above the general buzz of conversation; but after the first few phrases, the grins and smirks disappeared and they listened to him with rapt attention, eyes goggling and mouths gaping open. Fielding's favourite gambit was to gather the bar's unsuspecting mama-san in his arms as she walked by and clasp her tightly while murmuring a sugary love ballad in her ear. As this was one step further than any of the regular customers would have dared to go, it was always wildly popular.

6 | All Together Now

FIELDING AND KIKO lived in an old, six-roomed wooden house which backed on to a copse of stringy trees, many half-strangled by ivy. They had a modest patch of garden in front, large enough to sit out in when the weather was warm, and a few trees including two dwarf maples whose leaves now glowed a rich, deep red and a tall dogwood that appeared to be dying, although they said it still produced a fine display of feathery green foliage and soft pink flowers in the spring. In addition, there was a small rectangle of concrete on which they parked their battered Suzuki hatchback. Our two households began to see a good deal of each other. Sometimes at weekends we would get together to have a barbecue or play music while the children amused themselves with Fielding's one-year-old daughter or else settled down to watch one of the vast collection of videos which he had acquired as tax-deductible teaching aids for the English school. Occasionally we went to play tennis in the park, but even if we managed to get the one court with a net, our good intentions always degenerated rapidly into farce. For one thing, the surface of the court was hopelessly uneven, so that the balls darted unpredictably this way and that if we were incautious enough to let them bounce. For another, Fielding, who claimed to have taken a course in tennis at the University of Hawaii, was even more of a duffer than I was. Somehow the pinpoint serves, delicate drop volleys and looping topspin lobs with which I seemed to remember baffling my schoolmates had vanished with the years, while if Fielding had ever learned any techniques at the University of Hawaii he must have forgotten them by the next day; so that all our games amounted to was a lot of huffing and puffing interrupted by frequent breaks for beer.

But Fielding's gregarious nature provided a door through which we began to acquire new friends and enter into the life of the community. One of his suggestions, spun off from a remark of Hasegawa's, was that we should volunteer our two families to join a group of local residents and spend part of one Sunday morning patrolling the local streets in search of garbage. It was one of those well-intentioned ideas that look good from an armchair at a distance of a few days. The children would learn at first hand about participation in community projects. And they would see that their Mums and Dads were not afraid to get their own hands dirty.

At nine o'clock on the appointed day, we all mustered in the park. There were about 300 volunteers, at a rough count: children accounted for more than half of the total, followed by mothers, followed by about 30 or 40 fathers, several with visible hangovers. When the organisers showed up, they divided us into four teams and issued us with several strong brown paper bags, one push cart per team and a few brooms. Then each team set off behind a leader who carried a placard on which was written 'Yokohama Volunteer Group.'

I had imagined that our team would head for its assigned area and then split up into small bands and comb the streets separately. But it wasn't so easy. That arrangement would have produced a lot of sub-teams, and each of those would have had to have its own leader, responsible for deciding who should do what and where. Far too complicated to arrange without a series of preliminary meetings to establish the ground rules. So instead, we all worked the same street at the same time, proceeding in crocodile formation. As a result, the people at the front picked up whatever garbage there was to be found, while those at the back struggled along with almost-empty sacks.

In fact the sacks at the front were almost empty too, thanks to the efficiency of the regular garbage collection system. Three times a week, all the local residents sorted their trash into black plastic bags and stacked them at the nearest collection point, which was usually only a few yards away from their front doors. During the day, the municipal garbage service would come around, stop at each collection point and heave the bags into little trucks where they would be crushed by a machine. The few small scraps of refuse inevitably left behind by this operation would then be swept up by individual housewives who did the job in rotation, passing a municipal broom on to their next door neighbour when their turn was finished. Since this process was done so frequently, the streets were normally spick and span.

So what was our crocodile picking up? Well, cigarette ends of course, and wrappers from candy packets, mostly as fresh as yesterday, a few soft drink cans dropped on the verges and lots of ring-pulls, some of which had lain in the road for weeks, where the wheels of passing cars had flattened them so completely into the tarmac that they left a clear impression when we prised them off. Apart from that, there simply wasn't very much garbage to be found. And with everyone doing the same street, the workload was hardly arduous. Nevertheless, diligence paid off: even though I had taken up a position at the back of the crocodile, I still managed to find a few dog-ends and ring-pulls which had been passed unnoticed by those ahead of me. Not that everyone displayed equal zeal for the job. One middle-aged man in spotless white shirt and neatly-creased dark blue slacks, who had evidently just come along for something to do, engaged Reiko in conversation and plied her with the usual series of questions: what nationality she was (Thai? Malaysian?), how long we had been in Japan, whether the children spoke Japanese, what school they went to, whether they could eat Japanese food, whether we slept on beds or on the floor and so on. His interest in garbage, collected or not, was zero.

The same applied to the various children, who just dragged along behind their parents, looking vaguely to left and right but occasionally pouncing on tiny, pathetic shreds of paper that had once been part of a cigarette butt, or slivers of plastic blown from a homebound shopping basket. But the morale of the group as a whole was maintained at the requisite level by a man carrying a small portable cassette player from which there came, over and over again, a dreadful semi-martial song called 'Yokohama Ohayo' ('Good Morning Yokohama'). Every time the tape came to an end, the man rewound it and played it again. The volume was colossal, so that everyone in the neighbourhood who was relaxing at home, sleeping, reading the paper or otherwise enjoying their Sunday was made fully aware that in contrast to their contemptible selfishness, Some People At Least Had The Decency To Show A Proper Community Spirit And Go Around Doing Good.

Our procession kept walking, albeit very slowly, for just over an hour and a half, so that by the end, I calculated, we had walked a total of about three kilometers. Multiply by 300 volunteers, and you get the impressive total of 900 garbage-collecting kilometers. Did we amass the mountain of garbage that such a huge effort deserved? No, we didn't. Instead of filling a dozen large trucks, the total volume collected could have been comfortably accommodated in the back of an ordinary station wagon. The biggest waste in the whole exercise was one of effort, a fact that, on reflection, was no surprise at all: I had already noticed that it was the same in the commercial world, where although the average employee was required to put in unreasonably long hours, not much actual work got done. Instead there were daily group discussions of inter-departmental memos and interminable consensus-building meetings whose only real function was to rubber-stamp decisions already taken higher up the hierarchy. Here on our local streets, over-manning had the same effect as in an ordinary company: a low ratio of production to effort.

When we at last got back to the park, it was time for

a few short speeches from local dignitaries about the desirability of clean streets and the general value of community service. Then a small truck backed its way in through the park gates and a few people lent a hand to unload a *mikoshi*, or portable shrine, of the kind carried through the streets by crowds during festivals. This one had been specially made for a garbage-focused occasion out of discarded paper and cardboard, and then sprayed with gold and silver paint. Several of the smallest children eagerly rushed to form a procession and carry this object a couple of times around the park, in the appropriate festive manner. The man from whose truck it had been unloaded stopped to chat with me for a few minutes. Delving into a small sack which was dangling from his hand, he presented me with a cream-coloured baseball cap with the words 'Yokohama Volunteer Group' printed on it in small blue letters. Then someone else produced a wooden box whose lid and sides were cleverly made to unfold and convert into a tiny stage, on which a puppet show was given for the children. Finally, gifts were distributed to everyone who had taken part. The children received cans of drinks, packets of biscuits and the adults each got a box containing a small thermos flask. And then, garbage and social bonding duties completed, we all trooped obediently home.

*

Another of Fielding's sidekicks whom we came to know well was Mr Kimura, a man with sharp, intelligent features and a shock of black hair which stuck straight up from his skull like the bristles of a broom. Kimura was a welder and metalworker by trade: he rented a cramped yard a few miles away where he and a small team of employees worked to produce steel staircases for factories, balconies for apartment blocks and prefabricated sections of multi-storey car parks. On days when he wasn't working, Kimura went fishing or played golf. He was openly disappointed that I had little experience of either, but willingly offered to take us along on his next fishing trip. In the meantime, he invited us to take part in the forthcoming demolition of his house, planned for a few days hence.

Kimura's house was a white, flat-roofed building, only about ten years old and still in excellent condition. Its pending destruction was a matter for regret, but out of Kimura's hands. The actual owner was his wife's mother, who allowed the Kimura family to live in it for a peppercorn rent. But she had another married daughter whose husband had no prospect of buying into Yokohama's fiendishly expensive property market, so she had decided to demolish the house and replace it with a new one which would contain two separate apartments, thus providing both families with homes of their own.

Fielding and I were to play the role of general labourers in the grand demolition, and when we turned up at 8 o'clock on the appointed morning, we found that things were already well under way. Kimura had assembled several friends who were all busy hacking at the house with sledgehammers and iron bars, heaping the wreckage into piles and then loading it onto the backs of two trucks that were plying back and forth between the site and the nearest municipal landfill. As the flesh of cement and lath-and-plaster was gouged from the house in ragged chunks and clouds of dust, the wooden skeleton emerged: much of it was flimsy, but there were also many excellent and reusable lengths of timber, including one massive main beam of cedar, 20 feet long and at least two feet square. I was horrified by the thought of all this timber being thrown into a landfill and buried or burnt, an attitude which caused Kimura much amusement. 'Our job today,' he told me, placing his hand on my shoulder and grinning into my face from close range, 'is to get this house down and leave a clean, flat site for the builders to start on. If you see anything you want, take it. Otherwise it's all going. There's no market for old bits of wood from a demolished house, you know,' he added. 'Who would buy them? And for that matter, who would have anywhere to keep them? This is Japan, not America.'

So after laying a few pieces aside to take home, with the vague idea of finding some use for them in the future, I gave up offering suggestions and pitched in with the rest. Nothing was saved but the roof tiles, which were carefully stacked to one side, and the larger plumbing fixtures – these, apparently, could be sold or re-used. Otherwise everything was destroyed: sheets of veneer torn from the walls, doors kicked off their hinges, wooden staircase smashed to bits, beams and pillars cut up with a chain saw, garden wall hammered into manageable chunks, shrubs and small trees ruthlessly chopped down and their roots grubbed out. There were frequent stops for beer, and Kimura's brother-in-law, who had hired a mechanical digger for the day, soon found he could operate it with a can in his hand – although for especially tricky manoeuvres he had to wedge the can between his knees. By the end of the day the job was done and Kimura estimated that he had saved about 60 per cent of what a demolition company would have charged him. That night we all went out to celebrate, starting with a huge tub of raw oysters in ice and ending up, inevitably, doing the rounds of the karaoke bars.

How many people, I wondered, would have not only tolerated the idea of their home being destroyed so that the site could be shared with another couple, but also have participated so willingly – even cheerfully – in the very act of destruction? It was true that, strictly speaking, Kimura couldn't do anything about it since he was not the owner of the property, but it would hardly have seemed unreasonable to me if he had resisted the plan and sought some other solution. But Kimura was a strong believer in the right of senior family members to make decisions, which the younger members had then to implement without asking questions. This, he declared, was a traditional Japanese characteristic. So if his mother-in-law wanted the house torn down and a new one built, there was nothing to argue about.

Kimura was born the second of three sons but had inherited the rights and obligations of family heir on the death of his older brother, a well-known alpinist who had been killed in a mountaineering accident. He wore a chunky, old-fashioned wristwatch which this brother had once given him, and spoke with reverence of his achievements, which included scaling peaks in the Himalayas, Europe and Africa, earning the friendship and respect of noted foreign climbers and having two routes named after him in the Japan Alps. Under normal circumstances, Kimura should have taken on the traditional duty of the eldest son and settled in the original family home to look after his father. He was in fact ready to do so at any time, but the father, a crusty old widower who had sold his small engineering business and retired, insisted on living alone in his dilapidated country home a couple of hours' drive down the coast. When the old man became incapable of managing alone any more, Kimura would move in and care for him, but in the meantime he found Yokohama more convenient for his business affairs.

He and his wife, who spent most of her time running a coffee shop near the local station, had two children: a somewhat taciturn teenage daughter who liked to retire to her bedroom with the portable phone and pass long hours in conversation with her friends, and an extremely fashion-conscious son of about 20, called Toshi, who supplemented his already extensive wardrobe by borrowing anything of his father's that took his fancy. Toshi was popular with girls, much to his parents' satisfaction, and his job in a computer company, Kimura believed, destined him for a more success-ful and sophisticated career than his father's.

*

Still another valuable introduction I obtained through Fielding was to a former student of his called Wada. Wada lived a short distance away on the Shonan coast in Kamakura, which had been the national capital in mediaeval times, from 1192 to 1333. With its many famous old temples, gardens and his-torical associations, Kamakura has the status and reputation of a subsidiary Kyoto, a museum town, a showcase of old Japan. Swarms of visitors come at all times of the year to wander around its tourist sites, attend its ancient festivals, sift through its curio shops and wander along its shady lanes and stone-paved alleys, peering over tile-capped walls at the secluded gardens and private mansions of its many wealthy inhabitants. Wada, who was married to the daughter of the head priest at one of the principal temples, liked nothing better than showing people around, and we went together to Hachiman-gu, a famous shrine to the tutelary god of the Minamoto, one of the clans that battled for supremacy in the Kamakura era, and also to the Daibutsu, the great bronze statue of Buddha on the western side of the town. This, he told me, was cast in 1252 and was originally housed in a large wooden hall: but in 1495 the hall was destroyed by a tidal wave, since when the Buddha has remained in the open. The technical term was *roza*, which Wada translated as 'seated amidst the dew.'

Wada also liked to talk about his work, and I was very much interested when he told me that his job was producing TV commercials. I described how my brief encounter with narration work had already brought me into his professional territory, and explained how eager I was to explore it further. Pleased by the coincidence, he willingly offered to give me some tips on how to proceed. To begin with, he assured me, there was no point in approaching film production companies directly. The procedure, which had no formal basis but was nevertheless commonly adhered to, was that when producers required the services of foreign models, narrators, singers, actors, jugglers or any other performers, they obtained them through the medium of so-called 'talent' agencies. There were several such agencies in Tokyo, but he himself only used two. Certainly he would give me their names, and an introduction.

The first one I went to see, bearing a cassette tape on which I had recorded demonstration samples of my voice, was called StarTalent and was managed, Wada told me, by a certain Mrs Kawaguchi. The office, at the top of three unlit flights of stairs in a grimy, ramshackle building in central Tokyo, contained a wizened old man hunched over a typewriter and a woman of about 50, presumably Mrs Kawaguchi, who was sorting through a large pile of black-and-white photographs. Speaking excellent English in the gruff tones of a long-time chain smoker, Mrs Kawaguchi received me affably, listened to my tape, made some appreciative remarks and then got me to fill in a printed registration form. When I had finished, she put on a pair of pink-framed spectacles and studied it carefully, grunting at intervals and asking once or twice for clarification of certain points in my answers, which she then corrected with a gold ballpoint pen.

'The only problem,' she said, laying the registration form down on the desk, leaning back in her chair and looking me slowly up and down, 'is that we don't get all that much demand for narrators. Most of our clients come to us for models. How do you feel about doing modelling work?'

'Modelling? Me?' I was astounded. My idea of a male model was a slim, handsome clothes horse in his mid-twenties. 'It's very kind of you to suggest it, but I don't see how I could. I have no experience. And aren't I a little too old?'

'Not in the least,' she replied, waving her hand dismissively. 'Look here, at these pictures.' She spread out some of the photographs she had been studying when I came in. Some were of young models, but there were also several of older people, both men and women, and some of children too. 'There's plenty of work for people in your age group,' she went on. 'You might be picked to be a businessman in a company brochure, a father in a family situation, a taxi driver, a member of a crowd in a poster . . . anything at all. We don't just handle fashion modelling you know,' she added a little severely. 'Nor even just photographic work. There are bit parts in TV shows, acting jobs in movies or commercials, all sorts of things.'

As I had never considered this kind of work in my life, it took a few moments for the idea to sink in. Modelling? Acting? Well – why not?

'Well,' I said, 'why not? I mean, thank you very much for the suggestion. If you think I might be able to get work, I'm willing.'

'Good, good.' Mrs Kawaguchi stood up and pushed her chair back abruptly. 'We'll need some photographs of course. We can take them here.'

There was a tall grey curtain behind her, which she drew aside to reveal a chair, some simple lighting equipment and a camera set up on a tripod.

'Look, there's a toilet over there, through that door. Go and comb your hair. And take that tie off while you're in there, and tie it again – neatly, please.'

The wizened old man, who had continued slowly pecking at his typewriter throughout this interview, now joined us to operate the camera while Mrs Kawaguchi stood to one side and gave directions.

'Do that one again – look more serious this time. That's better. Now turn your head the other way. No, the other way, towards the window. Right, now let's have one with a smile. A big smile. I want to see your teeth. All right, now stand up. That's right, unbutton the jacket. Relax! This isn't a wedding. Put one hand in your pocket. And your right foot forward a bit. You know, casual. Now look away from the camera. Not as far as that! Just slightly. Good, that'll do.'

We sat down at the desk again and Mrs Kawaguchi filled me out a model's form. Age, height, weight, chest measurement, waist, hips, inside leg, shoe size, hair colour, eye colour, special talents. Special talents? Well yes, because there's no limit to what clients may have in mind. Frequently they don't have anything much in mind at all, and may ask the talent agency for suggestions. So that if a model can play tennis, drive a forklift truck, swim under water, ride a skateboard, sing Swahili folk songs, strum a banjo, swing on the trapeze, perform the bellydance, suck a raw egg out of its shell or demonstrate any other oddball skill, that alone may be enough to secure a job.

'Thank you for coming in,' boomed Mrs Kawaguchi, vigorously pumping my hand as she showed me out of the door. 'We'll be in touch. And don't forget – give my regards to Wada-san!'

Buoyed up by what appeared to be the opening of a completely new line of work, I went straight round to see the other agency Wada had told me about. This one was the opposite of StarTalent in every way: it had a spacious, well-lit office whose picture windows looked out onto a small, neat garden, and was run by a softly-spoken, elegant man assisted by a thin, fragile-looking secretary with long straight hair and a pale complexion accentuated by her chilling choice of mauve lipstick. They handled a little modelling work, they said, but their main business was providing 'voice artists' for TV commercials, product videos, PR films and language-teaching tapes – which was why they had decided not only to name their company 'Speakers' but also to divide the males and females on their books into two categories called, horribly, 'Woofers' and 'Tweeters' respectively. The manager seemed a little stiff and formal, but pleased to meet me because, as he explained, he was getting more and more requests for British voices. Americans were still specified for something like 70 per cent of the narration work in Tokyo, he said, but the ratio was slowly changing. It depended on the target market. If the video was being made for North America, as most of them had been hitherto, they used an American. If the target was South-East Asia, or 'Oceania' (Australia plus all those specks on the map down there) or, increasingly, Europe, they tended to prefer a British voice. 'Don't expect too much too soon,' he told me. 'It will take some time to get your tape around and get your name known. But I'm sure we'll get something for you. Oh and by the way – get some good photographs taken of yourself and put them in the post to us. You never know, we might be able to get you some modelling work as well.'

7 | Pure Garbage

FIELDING'S ENGLISH SCHOOL closed down. In fact, it now transpired that it was not 'his' English school in any sense, nor ever had been. True, he had been hired as the senior teacher when it had opened, and had lived with Kiko on the premises for a few months, but after they found a house of their own to move into he had quickly begun to drift away from the school and anything else to do with his former wife. He had skipped classes, fallen out with other members of the staff and generally lost interest. And with Sachiko's abrupt departure for the United States, there was no-one to manage the administration, receive the students' fees, pay the wages or settle the rent. The landlord had therefore issued a notice to quit and taken down the signboard on the side of the building.

'It doesn't matter,' Fielding said. 'It wasn't much of a school anyway. I'll find another job. But there's a lot of stuff in there! We've got to get it out before someone else does.'

By 'a lot of stuff' he meant books, tapes, video machines, furniture, filing cabinets and all the rest of the school's paraphernalia. But when we went round that evening to appraise the contents, we found that other hands – possibly belonging to the other teachers, or maybe to the landlord – had already been rummaging around for what they could scavenge.

'Dammit! There were four good video players here, and four TV sets too!' said Fielding bitterly. 'Now there's only one of each. Well, never mind. It's my own fault. I should have thought of coming here sooner. But whatever we want, we've got to take it now. Someone's on to this place and tomorrow may be too late.'

It was a cold night with a keen, gusting wind and fierce little squalls of rain that lasted for twenty minutes, then stopped, then started again. Back and forth we went in Fielding's little Suzuki compact, carrying loads of books and tapes, stationery, telephones, crockery and carpets. The computers were gone and so were both typewriters, the gas cooker and the fridge from the kitchenette, the pictures off the walls and quite a lot of the furniture. What was left was mostly junk, but there was a sofa and a large leather chair that Fielding decided he could use. We lashed them onto the roof of the car with rope.

'Listen, if there's anything you want, just say so,' said Fielding. 'All this stuff is mine. Well, okay, my ex-wife's. But that gives me the right to take it. And if we don't, someone else will. This is our last chance. So go ahead. And let's not forget the light bulbs! We'll take them last.'

Our house was still seriously under-furnished, so I picked out a couple of tubular steel chairs, some cushions, a coffee pot, a bookcase and a small desk cabinet with shallow drawers. There was also a long, L-shaped reception counter, which gave me an idea.

'Look,' I said, 'this counter would make just the desk I need to work on. We can't take it the way it is, because it would never go up my stairs, even if the Suzuki could carry it. But if you help me get the top off, we can cut through it with a saw and take it in two sections. I can make the legs at home, out of the wood I saved from Kimura's old house.'

Obtaining the various household objects we needed was a considerable problem, since I still wasn't making enough money for the family to live on and our savings were still steadily draining away. There were two local secondhand shops which sometimes yielded useful items, although both were of more interest for the curios that crammed their shelves – old chests made of a light, durable wood called *keyaki* (pawlonia), various ceramics, several weathered stone Buddhas (probably stolen from rural temples), carvings of bears and fish from the northern island of Hokkaido, flower vases in a hundred different shapes, gleaming lacquered boxes, and on one occasion, a large, cumbersome wooden contraption with a funnel at the top and a cranking handle on the side, which turned out to be an ancient machine for threshing rice. But there was something furtive about both the secondhand shops. Both were run as 'side' businesses by women whose husbands had some other work. Their premises were shabby and cramped, and we rarely saw any other customers. It was as if people were somehow ashamed to be seen patronising them.

In fact, a much better selection of secondhand goods could be had for nothing by browsing through the neighbourhood garbage, or *gomi*. There was a specially designated 'Gomi Day' every month, on which local residents could put out on the street any household items which had been replaced or otherwise outlived their usefulness. These were piled up on specified street corners and taken away to be dumped by the city authorities. The range and quantity of what our neighbours discarded was simply staggering: everything was heaped higgledy-piggledy on top of everything else, and some of the piles stretched as much as 50 yards. There were bicycles, birdcages, tables, chairs, tools, clocks, school trophies, car tyres, paraffin heaters, electric fans, fishing rods, sewing machines, rice cookers, ornaments, 50cc scooters, toys, baby buggies, speakers and stereo equipment, electronic keyboards, tennis racquets, desks, skis, thermos flasks, broken air conditioners, faded carpets and unwanted umbrellas. Some of it, naturally, was plain junk, beyond any hope of repair or recovery, but plenty more was in or close to perfect working order. Fielding's house was almost entirely furnished with objects retrieved from the *gomi*, but he continued to conduct careful searches in the hope, often realised, of turning up even better editions of things he already possessed. In many cases, objects were discarded for reasons that were barely credible: Fielding had one enormous television set whose sole defect, when he found it, was that the on-off knob had come loose and fallen off. Who could have decided to buy a completely new TV when replacing the missing knob would have been so cheap and so easy? Come to that, who could have thrown away that full set of almost-new golf clubs? Or that expensive guitar, kept in pristine condition inside its leather case?

The answer was 'almost anyone.' Readers of the many chilling foreign press reports about Japan's famously astronomical cost of living could be forgiven for imagining that the wretched Japanese consumer has a hard time acquiring even the basic necessities of life, let alone the luxuries. Only a millionaire, surely, would dream of incurring unnecessary new expenses by throwing away anything that was still serviceable. But the number of *gomi* items still in good working order proved that their owners had got rid of them out of choice, not necessity. Every Gomi Day illustrated the phenomenal rate at which consumer goods are bought, used, discarded and replaced in Japan. Relatively high disposable incomes are not the only reason. Another is that the country's manufacturing base is so huge, and the quantity of goods produced is so enormous, that there is a correspondingly wide variety of price and quality in most product categories. Discount stores proliferate like mushrooms and many cheap items can be bought from open stalls on the streets. Some manufactured goods are priced at absurdly high levels – cameras are particularly notorious, with identical models often retailing in Japan for twice or even three times as much as on overseas markets – while others, such as clothes, shoes and cars, can easily be found for less money than in other industrialised countries where real wages are lower.

At the top end of the scale, like anywhere else, the much-vaunted attribute of 'quality' maintains prices at an astronomical level, and there is a large pool of wealthy consumers to keep them that way: but at the bottom, sheer volume guarantees wide choice at low cost. It stands to reason that this should be so: any economy with a massive input of new products at one end must have a correspondingly massive discharge of discarded goods at the other. Allowing for differences in content, the same is true of the secondhand market in America, and for the same reason.

During the first two months we were in Japan, the *gomi* provided us with a fridge, washing machine, a complete stereo system, an answering machine, three electric fans (which we would need during the hot days of summer), an electric oven, an extra paraffin heater and two TV sets. Everything was in perfect working order except for one of the TVs, which had something wrong with its picture reception. The red end of the spectrum was all washed out. But fixing it was a simple matter of replacing the defective circuit board. Our friend with the electric appliance shop did the job in ten minutes, and when I made him the first gin-and-tonic of his life – and then the second – he was so pleased that he waived the service charge.

The realisation that objects discarded by other people were considered to have no value opened up other opportunities as well. Down on the main road, close to the shopping centre, was a place that sold and repaired bicycles and small motorbikes. Out at the back were a dozen or so rusted wrecks leaned together in a pile, waiting for the next visit from the scrapyard truck. Except that . . . just a moment here . . . one of them didn't look all that badly wrecked. It was a black Honda 125, and when I inspected it more closely, I couldn't find anything to justify junking it. It was the brakes, the shopowner told me. They needed a complete overhaul. And he was going to scrap the bike just for that? Well, yes, because it was several years old: no-one wanted that kind of bike nowadays. But did it start, I wanted to know. Certainly it did. With the electric starter or with the kickstart. He demonstrated both. And how much would it cost me to buy it and have the brakes fixed? A pittance. A couple of hours later, the necessary repairs had been done and I was mobile.

During the course of our explorations around the neighbourhood I had more than once passed by a junkyard with the lofty title 'Recycle University', where old industrial machinery, water tanks, air conditioners, washing machines and other metal objects, including dozens of motorcycles, were dismantled for spare parts or cut up and melted down for scrap. Here I found another example of the same Honda model, which yielded a front mudguard that still had nearly all its chrome, a set of crashbars, a back tyre with plenty of tread and a luggage rack.

In one corner of Recycle University's yard, obviously newly delivered, were four white police motorcycles. I examined them to see if any components could be rescued, but the owner strode quickly over and told me not to touch them. It was against the law for him to sell any of the parts. This rule had been introduced in the wake of a robbery which had occurred some twenty years ago in a Tokyo suburb called Fuchu. The robber, working alone, had dressed himself as a policeman, disguised his motorbike to look like a regulation police model and stopped an armoured truck full of cash on the pretence of checking a report that a bomb had been planted inside the cab. The driver and guard had obligingly stepped out onto the road while the check was made, and the robber had simply started up the engine and driven away. Neither he nor the money had ever been seen or heard of again. The speed and effectiveness of the crime, which was accomplished in a few minutes without any threats or violence, had made the Fuchu Robber famous. But for the police, the humiliation was almost intolerable. It was just the kind of crime – swift, well-planned and above all individual – which was guaranteed to baffle them. And unless the thief made some stupid mistake, like drawing attention to himself by spending the money too freely, they had no hope whatever of solving it. One result of their confusion and rage was a decree, supposedly designed to prevent any such thing from happening again, that when police motorbikes were scrapped, they were to be scrapped completely. Everything had to be cut up and destroyed, regardless of its condition, even the tyres. Even to be permitted to do the job required special official clearance.

*

As Christmas approached, the sunny days of autumn began to turn cold. We made regular use of our paraffin heaters, buying the fuel at the front door from a man who drove slowly around the neighbourhood twice a week with a tank mounted on the bed of a small pick-up. In the park, the gingko trees shed their yellow, fan-shaped leaves and gusts of chilly wind swirled them in eddies across the children's playground. Most of the trees were bare, their gaunt limbs stark against the blue sky, but the camellia bushes were coming into bud and from the orange trees in people's gardens hung globes of ripening fruit that looked as if they had been strung up for decoration.

In Tokyo, all the signs pointed to an upcoming orgy for retailers, cheerfully unencumbered by any tiresome religious sentiments. As one of the English-language newspapers succinctly put it, 'Ho! Ho! Ho! 'Tis the season to be jolly. 'Tis also the season to rush to the shops and buy gifts.' Department stores hung out carload lots of tinsel, streamers and scarlet banners trimmed with white fluff, and concocted window displays around life-size models of Santa Claus which slowly nodded their heads, rolled their eyes and gestured mechanically with rigid arms at piles of gold-wrapped boxes scattered around their feet. Other shopfronts festooned themselves with coloured lights, and some of the major shopping thoroughfares were decorated from end to end with lengths of crimson and gold polyester tied into the shape of enormous bows and hung from the tops of streetlamps. The sound of traffic faced new competition from a barrage of supposedly traditional music – carols like 'Silent Night' hideously processed into sugary pop versions, synthesised renditions of 'Rudolph the Red-Nosed Reindeer' and feeble, hypnotically repetitive ditties with titles like 'All I want for Christmas is my baby.' Theme displays, carefully planned in busy advertising departments through the long, hot days of summer, now sprang up in the bigger department stores like toadstools. There was a Kid's Farm, where children could buy candy from a slot machine disguised as a giant stuffed teddy bear disguised as Santa Claus. There was a Cinderella Castle with a full cast of Disney characters to act as hosts and hostesses. And, for people who liked to skip the subtle parts and get right on with the entertainment, there was

Package City, which was filled with hundreds of wrapped-up gifts waiting to be claimed by patrons who could guess how many there were in the pile.

Also quick to cash in on the festivities were Tokyo's leading hotels, which competed fiercely for the theme dinner market with unbridled vulgarity and ostentation. Amidst a general chaos of sparkling champagne, gleaming tableware and twinkling wine glasses, one hotel proposed a 'sacred Christmas night' during which diners could look forward to 20-minute recitals by the Acapulco Jazz Chorus alternating with the festive plunking of 'European and early American antique musical boxes to make your Christmas night joyful and holy.' Another promised a 'menu to delight the palate and warm the heart,' served up with performances by pantomimists and musical interludes from the Diamond Herd Orchestra. Christmas trees were much in evidence, mostly artificial, although for those who insisted on the real thing consignments of young Noble Firs had been imported from the Pacific Northwest and could be had for a small fortune, or two small fortunes if the customer expected decorations as well.

Our own preparations also included the acquisition of a tree – actually a suitably-sized branch of some evergreen which I sawed from the parent trunk one night in the copse behind Fielding's house and carried home strapped to the back of the Honda so that its densed clusters of waxy needles dragged along the ground like the bushy green tail of a motorised fox. Sumiko from next door continued to come round with a small army of friends, all of whom were eager to join in making paper chains and other decorations out of paper, some of which they took home for themselves. None of them had ever had a real tree in their own homes, nor had they ever tasted a proper Christmas cake: those made by the local bakeries tended to be light, gooey sponges topped with swirls of soft cream and decorated with slices of strawberry. Christmas Day itself was theoretically just another working day on the national calendar, but since I had no jobs we stayed home and invited Fielding and Hasegawa to bring their families round in the evening and try a little inexpertly mulled wine.

Treating Christmas as a strictly commercial event makes sense in Japan for two reasons. One is that it coincides with the distribution of winter bonuses to company employees, who then need active help to return as much of the money as possible to general circulation. The other is that it immediately precedes New Year, Japan's own traditional winter holiday season. Thousands – in fact millions – of city dwellers depart for a few days to their ancestral homes around the country, jamming the roads, choking the airports and filling hundreds of special 'extra' trains to capacity and beyond. Despite the ordeal this exodus guarantees, we joined it to spend a few days with Reiko's family on the other side of the country, in a small village set among mountains close to the Japan Sea.

In winter, the journey is dramatic. For the first hour or so, the bullet train hums smoothly north from Tokyo across the flat Kanto plain, with the sun blazing brightly out of a wide blue sky; and then suddenly plunges into a succession of long tunnels through the rugged mountains of the Japan Alps. When it emerges, it is as if the passengers have been carried into another world entirely, a world blanketed in heavy snow and with no sky at all, just a great grey mass of cloud hanging so low that you feel you could reach up and touch it. This instant Siberia continues all the way to the Japan Sea coast, first passing through narrow valleys with precipitous white slopes hemming in the track on both sides, and then coming out onto the snow-covered Echigo plain beyond the mountains. If you look carefully from the train window at the passing towns, you can see the little flares of occasional neon signs, the winking traffic signals and the moving beams of car headlights that prove you are indeed still in the modern world; but if you narrow the angle of view, confining yourself to brief glances at the identical snow-covered roofs of the tightly-packed houses and the thin wisps of smoke rising from their chimneys, you can easily believe that you are looking straight back into a bygone era, at the Japan of woodblock prints, of rustics wearing straw coats and lampshade hats as they trudge through the narrow streets carrying bags of vegetables or trundling barrows loaded with firewood.

This impression is suspended at Niigata station, the bullet line terminus, with its bustling efficiency, its grandly-uniformed ticket inspectors, its brightly-lit restaurants and its well-stocked souvenir shops; but is restored again after you have waited for half an hour on some other platform, stomping icy feet and clapping gloved hands, for a chance to board one of the small, old, local trains that trundle their slow way from the heart of the city to a string of remote rural destinations. Ours set off at an almost Soviet pace, creaking and rumbling through the industrial sprawl of the suburbs, all slag heaps and narrow roads furrowed with grey slush, past little factories and tin shacks looking gaunt and pathetic in the cold, gloomy semi-darkness of winter, and then rattled painfully across a big river estuary where wavelets of brown water, driven by an icy wind from the sea, lapped at the clumps of scrubby, dirty-looking reeds along the banks. Every carriage was packed with passengers heading home for the holidays. They huddled together with bags and parcels on their knees, all muffled up in coats and hats and scarves, all smoking cigarettes or eating snacks like dried fish from spread-out paper packages. Outside, flakes of snow fell and clung to the windows, lingering for a moment before melting and leaving grimy streaks on the glass. As the city receded, the timber yards and power plants gave way to bare fields on either side of the tracks. Bordered by ragged tufts of coarse grass, they lay under a thin covering of snow which was pierced here and there by clumps of thin brown rice stalks left from the autumn harvest.

For an hour we proceeded through this bleak and miserable landscape, heading north along the coast, until a wide gap suddenly appeared in the forbidding wall of mountains to the east; here the train swung slowly to the right and entered a broad valley. As the valley narrowed, we passed one little station after another, each one smaller and more snow-bound than the last, yet softer, warmer and more friendly in aspect than the gloomy precincts of the city. Village graveyards loomed out of the darkness, their stone lanterns crusted with snow, and wooden houses appeared with thick tiles along the edges of their roofs and warm, yellowy-orange lights discernible through misted windows. Some had simple wooden shelters attached to their sides to offer a little protection from the elements to pick-up trucks, farm machinery or piles of firewood roughly covered by bright blue plastic tarpaulins. And when we reached our destination and stepped out of the train onto the snow-covered platform, I found that nothing had changed in the years since my last visit: it was still one of those story-book country stations where only two other passengers get off and the stationmaster looks about 300 years old. We handed him our tickets, which he accepted with a bow, and then, shouldering our bags and holding hands to keep our balance on the icy streets, walked the last half mile to the family home at the end of the village.

At the head of the household hierarchy was Grandfather, now retired but still directing family affairs from a wheelchair, where he had been confined by a progressive bone disease that had already resulted in the loss of both legs. Despite this affliction he was still a handsome, upright man with sharp, almost aquiline features, who spent his days reading, watching television and writing letters in an elegant hand with a gold-barrelled fountain pen. His modest needs were met by Grandmother, who was severely crippled by arthritis but still managed to accomplish a long list of domestic tasks, punctuated by breaks for green tea beside the old iron stove and slow, quiet conversations with friends and neighbours who dropped by to pass the time of day. Much of the practical work of running the home had become the responsibility of the next generation, who lived under the same roof: Eldest Brother, a tough, wiry man in his late forties who tended the family fields in summer and found sporadic work operating a mechanical shovel during the winter, and his wife, Eldest Sister, who tended a factory production line by day and took seasonal breaks to help her husband with the farming chores. There were also three grandchildren living at home, all grown up and working nearby.

The practical improvements brought by modern life, especially good roads and efficient transportation, meant that the people of the village could now go to work throughout the year like anywhere else. But before the economic advances

of the postwar years, there was little or no winter work to go
to in this part of the country: adult men from farming families
moved to cheap company dormitories and tough, poorly-paid
labouring jobs in the cities (many still do this) or else simply
stayed indoors during the long weeks and months of snow,
only going out to make purchases, collect firewood or take
part in collective village undertakings such as clearing snow
off each others' roofs.

Outside, the wind blew steadily from the north, from far
away in Siberia, across the Japan Sea where it picked up
moisture and then dumped it on northern Japan in the form
of prodigious quantities of snow. Huge drifts piled up everywhere, so that walking was difficult away from the roads,
which were cleared twice a day by a municipal snowplough.
The children had never seen so much snow before, so we went
out every day to build enormous snowmen and replicas of Mt
Fuji, and to exercise an old plastic toboggan that Eldest Brother
recalled his own children using and dug out from the depths of
a shed. We also went for long, slow walks by the river, plun-
ging at times thigh-deep into gargantuan drifts, rolling down
embankments and slinging snowballs up into the grey sky.
When we returned, tired and cold, we collected plastic bowls
and towels from the house and then walked a little way down
the road to the public baths, where the tubs were constantly
fed with hot water piped in from a natural spring from the
next village. After the loss of his second leg, Grandfather had
conceded the need for a modern bathroom in the house, but
the healthy members of the family still followed the old habit
of going every day to join their neighbours in the fiercely hot,
slightly sulphurous water of the public bath.

Afterwards we crunched back over the frozen snow to
the house, pink and glowing, and settled down to eat long,
slow meals and drink hot *sake* with friends and relatives who
dropped by to bring gifts of seasonal food, to hear the news,
meet the children and tell about the latest development in their
own affairs. And late at night, when everyone else had gone
to bed, Reiko and I sat up round the stove drinking tea and
listening to Grandmother, who slept little, talking of family
matters and reminiscing about the past. She liked to tell the

story of how she and Grandfather came to be married (it was a case of mutual attraction, not an arrangement made by the parents) and to speak of the brief time they had lived together as a young couple, before the war broke out. Then one day Grandfather had received the 'red paper', which summoned him for military service, and was dispatched to a city far away where he first underwent his own training and then supervised the training of new recruits, a job he held until the war's end. During those four years they saw each other only twice. For the rest of the time, Grandmother had to stay at home, care for her husband's elderly parents, raise her firstborn son and do all the work in the family fields, alone and entirely by hand. Once I asked if she had any photographs from that time, but she smiled and shook her head: no-one around there had owned a camera nor knew anyone else who did.

Another subject she liked to talk about was Yamamura-tei, a large and very distinguished-looking old farmhouse that stood in its own walled grounds alongside the main road that passed through the village. It was built at the end of the 18th century by an enterprising farming family that had branched out into *sake* brewing, haulage and moneylending and had ended up by becoming the biggest landowners in the district. At the height of their fortunes they employed 75 servants, administered 1000 hectares of forest and leased out a further 700 hectares of rice fields to local tenants. In those days the rent was paid in rice. Yamamura-tei received some 10,000 *tawara*, standard-size straw bags which each contained about 60 kilos of rice.

Although the family which had owned Yamamura-tei was still in existence – the present owner made regular visits from his home in Kyoto – its members were now dispersed and most of the house had been converted into a museum. There was a main living area with a wooden floor and a large platform covered by *tatami* mats, with a square firebox in the middle where an old kettle on a small iron tripod was kept steaming over a charcoal fire. The huge roof, made of cedar shingles weighted down by heavy stones, was supported by an interlocking structure of massive pillars and beams of smoke-blackened timber, some so large that an adult lying lengthwise along them could not be seen from the floor below. An additional network of spacious rooms filled with old furniture and art treasures in glass cases, many made or painted by artists who had once enjoyed the family's patronage, led through to a broad veranda that curved in a rough semicircle around the edge of a formal garden, the creation of an expert brought in from Kyoto at the time the house was built. There were several other buildings elsewhere in the grounds, including separate warehouses for *miso*, rice, money and artworks.

The family that built up this estate may have been rich, but its members lived by a set of strict rules which were carefully designed to discourage any arrogance or displays of lordly behaviour. On one wall of the main living area was displayed a facsimile of the family code, which had been promulgated in the 18th century and laid out very specific instructions about what the members of the household could and could not wear, eat and do, along with precise definitions of their rights and responsibilities. The head of the family should always wear cotton at home, keeping silk clothes for occasions when he had to conduct business. The eldest son could wear silk up to the age of ten but had to switch to cotton thereafter. In order to prepare him for succeeding his father, his education was planned as a mix of farming, business, household management, self-discipline and the knowledge and maintenance of family traditions. He was forbidden to change or neglect any part of the family business on pain of being disinherited.

His younger brothers were only permitted to wear silk until they turned seven. Their education was more restricted, consisting of reading, writing and the use of the abacus; after they had mastered these skills, they had to work the family land to earn their keep. Family meals were normally to consist of soup, rice and one vegetable dish, with relatives and servants eating the same. Servants, the code declared, were 'the hands and feet' of the head of the family: their good work should be rewarded with praise and their errors should not receive severe punishment. The family should care for them in old age if they had no-one else to look after them. All the rules of the code, formulated at length and in great detail, were to apply to all future generations of the family.

Just over a century ago, in a little hamlet a few miles to the north of Yamamura-tei, there lived another family which made its living by selling firewood and charcoal. The business prospered as the years went by, but trouble flared when the eldest son, Fukusaburo, announced that he intended to marry a woman who had already divorced or survived three previous husbands and was regarded locally as having an immoral character. Refusing to reconsider his decision in spite of the pleas of his relatives, Fukusaburo went his own way: he married the woman, was formally disinherited in favour of his younger brother, and left the area with his new wife. For several years they wandered around rural Niigata, living in rented rooms and humble cottages and doing any odd jobs or seasonal labour they could find to make ends meet.

One day, Fukusaburo heard that there was a vacancy for a servant at Yamamura-tei. He applied for the position, was taken on and rose eventually to become a sort of major-domo in charge of the other servants and a special adviser to his master on various matters of importance. The master owned dozens of properties, and when one of these became vacant (the previous occupants emigrated to Brazil), he gave it to Fukusaburo to live in with his wife and growing family. In due course, the master died and so, a few years later, did Fukusaburo. Both were succeeded in their respective households by their eldest sons. Friendly and respectful relations were maintained, but the master-employee relationship between the two families came to an end.

During the years of the Occupation, after the Second World War, many of the semi-feudal practices of Japan's old social structure were abolished or reformed. As part of this process, it was decreed that everyone who owned property of any kind in the area should present himself to the local authorities to have his claim confirmed and registered under the new administrative system. So Fukusaburo's son Tamotsu went along to record the ownership of his house. But when the relevant papers were brought out for inspection, he found to his dismay that the house did not belong to him but to the family for which his father had worked. Fukusaburo had been permitted to live in it but the registration papers had never been formally changed to his name. Considering the circumstances under which he had come to occupy the house, it had probably never occurred to anyone to make any such change.

This discovery came as a bad shock to Tamotsu. The war was over and work was scarce. He had three children, and a fourth on the way. Feeding them was already difficult enough: he raised rice and some vegetables in a few small fields that Fukusaburo had left him but he had no other job and no savings. The situation, he decided, called for bold action. So he put on the best clothes he had, went along to Yamamura-tei and applied to see the owner. An interview was granted, at which he explained the position. He was willing to make an offer to buy the house, he said, but was unable to do so because he had no money. He therefore asked, with great respect and in consideration of the circumstances, that it should be given to him for nothing.

Some days went by while this daring request was considered, and then the owner summoned Tamotsu and announced that he had decided to accede to it. However, to make it a proper legal transaction, he asked for a token payment of two *tawara*, the 60-kilo straw bags of rice with which tenants in the old days used to pay their rent. Over time, Tamotsu paid up and the house became his. And that, Grandmother explained to us as we sat with her around the stove, was how the house in which we were now sitting, the house where my wife had been born, had come into the possession of the family.

On New Year's Eve, just after midnight, we shook off the lethargy brought on by the warmth of the house and the endless cups of *sake*, hauled on our boots once more and set off into the forest on the side of a nearby mountain. The snow had stopped falling and the sky had cleared: shafts of moonlight falling between the branches illuminated a footpath that led up a steep slope to a clearing where there stood a tiny, ancient wooden shrine. In a space on one of its ledges we lit some candles and arranged the offerings we had brought: little cakes, some rice in a small bowl, glass jars of *sake* and a few pieces of fruit, together with some freshly-cut evergreen branches. Then we stepped back, clapped our hands, bowed and said a brief prayer. With no-one there but members of the family, the year came to an end. Old successes faded from prominence, old mistakes were forgotten, old slights forgiven. The wheel had turned all the way, the annual cycle was complete. Tomorrow we would all start again from the beginning.

8 | Thus It is Written

THE NEW YEAR saw the arrival of some new neighbours. It started with a phone call from someone we knew in England. Would we take care of a pal of his who would be arriving in Japan shortly – show him the ropes, find him a place to stay, maybe a job? I didn't feel especially enthusiastic, but Donald sounded like he might not be too much trouble. He'd done a bit of travelling of his own, knew how to make his own way. Was an accomplished musician, too. I said we would do what we could.

Three days later Donald called – from Bangkok. Having spent the previous year in India, he and his girlfriend had been relaxing for a few weeks on some beach in Thailand. Now the R & R was over. They were ready to come to Japan and get jobs. I told them how to take the airport bus from Narita to Yokohama and said I would meet them at the terminal.

Although we had never met, recognising them was no problem at all. They stepped off the bus looking as if they had been frozen in some late 1960s' time warp. Donald was small and slight, with round, steel-rimmed glasses, a mass of black hair trailing over his shoulders, a bushy beard and vast quantities of luggage in red and yellow cloth bags. The girlfriend had a large, battered nylon rucksack and was struggling under the additional weight of some long-necked musical instrument made of varnished rosewood. Her hair was decorated with glittering beads and she was dressed in what looked like a random assortment of brightly coloured rags.

On the way back to the house, Donald explained that they were disciples of some Indian guru, and had divided their time over the last several years between sitting at the feet of the Master until their money ran out and then saving up for the next stint by painting people's houses in the United States and drawing welfare. It didn't sound like a great way to get rich, but he assured me that they didn't need much money to survive in India, where the sustenance was more spiritual than material. With a faintly apologetic air he asked me to call him by his 'proper' name, the one assigned to him by his guru – Deva Donald. The girlfriend said her new name was Onara. 'I never did like being called Brenda,' she added, 'and anyway, someone told me that Japanese people would probably pronounce it "Blender." ' They had a good laugh at that. Japanese can't distinguish between Ls and Rs! Tee hee! They had obviously never played that game I remembered from childhood, where you had to repeat the words 'Red lorry, yellow lorry' over and over again as fast as you could and all the Rs dissolved and became Ls. Still, what Onara had said was quite true. In Japanese, her name would almost certainly be distorted to 'Blender.' But whether the new one would turn out to be an improvement remained to be seen. I decided not to point out that 'O-nara' is the Japanese word for 'fart.'

Back at the house, they unloaded their things and then sat down to have a cup of tea. I noticed that Deva Donald's eyes were dull and slightly bloodshot, and his skin, though tanned by the sun, was slack and pallid. Obviously it had been some time since they had eaten a normal human diet. When I asked what the food had been like in India, they spoke vaguely about endless curry and miserable, impoverished vegetables growing in dusty, depleted soil. They also mentioned the prevalence of diarrhoea. We decided that this problem at least could be rectified at once, so Reiko called to order a large dish of take-out *sushi*. When it arrived, ten minutes later, they stared at it for a few stunned seconds and then began to wolf it down as though it was their first food for a week.

After they had finished eating – the *sushi* needed to be topped off with a few thick wedges of bread and some sliced tomatoes – we talked about work. They had heard that there was good money to be made teaching English in Japan. Could I tell them how to go about finding a school? Bluntly I replied that neither of them would get any kind of job at all unless they smartened up the way they looked. They exchanged quick glances, but conceded that it might be necessary. Deva Donald hauled out a crumpled suit from the bottom of one of his bags and showed it to me. He had had it made by a tailor in Bombay, he told me, precisely with the trip to Japan in mind. Could he borrow an iron?

While he rubbed inexpertly away at the grubby cloth, I explained that teaching jobs were widely advertised in the *Japan Times*, which they could buy the next morning. They thought this was a good idea. Also, their guru's followers had a centre in Yokohama so they would pay a call there to seek assistance and perhaps a place to stay. Then they dropped their bombshell.

'By the way,' said Deva Donald, pouring himself another cup of tea, 'I've heard that it can be pretty expensive to get an apartment in Japan. Just how much money are we likely to be talking about?'

'Well,' I said, 'what you can realistically look for depends on how much money you've brought with you.'

He looked a bit sheepish. 'We don't have much, actually,' he admitted. 'I think it's about . . . 20,000 yen.'

20,000 yen would keep two newcomers to Japan going for a few days, if they were careful.

'20,000 yen?' I said incredulously. 'How long were you planning to survive here on that? And what do you think you'll do when it runs out?'

'We thought ... well, you know,' put in Onara. 'We just thought something would sort itself out.'

'That's right,' added Deva Donald cheerfully. 'We never worry. Something always turns up.'

Translated, that meant they expected to find someone to sponge off. It wasn't hard to figure out who they had in mind.

'You're lucky they let you into the country,' I said. 'Didn't it seem to you a bit risky to come here with so little?'

'It wasn't supposed to be that way,' said Deva Donald defensively. 'You see, Onara's mother sent us money from England. That was to help us get settled in Japan.'

'So what happened to it?' I asked, although I had already guessed the answer.

'Well, we met these people in Bangkok and they told us about this island we've just been to. So we went to check it out and just sort of ended up staying there for a while ...'

This was a serious problem. Having agreed to help them, I didn't want to sling them onto the street as soon as they arrived. On the other hand, having the Deva Donalds camping out as semi-permanent houseguests was out of the question. Finally we agreed that they would go to the guru's centre the next day, to see what help they could dig up, and I would make some enquiries locally.

When they returned the following evening, they had a downcast look. Spiritual solidarity among The Followers, it seemed, didn't extend to anything practical. They were all in Japan to make money too, and weren't about to share their contacts with anyone else. The Deva Donalds had cadged a meal but that was it. No-one had offered them a place to stay, a loan of money, or any ideas about finding a job. I could see that they had not been made particularly welcome, either.

With little hope that I would be able to do any better, I played the only card I could think of and went round to pay a call on Kimura. Amazingly, he came up with a promising line of enquiry right away.

'I'll speak to my brother,' he said. 'He's a real-estate agent.'

I explained that the Deva Donalds didn't have any money. 'What they need is a place to get started,' I said. 'If possible, somewhere where they could move in right away and come up with the money later.' Kimura gave me a hard look. 'Could a foreigner get an apartment in England if he arrived with no money, unable to speak the language?' he asked, with a hint of reproach in his voice. 'It doesn't work like that here. You have to pay before you can move in.'

That being undeniably true, there didn't seem to be much point in calling the brother. But Kimura waved the objection aside. 'We can ask,' he said simply.

The following morning we bought the *Japan Times* and started to call up some of the ads for English conversation teachers. First I called a few of the less promising-looking ones, while the Deva Donalds watched and listened. Once they had got an idea of what to say, they started to make their own calls. By lunchtime they had arranged a handful of interviews for a few days hence.

We also had an appointment for 3 o'clock that afternoon to meet Kimura Junior, the real estate agent. He was going to pick us up in his car near the park. Before that, I got Deva Donald to put on his Bombay suit and then took him off to have his hair cut. The hairdresser looked a bit shocked by the size of the task, like a garage mechanic being shown a completely totalled car and asked to straighten out the dents, but he quickly recovered and went to work. What with washing, cutting and shaving, it took nearly an hour and a half to do the job, but the final result was handsome. Even Deva Donald was pleased. He examined himself in the mirror with an affectionate smile, as if meeting up with an old friend after a long separation. 'It must be more than ten years since I've looked like this,' he said.

Kimura Junior was sitting waiting for us in his car when we showed up for our meeting. I climbed into the front beside him, where I could introduce us and do the talking, while the Deva Donalds got into the back. 'What they need,' I explained, 'is just a small place. Something not too expensive. In fact, something cheap.'

Kimura Junior nodded slowly. 'Something cheap,' he repeated. 'Well, something cheap around here means, say, 50,000 yen a month. One month's rent in advance, plus the deposit ... plus key money' – he mimed a quick calculation – 'yes, a layout of somewhere around 200,000 yen. It wouldn't be possible to do anything for less. Does that sound all right?'

'Yes,' I said, 'that sounds fine. There's just one problem. They don't have any money. They'll be getting jobs in the next few days though,' I added hastily, 'and in a month or two they'll have more than enough money. So we were wondering if the payment could be . . . you know, deferred for a bit.'

Kimura Junior already knew about the lack of money – his brother would undoubtedly have told him – so he looked grave and solemn rather than surprised. There was a long silence, during which he gripped the steering wheel with both hands and stared ahead at the road, obviously deep in thought. After a while he turned slowly round to examine the silent couple in the rear seat. They looked anxious, which made him smile. Then he reached down for the key and started the engine. 'Let's go to my house,' he said.

Kimura's place was an apartment on top of a white-painted concrete building surrounded by *danchi*, the huge, gloomy-looking blocks of apartments rented inexpensively to low-income tenants by Japan's local authorities. We climbed an iron staircase on the outside of the building and went inside. It was a modest-sized place, though clean and modern. The living room contained a dining table and four chairs, a piano, a chrome-plated stand for the TV and video, and a large, comfortable sofa placed beneath two west-facing picture windows which offered a view (on clear days, Kimura told us) out to Mt Fuji. There was also a small, narrow kitchen, a bathroom and two bedrooms, one for Kimura and his wife and the other for their daughter, who was studying English at a college in Tokyo. While Kimura prepared some green tea, Deva Donald asked me in a whisper what we were doing there. I whispered back that he should keep quiet and wait. Presumably Kimura was thinking about the problem and would announce his conclusions when he was ready.

After we had drunk the tea, Kimura announced awkwardly that what we had asked – to find an apartment without any money – was 'very difficult.' He did not want to say 'impossible', but that was obviously what he meant. I answered that we quite understood, that we apologised for burdening him with the problem and that we much appreciated his taking the time and trouble to give the matter his consideration. I then explained the gist of his remarks to the others, who nodded their agreement, and we all rose to go.

'So until they can save enough money to afford a place of their own,' said Kimura, 'they can stay here.' Knowing that he was only proposing this solution to save face, I protested that they wouldn't consider inconveniencing his family in such a way. 'Don't worry,' Kimura assured me, 'it will be no trouble.' No trouble? His wife wasn't even home. Wouldn't she have something to say about it?

'But Kimura-san,' I said, 'they would have to sleep here in your living room. It would completely disrupt your family life.'

'No it wouldn't,' replied Kimura. 'They can have my daughter's bedroom.'

I looked wildly round at the small apartment, as though there might be a broom cupboard I had overlooked. 'But where would she sleep?' I asked.

'She can share with my wife,' he said.

'But what about you?'

He looked vague. 'I am often not here,' he said. 'Stop worrying. If my proposal were not possible, I would not make it.'

I translated all this for the Deva Donalds, who also began to protest that such an arrangement would inconvenience the family too much. Kimura continued to insist. After a while, seeing that he was not to be moved, I began to give in. Perhaps there was more to this than met the eye. Perhaps Kimura had his own reasons for wanting them to stay – to expose his daughter to free English conversation practice, for instance. Or possibly to defuse some domestic situation I knew nothing about. Meanwhile I could see that the Deva Donalds were also warming to the idea. Onara kept getting up and looking out of the window, as if she hoped Mt Fuji would suddenly appear.

'Look,' said Deva Donald. 'All we would need would be to sleep here. We'll be out all day working in any case. And if we can get a salary advance, we might be out of here in a week. If he really means it, let's stop arguing with him and accept.'

So we stopped arguing and accepted. That evening, I helped them take their stuff round to Kimura's apartment and we met the wife. She behaved as if nothing unusual was going on. Having the Deva Donalds to stay would be a pleasure . . . and so good for their daughter. No, really, no trouble whatsoever. On the contrary, she regarded their presence as a rare stroke of good fortune, a privilege even. Knowing that they were there because Kimura Senior had interceded on behalf of supposed friends of mine, I still felt uneasy. But apart from voluble thanks, there was nothing more to be said. I left them to it.

*

Every ten days or so there would be a knock on the door in the early evening and one or other of our neighbours would drop round to deliver the *kairamban*. This was a foolscap-size clipboard to which were attached various documents, forms, brochures and announcements of immediate concern to the community. The *kairamban* was passed from house to house so that the occupants in each case could take note of its contents and, when appropriate, register their agreement with some proposal or sign up for involvement in some group activity. If a new shop was opening up, or a new service had become available, that would be included. Perhaps a local travel agent was seeking participants in a 'special offer' holiday. Or a nearby store had begun to stock a new line in gardening tools. Or a neighbourhood clinic was planning to offer free screening for breast cancer.

Upcoming local events would also be announced: the hour and location of festival celebrations, a sports event, a community walk for charity or a cooperative venture to clear litter from the streets, such as the one we had already taken part in. Announcements concerning children were especially frequent, so much so that there was a separate *kairamban* to deal with them. That one was the conduit for a relentless stream of good intentions, including notices about new inoculation programmes devised by the local authority, suggestions about the adoption of healthier eating habits, exhortations about the prevention of tooth decay, warnings about the harmful effects of wearing cheaply-made shoes or drinking chemically-produced orange juice, invitations to participate in nature rambles, quizzes and competitions and lists of individuals in the area who were available to give private tuition in piano-playing, English conversation, calligraphy, maths, pottery, woodcarving, flower arrangement and a dozen other subjects.

The education of their children was the principal interest of most of the housewives who lived near us, and many pursued it with a commitment that bordered on obsession. The preferred launch-pad, income permitting, was a place in a private kindergarten, for which the uncomprehending tots were made to sit formal exams and large sums of money were sometimes discreetly passed to persons in a position to ensure a favourable outcome. Entry to the right establishment launched the child on the fast track to success, as there were private primary schools which gave priority to children from the top-ranked kindergartens; private middle schools which gave priority to graduates of those primary schools; and so on up the educational ladder to university level and beyond, where fabulous career opportunities of an unspecified nature awaited the individual who had succeeded in passing through each stage of the process. Naturally, this hysterical pursuit of the 'best' private education was less common in suburban Yokohama than among the wealthier inhabitants of Tokyo. But even among our neighbours, most of whom would be obliged to send their children through the state school system, lack of wealth was no excuse for dragging their heels in the race for educational achievement. On every street, sprouting like toadstools, were *juku*, Japan's ubiquitous crammers, which children of all ages attended as a matter of routine when their normal school day was over. Right from the start, being a student was a full-time job, just as much as being a bus driver or a secretary was for an adult. The job of the crammers was to amplify and reinforce what the children were learning at school; and since every subject was taught at school according to a Ministry-prescribed formula, to which every teacher was obliged to adhere, the question of whether or not it was desirable for children to be taught the same thing by two different instructors at the same time never arose.

The crammers varied a lot in quality, ranging from large, well-organised institutions employing trained teachers and dedicated to attaining specific academic goals to squalid one-room operations in which a person of dubious qualifications offered vaguely-focused instruction in some subject in high demand, such as English grammar. The mothers, by and large, were malleable customers, partly because of the awe in which they automatically held anyone who laid claim to the magic title of *sensei* (teacher), and partly because they perceived education to be nothing more than a relentless accumulation of knowledge and would therefore be satisfied if their children came home from class with even one more fact – any fact – drilled firmly into their brains.

This idea of education was behind the operation of the *Kumon* system, which was offered by a network of crammers throughout the country. It had originally been devised by a former high-school teacher in Osaka for improving his pupils' maths comprehension and had now begun to be extended to cover other subjects as well. It worked on the oldest educational principle in the world, Constant Repetition. First of all, tests were conducted to discover what level the prospective student had already attained: this might be, say, the ability to perform additions of three-digit numbers. The teacher would then prescribe not 10 or 20 such sums to practise on but literally hundreds. After that, the student would proceed to the next level of difficulty and go through the same process again. The basic idea was that when the child has done the same thing 500 or 1000 times, the message is sure to have got home. In terms of educational sophistication, this was about as advanced as obtaining flour by grinding corn between two stones, but there was no doubt that, within its own limits, the system worked. Many adults also felt that it was good for a child's confidence to have homework of 50 sums which he/she could do easily as opposed to three sums which were all completely baffling. Even the ordinary schools applied a similar method to certain subjects: multiplication tables, for

instance, were still taught the old-fashioned way, with everyone in the class reciting them in unison until they knew them
by heart.

Naturally Reiko and I were extremely curious to see how
our own children, who had already spent one and three
years respectively in an English primary school, would adapt
to their new educational world. The answer soon became
clear: they loved it. Every morning they woke up bubbling
with enthusiasm, ate their breakfast, shouldered the regulation burgundy-coloured knapsack full of books, pencils and
other items, plonked on the regulation bright yellow hat (easily
visible to traffic) and went outside at the appointed time to
join Sumiko from next door and set off on the 15-minute walk
to school. Parents never accompanied their children on this
journey, no matter how young they were: ours had Sumiko
to show them the way, but if there had been no Sumiko, the
school would have assigned some other older child to act as
escort. Even so, there were a number of roads to be crossed
at a time when morning traffic was heavy, so adult supervision
could not be dispensed with entirely. I remembered the same
problem arising at our children's school in England, and how
the local authority had advertised for a lollipop man or lady,
without success, and the fuss and anger and criticism that this
failure had provoked among the parents. Here in Yokohama,
the same problem was solved the same way as everything else:
the mothers took turns to do the job. Just as the *kairamban*
and the municipal broom made their regular appearances at
our front door, so did a large yellow flag which Reiko would
carry to one of the crossings on the walk-to-school route and
use to stop the traffic and let another batch of children pass
over to the other side. When her turn was over, she delivered
the flag to the home of the next mother on the list. Everything
was terrifyingly simple and well organised.

To begin with, of course, our daughters understood virtually nothing of what took place at school. Flora, who was
six, was placed in a class in the first grade, where she had
missed the first six months of instruction and therefore had
that much ground to make up. But much of the first-graders'
time was spent on painting, singing and other activities which

straddle the border between work and play, so her absorption into the system threatened relatively little hardship. Bonnie, by contrast, who was eight, was inserted into a class in the third grade, by which stage the steel teeth of Japan's educational cogs have already begun to bite. She was two and a half years behind her classmates, in addition to not knowing the language. Whether the catching-up process would be impossible remained to be seen. The principal, Mrs Hattori, had counselled us to rely on the power of *gaman*, and since there was no alternative, we followed her advice.

Apart from the academic work, the children were involved in other activities for which verbal communication was less important than simply copying what they saw their classmates doing. One was the serving and clearing away of school meals. Another was *soji*, cleaning the classroom, which was done every day after lunch with brooms, dusters, buckets of water and *zokin*, or heavy washcloths. Each child brought its own *zokin* to school and kept it there for use when floor-cleaning time came round. From time to time the whole school would embark on *O-soji*, or 'Big Cleaning,' when they would do the corridors, staircases and so on, as well as their classrooms.

The cleaning routine was only one feature of another area of complexity which demanded the children's attention, namely remembering which items of regulation equipment they had to take with them each day, where to keep them and what to use them for. There were special indoor shoes, special bags for this and that, special clothes for PE and other sports, special lunch mats and even special quilted earthquake helmets that covered the head and shoulders and were supposed to be donned during the regular drills held to prepare everyone for the next big tremor. Accurately remembering the sequence and combinations in which these items came into use on any given day helped to cultivate the habit of automatic compliance – acting correctly without thinking about it – which was mirrored in the children's response to schedules, duties, rules and instructions. Academic work, too, was to a large extent a matter of absorbing instruction and then regurgitating it, on demand and without alteration. In art classes, everyone drew the same subject. In music, everyone played the same tune. All the teachers, it seemed, shared the same dream: to extract an identical response from each of the pupils in their charge.

The toughest problem, for Japanese children as well as ours, was the language. Speaking was relatively simple, and could be learned by mimicry and memory, like any other language. But the writing loomed before them like the face of an unscalable mountain. To begin with, schoolchildren learn the two systems of *kana*, by which Japanese words are written syllabically. But soon they embark on the study of *kanji*, the Chinese-derived characters with which the bulk of any normal sentence is written. Each *kanji* has one or more meanings and one or more pronunciations, depending on the context and combinations in which it appears. Learning them is a process that continues throughout the academic career and beyond, for the simple reason that they are so numerous. A few are quite simple, but many others are staggeringly complex, involving twenty or more individual strokes of the pen, all of which have to be executed with the right weight and in the right order. There is a set number of *kanji* a person must know to qualify as literate and to be able, say, to read a newspaper, and these are taught in sequence, one batch at a time, during each year of school life. During the six years of primary school, the syllabus called for 960 of them to be learnt.

To grasp what this involves, an approximate comparison might be made with the road signs contained in the Highway Code. Some of the signs are self-explanatory, such as the picture of a knife and fork that's used to inform drivers that they will shortly arrive at a rest area. Others, such as the white bar on a red circle used to mean 'No Entry', are not obvious at first sight and can only be learned and remembered by study and repetition. *Kanji*, though much more complicated, work the same way: sentences are created by stringing them together in different combinations. It is as though the warning 'No Smoking' were to be expressed in English by placing two signs – one meaning 'smoking' and the other meaning 'forbidden' – side by side. The potential complexity of this system when applied to literature or abstract discussion is enough to make the mind reel.

The immediate effects of the use of *kanji* are numerous and striking. One is that children, even teenagers, are restricted in what they can read in the newspapers, which is one good reason why they don't appear to take much interest in current affairs. Another is that they are hindered from reading their country's literature, unless it is published in simplified editions: this helps to explain the national love of comic books, in which the text is largely exclamatory and always elementary. Another is that many adults cannot read place-names on a map unless they are familiar with the district, since they either do not recognise the *kanji* in question or else cannot pronounce it in the combination in which it appears.

But the effect with the deepest cultural impact is that the difficulty of writing lies in the act of forming the right characters, not in composing the intended message. How something is written – the proper execution of the *kanji*, the weight of the strokes and their mutual balance – often takes precedence over the idea or statement being expressed. This artistic dimension has no proper equivalent in languages based on an alphabet: even the old days of copperplate handwriting were nothing by comparison. But the extent to which calligraphy is studied – many adults practise it as a hobby, and it is part of the formal primary school curriculum from the first grade – clearly shows that it is still highly valued and widely appreciated.

Meanings and concepts, too, are sometimes quite different in kind, so that what is clear and simple in Japanese may seem clumsy or convoluted in English, and vice versa. Thus, for instance, the expression Wada-san used about the Great Buddha in Kamakura, *'ro-za'*, is made up of two *kanji*, meaning 'dew' and 'sitting': he translated this to me as 'seated amidst the dew', which I took to be a delicate, poetic description of the setting, as indeed it is. Later, however, I learned that the expression 'seated amidst the dew' not only has poetic sense, but also alludes specifically to the absence of protection from the elements, so that it could be just as correctly translated as 'out in the open.' This conceptual difference in the languages, with English esteeming precision and clarity, and Japanese esteeming subtlety of allusion, continues to sustain two impressions which date back to the earliest encounters between East and West: the Occidental perception of Orientals as devious and untruthful, and the Oriental perception of Occidentals as crude and stupid. In their own cultural context, *kanji* are felt to express much greater depth and refinement than words made up of Roman letters. But as a tool for learning and interpreting a modern academic syllabus, for communicating clearly and efficiently, they have serious disadvantages. The worst is their sheer number, which means that children must learn them in the same way they learn the multiplication tables – by repetition, repetition and more repetition. Few elements of Japanese education so effectively hinder the development of the 'creativity' and 'individualism' which both domestic and foreign critics so urgently propose.

Then there were the school rules to learn, although these were generally unremarkable – things like not being allowed to bounce a ball indoors, or not playing in the teachers' car park. According to what the children reported, the rules were seldom broken and punishments hardly existed at all: an unruly child might be sent to stand in the corridor for the rest of the lesson, or the teacher might shout angrily, but there was no physical punishment, no detention and hardly any unpleasant private chats with the Principal. When the class was to go on an outing somewhere, the pupils drew numbered slips of paper from a box, which assigned them to groups of manageable size. Any imbalance between boys and girls led to positions being bartered, with disputes settled by the teacher. Other schools, we learned, left these matters entirely to the pupils, in which case bartering might go on for hours, or even days.

Another problem we expected to have to deal with was exclusion or prejudice of a racist character, but this fear, by and large, proved unjustified. Finger-pointing, taunts of 'Gaijin! Gaijin!' (Foreigner! Foreigner!), intentionally insulting questions (Do people in your country wear clothes?) and the like were mostly confined to the youngest children or those below school age – although gangs of boys in search of ways to annoy girls sometimes availed themselves of the handy ammunition provided by un-Japanese features and different-coloured hair. But the fact that such taunts only issued from the safety of a group, never from a single individual, told its own story.

One teacher advised us that taunting foreigners with their foreignness was an expression of Japanese children's secret admiration. At first I discounted this as a piece of idiocy, but a curious incident led me to at least consider it as a possibility. One day Sumiko's mother from next door came round in a state of some distress and showed us an insulting note written to her daughter and signed by Flora. She wanted to know what had occurred to cause a problem between the children, as Sumiko professed to know nothing. An examination of the note showed at once that the writing ability was well beyond what either of our children could manage at the time, so some other child must have written the note and signed it with Flora's name. Eventually the culprit was found to be another girl in the neighbourhood who had concocted the note as a device to disrupt relations between our children and Sumiko, who lived next door to the foreigners and thus had the best chance to play with them. The child hoped that once Sumiko was out of favour, she herself would be able to replace her. The same evening, she was brought to our house by her embarrassed mother, who made her stand in the hallway, give an account of her actions and deliver a well-phrased apology accompanied by several deep bows.

But there was no reason to suppose that our children were the object of such intrigues and jealousies any more frequently than anyone else's. Others earned their playmates' dislike for equally obscure reasons: one unfortunate little boy was universally shunned because his parents' house stood close to the local crematorium. Over time, it became clear that anything in a child's appearance or behaviour that attracted the wrath of his or her classmates was being seen as an example of the one and only, all-encompassing crime: deviating in some way from the narrow norms of the group. This is the only consistent source of Japan's famous problem with school bullying. When particularly serious cases result in death or serious injury, and are reported in the press, the teachers at the school involved invariably deny knowing that anything was going on: but few people with experience of how a Japanese school operates believe them. A teacher is much closer to the pupils than in the equivalent situation in Europe or America, being not only their instructor in lessons and sports but also the accepted arbitrator of their conflicts and the enthusiastic supervisor of their moral development. Group bullying is certainly less common today than it was in the past, but there are many Japanese adults who can recount stories from their own schooldays in which teachers not only knew of bullying campaigns but encouraged or even orchestrated them. In one case that made the papers soon after our arrival, a wretched Tokyo schoolboy was forced to 'play dead' while his classmates – and the teacher – held a mock funeral and wrote their names on a list of 'memorial signatures.' When the boy subsequently committed suicide, the Tokyo District Court rejected his parents' claim for damages against the authorities.

At the same time, there is little doubt that such instances of organised bullying are declining, in proportion to the general relaxation of other aspects of social discipline, slow though that process is. Teachers are becoming more enlightened, children more tolerant of each other's idiosyncrasies, and parents more willing to take an open stand when they come to know of cases of victimisation. We were surprised and touched when the mother of one of Flora's classmates rose to her feet at a PTA meeting and said her daughter had told her that Flora was sometimes taunted with being a foreigner. Her proposal, greeted with solid approval by the assembled mothers, was that they should all sternly warn their own children against taking part in such behaviour.

Of course persecution to enforce group norms is only necessary if the individual concerned is unable or unwilling to conform. In many cases, the individual quickly recognises his own fault and takes steps to rectify it. Thus two boys who joined the school a month or two before our daughters, having spent a few years in California where they had learned to speak English perfectly, reverted in a matter of weeks to the monolingualism of their classmates. When addressed in English, they were no longer able to answer. All the beloved books and videos they had brought home from America were cast aside. They had quickly perceived what their classmates were thinking: that for a Japanese-born child to be able to speak English fluently was not merely an attempt to put on airs, but actually a violation of the laws of nature, as though an orange tree had suddenly started to bear apples as well. Perhaps they were not really Japanese at all? Suddenly, their very national identity was in doubt.

For a foreign-born child it was different: bilingualism was irritating but at least comprehensible. It would be wrong to think that only children feel that way. The same perception is so deeply ingrained into adult society that while young returnees from abroad can be absorbed back into the Japanese primary school system, albeit with difficulty, teenagers in the same position often have to attend separate schools, many of which have been established in recent years precisely to ease and direct their re-assimilation into society. Even Japanese adults who have lived for extended periods abroad are regarded as tainted: Wada-san told me that in his company as in many others, most of the executives who had been posted to overseas offices for more than a couple of years were demoted, in fact or in effect, after their return.

Yet although there were plenty of cultural rocks to run aground on, Pine Hill Primary School also offered our children much that was good. One was their rapidly-growing independence: from walking to school without parental supervision they soon progressed to going out with their friends at weekends, taking a bus to some other part of town, having a burger somewhere and doing a little window-shopping, all at a much earlier age than would be considered safe in other countries. School activities also taught them valuable disciplines of behaviour: to participate, to share, to be cheerful, to turn up on time, to be willing to learn, to remember instructions, to practise *gaman*. Another thing we liked was that all the children learned to play at least one musical instrument and all of them learned to sing. That's not to say they hung around in the crowd and went through the motions. They were actively taught. The ability to teach music is a compulsory requirement for getting a position on the staff of a primary school. None of the teachers were above standing up and singing, alone and unaccompanied, in front of the whole school. It was all quite different from England. And by and large, the children liked it. They eagerly looked forward to school every day. Whatever faults the system may have had, that said something.

9 | Coming of the Snow Baby

AT THE END of January, we calculated that we still had enough capital, living at the present meagre rate, to last another five weeks. But before those were up, my first invoices would have fallen due for payment, and there were others coming along behind. It looked as though things were going to work out. Most of the jobs I was getting were still rewriting texts translated from Japanese, but once I had rented a fax machine I could do most of this work without leaving the house. Hi-Life Advertising was my principal source, but I was on the books at half a dozen other small agencies, all of which had begun to give me occasional assignments. The rewriting itself was rarely difficult, but the subsequent revision of my work by clients with a poor command of English was harder to put up with. In most cases their intentions were good but they could not abide the idea of a finished text to which they had made no contribution: these I classified as being under the spell of the Big and Large Syndrome. If I wrote 'big' they would politely enquire if 'large' could be substituted without radically altering the meaning of the sentence. If so, they had other semantic suggestions to make as well. How about 'lower in weight' for 'lighter'? 'More sporty' for 'sportier'? 'Optimised' for 'best'? This kind of well-meaning interference tended to come from dedicated self-improvers, the kind of people who studied the thesaurus in the train on their way to the office.

More serious disruption came from Tokyo's many sub-scribers to the Mechanical Theory of Foreign Languages. These pests remembered every grammatical rule they had ever learned at school, and were convinced that it was possible to remove words from an English sentence, as though with a spanner, and bolt substitutions in their place. As long as some simple rules were followed – a noun had to be replaced by another noun, a verb by a verb – the grammatical structure would be preserved and the sentence would therefore still be 'good English.' Thus, if I submitted half a dozen ideas for the corporate slogan of, say, a company making household cleaning products, I had to expect the client's committee of supposed English speakers to dismantle my proposals, select words at random from the resulting pile and then reassemble them to form the final choice: 'For Spick And Clean Kitchen Life Today.'

The Mechanical Theory of Foreign Languages also explained what appeared at first sight to be the widespread abuse of English, especially in the adoption of the meaningless slogans seen everywhere on T-shirts and department store shopping bags, or heard at the conclusion of TV commercials. The lat-ter category included idiocies like 'Coffee Communication,' 'Beer's New' and, for a property company selling new homes and apparently determined to drum up business at any price, 'Sexy House.' On the face of it, such slogans showed contempt for the real meaning of English words and expressions, but I soon came to realise that no contempt was involved, nor even ignorance. It was simply that the words and phrases so appropriated ceased to be English at all and became Japanese-English, which is not a subdivision of English but a subdivision of Japanese, exclusively directed at an uncritical Japanese audience for whom 'meaning' has little or no importance. It was the foreignness of the words that made them attractive and gave them the power to carry conviction, not their meaning.

But whether the client was receptive or awkward, rewriting remained hack work by any standards, and therefore gave me plenty of incentive to continue trawling Tokyo's murky commercial waters for something better. To this end I worked my way methodically through a long list of advertising agencies, high and low, making might-be-useful-sometime contacts among harassed account executives in suits and ties, bespectacled editors lurking among dictionaries and reference books, graphic artists engrossed in the latest design and page layout software imported from abroad, and, of particular interest to me, the foreign copywriters. Some were young and keen, with sensibly-managed career backgrounds that included a few years' experience with some prestigious agency in their home countries; others had simply drifted into the trade by accident and stayed in it through inertia. Some preferred the security of a regular position at a single agency, content to pass the daylight hours occupying a cubbyhole in some creative department, composing texts for a regular list of clients, drawing a regular salary and plodding sporadically on with their unpublished manuscripts in the empty spaces at weekends. A few, tempted at some time in the past to strike out for responsibility and serious wealth, had teamed up with partners, set up their own companies and now occupied the presidential office, from where they stared out over the wall their own hands had erected and wistfully contemplated the lost freedom of earlier days.

And then there were the freelancers, optimists who preferred irregularity of work and pay because it held out the hope of stumbling on a jackpot or, as they vaguely hoped, having their circumstances transformed by some marvellous miracle: a tidal wave, perhaps, which would destroy everything else but save them, carry them to some tropical paradise with abundant fruit and a bevy of adoring island girls; or perhaps an impressionable employer whose generosity would be matched by an endless supply of undemanding demands which could be met by word processor and modem from the balcony of a spacious villa, furnished with embroidered cushions, Indian rugs and wicker chairs, overlooking a quiet cove in some select part of Hawaii; or a famous film director's impulsive and wildly enthusiastic acceptance of a script they had not quite finished writing, its purchase for tens of thousands of dollars, its casting with three or four of Hollywood's biggest names, its shooting in some exotic location with themselves on retainer as beer-drinking advisers, its successful showing at Cannes, its admiring reviews in *Time* magazine, its storming triumph at the box office, followed by royalties, contracts, lucrative new commissions, affairs with famous actresses . . . And in between times, while waiting for this miracle which would rescue them from commercial drudgery and win them the recognition they yearned to deserve, they lived from day to day and job to job, pausing at frequent intervals to wonder if maybe after all they were just treading water and would be better off if they moved to live in some other country and took up some completely different line of work.

Slogging around the agencies was hard, tiring and repetitive but ultimately rewarding. Making one's way in Tokyo is all about introductions, connections, recommendations and referrals; and at least half the places I visited generously gave me the name of at least one other place to try. This was how I came across Word House, a small writing farm that thrived on a lucrative supply of work subcontracted from major agencies and, in some cases, directly from the clients.

Word House was able to charge high prices, because both its American partners could read and write Japanese fluently as well as speak it. This obviated the need for the usual intervening layer of translators, which allowed Word House to get that much closer to the source of its work and thus offer what was perceived as a superior service. My Japanese was nowhere near the same level, but the two partners, who were called Jesse and Irving, were glad to find someone like me – a newcomer in town, with no established links to any of their competitors – to handle some of the overflow. We found we could work well together, and I began spending a couple of days a week at a table in their office.

Irving was the contact man, which meant that he spent much of his time at meetings and presentations elsewhere, but Jesse was in the office all the time and we soon became friends. Apart from a few years' break to attend university in New York, he had spent nearly all his life in Japan, and now lived with his wife Kazuko in a small apartment that was furnished with a mixture of high-tech gadgets and a carefully accumulated collection of valuable antiques. Jesse did everything slowly: he wrote slowly, talked slowly and took forever to get ready to do anything, so that he was invariably late for any appointment. Despite the problems this caused, he could never be hurried: he liked to consider things in depth before passing judgment or committing himself to action. He took infinite pains to get things right. To track down a certain type of wax needed for the care and upkeep of his three-legged Chinese table might take days. To obtain a particular brand of shoes he had heard about might take weeks, involving long descriptive faxes to specialist stores in America and the careful perusal of several different catalogues. Even a menu required meticulous study before he could make a selection. But the corollary was that when he had something to say, it was never dull. He could discourse for hours on aspects of Japan, on his favourite novelists, on the use of bamboo in musical instruments, a subject in which he was also an expert, and always have something interesting to say. When we were together, the line dividing work from talk became blurred. We often went out for dinner in the evening, outings which usually ended up with me missing the last train home to Yokohama and staying the night at his apartment instead.

Jesse and his wife, a dynamic, bubbly, fast-talking girl who worked as a fashion designer, liked to think of themselves as sexual gourmets. They gave each other plenty of space to pursue independent adventures, and would then get together and compare detailed notes. Neither of them exactly looked the part: Kazuko dressed well but was no more than average in looks, while Jesse, like many lechers of life and literature, was far from handsome, actually rather like a bespectacled gnome, small and spare and lean and slightly hunched, as though his mother never made him sit up straight at table, with short blond hair cropped close to his skull, a pasty complexion and a sartorial taste best described as 'casual.'

Not that any of this worked against him. His approach to women was not flamboyant or overtly predatory, but slow and deliberate. He collected them with the same care he showed in tracking down antiques. Where others surged through Tokyo as through an ocean, Jesse saw it rather as a tankful of tropical fish, each one resplendent with its own special colours, fin shapes and habits. Anything was capable of attracting his interest, provided it had something colourful, something exotic, something distinctive. Gentle and mild-mannered, he swam smoothly from pretty little nurses and simpering secretaries to lonely widows, from wide-eyed students to hard, seen-it-all-before executives, from the unhappily married who despised their husbands to the happily married whose husbands were about to go away on business trips and who had not realised, until the idea was tactfully broached, how ready they were to spice up their lives with a little harmless adventure.

In all of them without exception he took a genuine interest: no heartless bastard, eager to tear off a quick piece and have done with it, he passed contented hours in the enjoyment of their company, studying their eyes and their nails, watching while they brushed their hair and put on their jewellery, noting the colour and style of their clothes, buying them dresses and records, escorting them to intimate, candlelit restaurants, listening to their opinions and coaxing out their secrets. The idea of sexual fidelity brought out an almost allergic response. He was a self-confessed love addict, in constant need of refuelling by the first sweet ecstasies of another new affair. To that extent, his was a neurosis gone completely to seed, but it was quite unspoiled by cynicism. He remained on good terms with his ex-lovers and cherished the memory of their affairs. Each one was preserved and treasured, never flaunted like a notch on his gun butt.

In the same way, when he recounted his exploits, it was never in isolation, with the triumphant pride of a conqueror, but always as an organic part of some other story, usually connected with work. Because of his fluency in Japanese he was occasionally asked to act as an interpreter, and thus one day found himself at the Okura Hotel, supposedly the best in Tokyo, to interpret an interview between a Japanese surgeon and two American doctors, a husband and wife team who were experts in genito-urinary diseases. For two hours he sat there and assisted at a dispassionate discussion of micturition, the passing of bloody stools, the peculiar deformities that appear on the inside surface of the urethra if certain conditions are not treated promptly, and exactly where surgical incisions should and should not be made in the male and female genital organs. That evening he was supposed to go and have dinner with a friend and his family, but after that conversation, he said with an icy shudder, nothing would do except to go straight to the bar of the Okura Hotel, order a large dry Martini and try to think about something else. And while he sat there, brooding in the half-darkness of the Okura bar, a Japanese woman ('aged about 46' he remembered, with characteristic precision) came and sat down at the next stool. All the bar staff knew her and went through the grovelling bit they save for important customers ('Good evening Mrs Ozaki, how are you this evening? Your usual?'). She orders her drink and sits there turning the pages of a glossy English-language travel brochure. She is so elegant and smart and aristocratic, as marvellous as an expensive cream cake, like a countess or something, that Jesse begins to get interested. They start up a conversation, first in English, which she speaks fairly well, and later in Japanese, and they talk about . . . well, I never found out what they talked about, as I made him skip that part. Given a free hand, he was capable of wandering off in any direction, introducing complicated sub-themes about the general ambiance, the colour of the wallpaper, was the music Brahms or Rachmaninoff, the bartender had this curious ring with a blue stone in it, how he wanted to go and take a leak but didn't want to break the spell of the conversation, and how that gave him a tight, uncomfortable feeling in his bladder, which had the effect of concentrating his mind . . . GET ON WITH IT . . . all right, so one thing led to another and he's managed to make it clear to this lady that he wants to spend the night with her. But it's not actually arranged yet, because after all they've only just met and it wouldn't do for her to seem too willing . . . so she says let's go up to the Starlight Bar for one more drink.

The Starlight is on the top floor of the hotel, so up they

go and the waiters go through their routine again – what a pleasure to see you again, Mrs Ozaki, will this table be all right for you this evening? – and they order more dry Martinis and the night ticks on and finally it's settled, she agrees to stay the night with him. So Jesse goes down to the front desk and books a room, whose price makes him gulp more than a bit, and then goes back up to the Starlight, where he half expects the countess to have vanished, but no, she's still there, waiting, so they take the elevator and go to the room. But before getting down to business they each think they ought to make a phone call. Jesse calls his wife to say that he won't be coming home, which normally wouldn't matter in the least, but by chance Kazuko's horns are out: she is just back from a date of her own which obviously didn't work out because she's breathing fire and brimstone and where-the-hell-are-you and whichever cow you are with you can sling her in the can right now and that sort of thing, so Jesse hangs up on her and passes the phone over to the countess.

She calls home and gets her 23-year-old daughter, to whom she says that she has checked into a health clinic, one of those places where the fat-walleted go in at night and get an enema and then the next day the barium meal and a full check-up. When she puts the phone down she admits that it wasn't a very convincing story, but it doesn't matter, she adds, because her daughter is an airhead (the Japanese expression, Jesse takes time out to inform me, is *piman*, which means 'green pepper' – hollow inside except for a few useless seeds) and not only that but a virgin to boot. Jesse doesn't believe that for a moment. 'She only tells you that because you're her mother and she doesn't want to let on.' 'No, you're wrong,' says the countess, 'she's a virgin all right.' 'Well, that's terrible,' says Jesse, to whom virginity is something that should be torn down wherever it is found, like ivy damaging a precious old wall. 'I know it's terrible,' says the countess, 'but what can I do? I'm the mother, I'm not allowed to tell her to go out and get herself a man.'

For a moment, Jesse thinks of suggesting that the countess call back and bring the daughter round as well, but then he realises that it's already 2 o'clock in the morning and there's no more time to waste. The situation is ideal, not only now but also in view of possible repeat performances in the future, because the countess has a husband who's a successful businessman and never home, and she therefore hasn't had any attention for a year, not since her long-standing lover of 20 years, a Scotsman called Alistair, dropped dead of a heart attack.

So everything was fine until the next morning, when the countess started to worry about how to get out of the hotel without being recognised – God, what a fool I was to do this in the Okura, of all places – but Jesse knew an exit via the hotel garage, so there was nothing for her to worry about. And before going their separate ways they dropped in at a coffee shop for breakfast, where Jesse discovered that the countess's brother had a business selling old musical instruments, including various bamboo flutes. And by chance he was looking for a certain type of flute at the time, and there seemed a good chance that this brother might be able to help him. So that the story of the countess came to an end, not abruptly, not with a punchline or a conclusion, but just fading out in a smooth, seamless transition that led equally unremarkably into the beginning of a discourse on flutes. The real mystery was how someone whose natural thought processes ran on and on like a river could ever get focused enough to write advertising copy.

*

The mountains that run up the middle of Japan's main island provide a natural barrier that keeps most of the snow on the northern side, but the Tokyo-Yokohama area usually has a few brief falls in winter, and one February morning we woke up to find everything buried under a blanket of white. We threw out some bread for the birds and watched as half a dozen tough starling lookalikes called 'bulburs' swooped down out of nowhere and gobbled the lot, occasionally raising their heads to scream in a menacing manner at the sparrows and greenfinches which huddled together in chirruping clusters and watched enviously from a nearby gutter.

After school finished in the afternoon, the hilly roads quickly became scored by the narrow parallel tracks of toboggans or the broader mark left by the local toboggan-substitute, a sheet of cardboard torn from a grocery box. A few snowmen sprang up here and there but other children had more advanced ambitions: one group heaped up a mound as tall as a man and then excavated a very impressive igloo from the middle. When I had finished work for the day I stumped across the park to Fielding's house, to find that he had departed the day before for a short visit to America. It didn't seem the ideal time for him to be away, as Kiko's pregnancy was now close to an end, but Fielding had only gone for a few days, assuring her that he would be home before the date on which the doctor had told them they could expect the new baby to arrive.

Japanese doctors tend to be right in their predictions of birth dates, and for a very good reason. First they calculate the likely delivery date according to the usual method, and then make a reservation for the expectant mother to be admitted to their clinic on that morning. If she isn't in labour when she arrives, they immediately administer drugs to induce the birth. This is called 'delivery time control' and is practised because deliveries outside the normal 9-to-5 working hours, when fewer staff are available, are inconvenient and therefóre to be avoided. More than half of all births in Japan are said to be induced for this reason. Other maternity practices are less shocking but still years out of date. Fathers are rarely allowed to be present at the birth. Infants are taken from their mothers as soon as they are born and kept in separate baby wards: mothers get to see and hold them at feeding time but otherwise have to be content with peeping at them through a glass screen. Five or seven days of bed rest is all the post-natal care the average mother can expect. In this as in most medical matters, the doctor is presumed to know everything and expected to explain nothing.

Fortunately for Kiko, the birth of her son did not require inducing. She went into labour the natural way – the very next morning after the snowfall. At 7 o'clock she called us on the phone to give us the good news, and to ask us to please get there quickly and take her to the clinic. Considering that we were still in bed, we did well to be on the motorcycle and skidding round to Fielding's house in about two minutes flat. While Reiko took charge of the two-year-old and walked her back to our house, I bundled Kiko into Fielding's Suzuki compact and set off for the clinic.

Kiko was having a hard time, with the space between contractions down to less than two minutes, but I couldn't pay much attention to her. The snowbound roads were already difficult to drive on, and no sooner had we set off than it began to rain as well. The wipers didn't work, so I wound down the window and drove with my head sticking out at the side. As luck would have it, the clinic was located right on the main road, which was blocked solid in our direction by traffic carrying people to work. However, we had no time for traffic jams. Judging from the sounds coming from the seat beside me, my deadline in minutes could have been counted on my fingers. There was only one thing to be done. I pulled out into the oncoming lane, leant hard on the horn and went for it. Alarmed drivers pulled abruptly in to the side, mounted the pavement, blew their horns furiously and even shouted insults out of their windows. But craziness succeeded where good sense would have failed. I skidded to a stop in front of the clinic, jumped out of the car and banged on the front door, shouting for immediate help. Two anxious-looking nurses ran out and half-pushed, half-carried Kiko inside. I flopped down in the waiting room for a breather. And I had only just stopped panting, five minutes later, when a beaming doctor came in with the good news that my wife had borne me a son. It was a pity to have to disillusion him.

10 | Way Stations

MEANWHILE, DEVA DONALD and Onara had started full-time teaching jobs and were well on the road to financial recovery. When they were still 10 days or so away from their first paychecks, Kimura Junior came up with an apartment for them that looked ideal. Half a mile from our house there were two adjoining corrugated iron bungalows jammed into a small space between a concrete apartment block and a deep, dark copse of closely-planted cedars. One of these bungalows had just been vacated, and the landlord had contacted Kimura's real estate company to find him a fresh tenant. Getting it required an instant decision, and although the Deva Donalds still didn't have enough money, their credit was looking a lot better than when they first arrived. Kimura was ready to lend them half the money if I (to show my confidence in the friends I had introduced) stumped up the other half. The following Saturday, the formalities were completed and the Deva Donalds had a new home. Word had got around the neighbourhood and several people came forward to help. Kimura Senior, glad to put some of his things to use while waiting for his new house to be built, provided a table and a gas water heater which he installed himself. His wife offered a selection of plates, cups and glasses. Fielding dug into his store of possessions and gave them a television and a microwave oven. Our friend with the electric shop found another paraffin heater and put in a new wick before bringing it round in his little Honda pick-up. The Deva Donalds were delighted. The basic expectation they had brought with them to Japan – that despite their lack of money, 'something would work itself out' – was coming true beyond their wildest expectations. Everything they had heard about the generosity and good-heartedness of Japanese people, which they had taken for exaggeration, was being shown to be literal fact.

For the first fortnight or so after they moved into the new apartment, we saw a lot of them. Onara was pleasant enough, though somewhat taciturn: she was finding it hard, she said, to adjust to the new living conditions, especially in unexpected ways such as being unable to read product labels when she went shopping. Getting up in the morning and going to work every day was another unfamiliar responsibility. She also found that Japanese food disagreed with her. Deva Donald, by contrast, gave the impression of ready adaptability. He displayed keen interest in everything, asking numerous practical questions about shops, bus stops, likely changes in the weather and promising places to visit and jotting the answers down in a small notebook. The new short haircut had revealed the shape of his head and exposed an alert, intelligent face which had previously seemed to be sheltering inside his thicket of hair, like a mouse peeping warily out from a hedge. Now he cut an altogether smarter and more upright figure, striding rapidly around the streets and giving every sign of enjoying the process of settling in. He quickly got to work putting up shelves and building a few basic items of furniture, and borrowed a neighbour's spade to dig a vegetable patch out of the narrow, sunless strip of soil behind their tiny bungalow.

Word of these home-making projects quickly got around, to universal approval, and local shopkeepers began to report to us, and no doubt to each other, on recent sightings.

'Donald-san came in for some bread this morning,' the baker would tell us, beaming with satisfaction at this latest addition to his international clientele. Or if we went to the chemist's, the old lady behind the counter might have some news. 'Onara-san was out shopping early today,' she would say. 'I saw her walk past. She had a cabbage in her basket.' Things had obviously got off to a good start, and there were strong hopes that the Deva Donalds would prove to be valuable and entertaining new members of the community.

Unfortunately, these hopes were not fulfilled. Once they had obtained the various things they needed, the Deva Donalds' sociability rapidly faded away. Far from being pleased by the good impression they had made, they found it alarming. Participation in the social affairs of an unremarkable little suburban community was definitely not what they had come to Japan for. Now that they had established themselves, they found they were more welcome at the meditation centre than they had been at first, and they began spending a lot of time there. A photograph of the guru was hung in a prominent place in their apartment and they agreed, after some initial reluctance, to lend me a book which summarised the Master's thought. Its general trend was that the world's problems were better ignored than resisted. Disciples were recommended to avoid unnecessary contact with conventional society, to put their own interests first and to concentrate on developing their inner selves. This breezy advocacy of the art of self-absorption was supported by various convenient reinterpretations of other religious teachings, mostly misquoted or taken out of context.

For the Deva Donalds, the book was not only a repository of spiritual wisdom but also a handbook of practical tenets by which to guide their daily lives. When they weren't at work or busy developing their inner selves through group meditation, they now remained in seclusion in their apartment, resolutely avoiding the various local events and get-togethers to which someone (usually Fielding) always made sure they were invited. While waiting for their neighbours to give up and leave them alone, they fell back on a battery of excuses: they didn't care for drinking, they had difficulty speaking Japanese, they were suffering from colds, they had another appointment, they were too busy. This reluctance to take part in local affairs at first caused bewilderment and then overt disappointment: it was known, for instance that Deva Donald was a musician and everyone wanted to hear him play. Something had gone wrong and no-one was quite sure what it was.

The confusion also began to spill over into their contacts with neighbours. One day, Deva Donald was engaged in earnest conversation by a lady who had a remarkably beautiful daughter: the way he understood it, the lady wanted him to teach English conversation to the daughter, who stood in the background smiling prettily and fluttering her eyelashes while her mother did the talking. A regular weekly appointment was agreed, together with a fee. But when Deva Donald turned up to give the first lesson, he found that the lines of communication had become tangled: instead of the beautiful daughter, he had been engaged to teach English conversation to the mother and her dragon-like friend, who were planning to go on a cultural tour of Europe and wanted to get a taste of the atmosphere in advance by equipping themselves with some basic conversation ability. The daughter had no interest in English. She was studying to become a piano teacher.

Naturally, the Deva Donalds were aware that this abrupt return to their familiar, reclusive way of life was causing some disappointment, so they decided to dispose of whatever obligations they might have incurred by hosting a one-time-only party. 'It's to thank all the people around here,' explained Onara when she called up to tell me about it, 'who have helped us since we arrived.' In honour of the occasion, she thought she would prepare some Indian food. Maybe a few Mexican dishes, too. Did I think that was a good idea? I assured her that it was a splendid idea and would be very well received.

The party was scheduled for the following Saturday. By chance, the karaoke-loving local politician Mr Hasegawa had also chosen to give a party on that day: his was slated to begin at lunchtime but, in the usual way of such gatherings, had no fixed ending. We therefore arranged that the relevant guests should go on from the Hasegawa affair to the Deva Donalds' place at five o'clock. Hasegawa thought this was an excellent plan. I could see that he was hoping that the evening would mark the start of a new chapter in relations and would end with all the social ice well and truly broken and everyone celebrating together at a karaoke bar.

Hasegawa's party was held in a large upstairs room at one of his favourite restaurants. There were about forty guests, seated on either side of a long line of low tables heaped with food and drink. As it was daytime, and therefore too early for whisky, most of the guests drank beer, although a few of the older men started the way they meant to go on, with *sake*. There were a number of children present as well, who came along at the behest of their parents and stayed for an embarrassing half-hour, during which they were cross-examined about their progress in school, complimented on their appearance and recent growth, and urged to say something in English to me or Fielding. Tongue-tied and blushing, they would stammer out a few words which would be greeted by raucous approval from the assembled adults. But the embarrassment of being the focus of attention was just another part of their social training. I had been at a birthday party with Hasegawa a few weeks before, at which everyone without exception had had to make a short speech eulogising the guest of honour, and had been amazed by the composure with which even 12- and 14-year-olds had accomplished this potentially frightening duty.

There were speeches at Hasegawa's party too. As a local political hopeful, the host had gained plenty of practice while pursuing the official position he coveted somewhere on the iron grid of social and professional relationships that's clamped over Japanese society like a mask over the face of a fencer. Every wire, strut and connection on this grid hums with the sound of obligations – obligations incurred, discharged, overlooked, deferred but never ignored and never forgotten. And at every intersecting point of the grid stands an individual, or a group of individuals, important or insignificant, whose function and responsibility is so to oil the wheels of the social machine with the oils of cooperation, negotiation, compromise and right behaviour as to ensure its smooth and preferably silent operation.

One minor though useful lubricant is the speech, which should ideally contain plenty of platitudes and definitely no controversy. So Hasegawa was keen on speeches, especially the safe and sanitised variety suited for delivery at a party. He stood up and waved his hands for quiet, then made a few flowery remarks that welcomed his guests and expressed his hopes for their prosperity and happiness during the coming year. He also emphasised that the presence of foreigners made this not only a gathering of good friends but also an auspicious occasion for the eager internationalists sitting around him. This drew a round of obedient applause, as everyone knew that the internationalisation of Japan was one of Hasegawa's favourite topics. Various other guests also spoke, showing a similar talent for saying nothing beyond formal phrases of gratitude and appreciation. Hasegawa requested me to make a speech too, so I got to my feet and haltingly explained how our first meeting at the Buddhist temple had been the key that had opened the local community to me and my family, and how grateful we were. This went down extremely well, so I took advantage of the mood to put in a plug for the Deva Donalds, also newcomers to the area, who were even now preparing a modest reception, complete with Indian and Mexican specialities, to convey just the same sentiments.

It was still only 4 o'clock when Hasegawa's party began to break up. Some of the guests were going on to another party elsewhere, while others, replete with food and drink, were being helped into their coats and hustled through the formalities of farewell by wives who were clearly ready to go home. Hasegawa, by now a little red in the face from drink, proposed that those of us who were going to the Deva Donalds' should now do so. I warned him that it was still early, but he just laughed and waved his hand dismissively. Matters were now moving under their own momentum, so I slipped downstairs to a telephone and called Onara to warn her that we might be on her doorstep slightly ahead of time. This didn't go down well. 'Please bring them at 5 o'clock, as we arranged,' she said and then hung up. Her voice had a distinctly nervous edge, which made me smile. Scratch even a cultist, I thought to myself, and there's a hostess worrying about her party just below the surface.

Eight of us – Fielding, Hasegawa, me and five others – emerged from the restaurant into the cold afternoon and set off to walk the short distance to the Deva Donalds' bungalow. First we had to make a short detour to buy presents, as no-one would have dreamed of arriving empty-handed. A couple of large bottles of *sake* were purchased and giftwrapped in special paper, along with a box of strawberry-topped cakes, a bamboo basket filled with tangerines lying on a decorative bed of leaves, and a presentation set of half a dozen kinds of tea from different parts of Japan.

As soon as Deva Donald and Onara answered our knock at the door, I knew that something was wrong. They were saying all the right things but also wearing the sickly smiles of culprits about to be rumbled, as though there were a dead body, or a set of kinky underwear or something else unmentionable in the room behind them. And when I had taken off my shoes and stepped inside, with Hasegawa eagerly crowding in behind me, I saw what it was.

The table was indeed laid for a party, with plates of samosas, bowls of guacamole and other dishes which Onara had prepared, and cushions scattered around on the floor for the guests to sit on. But the cushions were already occupied, by eight or nine people who were evidently fellow Followers, and the bowls and dishes of food were empty, with nothing but a few crumbs and smears to indicate what their contents had been. Expecting to arrive at the beginning of a party in their honour, Hasegawa and his friends found that they had arrived at the end of someone else's instead. For a moment, everyone just looked at everyone else, frozen with embarrassment. I wished that some painter could have been on hand to record the scene: the stunned amazement of the new arrivals contrasting with the awkward, goofy, caught-with-the-hand-in-the-cookie-jar expressions of the hirsute and bead-festooned Followers.

Still, there was nothing to be done but act normally. A couple of the Followers sprang rapidly into action, clearing away the used dishes, while the others huddled closer together to make room at the table for the new guests. Hasegawa, who had been half-drunk and boisterous a few moments before, was now quiet and icily sober. He and the other guests placed their gifts silently on the table. Bewilderment had temporarily robbed them of words.

I stepped out into the kitchen to try and find out what was going on. Onara gave me a hard look.

'I told you not to come early,' she said bitterly.

'I'm sorry,' I told her, 'but there was nothing I could do about it. Anyway, what difference would it have made? Everything's been eaten. Weren't you expecting us? Haven't you got anything left to offer these people?'

'We've got beer,' put in Deva Donald, 'and there's some whisky. And some snacks – you know, crisps and peanuts and things. We were having another party first, you see. We meant to get everything cleared up before you arrived and then have a sort of . . . well, like a cocktail party.'

'Oh God,' said Onara in a desperate voice. 'What are we going to do?'

'There's only one thing you can do,' I said firmly. 'Just get back in there with whatever you've got and make the best of it.'

It might have worked, but it didn't. First, all the Followers got up and left. Aware that some blunder had been committed, they were unable to shake off their sheepish expressions: only one of them even managed to say goodbye. This awkwardness only confirmed the new arrivals in their impression that some great error had occurred, as if perhaps they had come on the wrong day. Unable to decide whether they themselves were at fault or if the situation was designed to slight them in some incomprehensible way, they sat around speaking to each other in low tones and sipping gingerly at glasses of beer they no longer wanted. Conversational gambits flared and then fizzled out as quickly as damp matches. The electric appliance shop dealer said how nice the apartment was and expressed the hope that the paraffin stove he had given the Deva Donalds was working satisfactorily. His wife kept softly sniffing the air with a puzzled look on her face: she couldn't figure out why the place smelled of incense when there was no altar to be seen. Hasegawa indicated the picture of the guru on the wall and asked Onara if it was her father. Even Fielding, who characteristically refused to succumb to the general gloom, found that his efforts met with little success. It was at his suggestion that Deva Donald agreed to play a few tunes on the guitar, but no sooner had he started to do so than one of the strings broke. There were no spares in the house. This undeserved disappointment was the last straw: it seemed to carry the same finality as the sound of a clod of earth falling on a coffin. Fielding and I hung on, but everyone else had had enough. Less than half an hour after arriving, they had all departed.

The next few times I saw Hasegawa, neither of us alluded to the failed party. He wasn't angry about it, nor even personally offended; what got to him was having been humiliated in front of his friends. Given time, I thought, he would get over it. But I was wrong about that too, as I found out one evening when his mellow mood encouraged me to think that the time was ripe for a little damage repair. 'They didn't mean anything bad, you know,' I told him. 'They just wanted to express their gratitude to the people around here who helped them. But somehow, they got the timing a bit mixed up.' Hasegawa nodded gently but remained silent. Then he said 'I know, I know. Perhaps they do not understand our customs.' And then, after a pause, 'But I think they have got everything they wanted.' Case closed. As far as Hasegawa was concerned, the Deva Donalds had ceased to exist.

*

What the children liked best at the weekends was to go to Dreamland. This was the brainchild of some Japanese entrepreneur who had visited Disneyland on one of his trips to the US and decided to build something similar in the depths of suburban Yokohama. The site he chose was inconveniently located for public transport, so the project included the construction of a five-kilometre monorail, at phenomenal expense, from the nearest main line station to the site. Incredibly, after the line had been completed, it was discovered to have been built to incorrect specifications: the track gauge was a few centimetres too narrow to meet the required safety criteria and the city's Department of Transportation regretfully declined to issue an operating permit. Ever since, the line had remained in place but unused, a rusting monument to administrative incompetence snaking its ugly way past the upstairs floors of private houses and across roads and fields on giant legs of concrete.

The failure of the monorail was a crushing blow, not least because it was also intended to bring patrons to the specially-constructed Dreamland Hotel. This was an enormous building with 18 narrow aprons of upcurved roof protruding from each of its 18 storeys in a design that was supposed to resemble a huge pagoda. In fact, it looked ludicrous and cheap, and having never managed to fill more than a quarter of its rooms at any one time, forlorn and defeated as well. It was rumoured that many of the floors had been out of commission for so long that they were virtually derelict.

But somehow Dreamland itself, the centrepiece of the project, had survived the failure of its infrastructure and still managed to lure substantial crowds – at least, at the weekends. Among the attractions was a giant swing shaped like a pirate ship, which could accommodate a hundred or so people at a time, a Big Wheel of colossal proportions, visible from several kilometres away, and a Jungle River Trip, on which pleasure-seekers huddled in a small boat and were carried for ten minutes or so along a scummy canal. The journey took them past a family of concrete gorillas which roared mournfully at regular intervals, a display of mechanical monkeys which swung and chattered in poorly-lubricated steel treetops, and a few groups of fibreglass alligators which yawned grotesquely from scrubby banks choked with grass and weeds. There was also a maze, a ghost train, various roundabouts, five souvenir shops and a big restaurant which sold imaginative, fun-oriented dishes such as 'UFO Noodles' in which the round, fleshy core of a scallop (the UFO) floated on the surface of a bowl of noodles in savoury soup, along with a pickled baby octopus (a space-walking astronaut) and half a hardboiled egg laid on a slew of dark-coloured seaweed (the moon in the night sky).

The best thing about Dreamland was the skating rink. This was a walled channel about 5 feet deep and 30 feet wide surrounding a large swimming pool. In summer it would be filled with water to serve as a secondary pool, but in winter its floor was frozen and used as a circular skating course. Patrons who had no skates of their own could rent them on the premises and go round and round the rink for as long as they liked – a ticket was valid for the whole day – or else buy a hot drink from a machine and sit on the side and watch everyone else. The right time to arrive was 9 o'clock in the morning, when the place opened; by 11 it was crowded and the convention by which everyone proceeded around the course in an anticlockwise direction had become an inescapable obligation. Some of the skaters were showily skilful: youths with expensive racing skates who could go backwards and forwards with equal ease and delighted in skidding stops which sent sprays of ice chips flying into the air, and one elderly man we often saw who wore old-fashioned skates with long, upcurved blades and moved steadily through the throng with extraordinary precision, hands clasped behind his back, never looking to left or right and never slackening his pace. Others were hilariously incompetent: giggling teenagers clinging to the side rail as they inched their way round step by clumsy step, middle-aged mums staggering along five abreast, clutching each others' arms for support and shrieking discordantly, and not a few fathers, out to impress their families, who would get up a good burst of speed and then suddenly lose control, teeter this way and that, claw at the air with flailing arms and finally come a dreadful purler, thudding onto the ice and skidding a long way on their backsides before gingerly picking themselves up and heading back to their seats with sheepish smiles for a few minutes' break and perhaps a restorative cigarette.

Another diversion we learned of, just as winter was fading away and the first signs of spring were beginning to appear, was in a town further down the coast called Odawara. Around the station, there was little to distinguish it from its seaside neighbours: it had the same low-rise shopping centre, the same dingy concrete buildings huddled together in narrow alleys, the same confusion of traffic and the same long, narrow beach where the Pacific breakers rolled in below the concrete supports of National Route 21, the shoreline highway, onto smooth pebbles embedded in the dark sand. But on a little hill to the west of the station, from where the coastline could be seen curving southwards along the flank of the Izu Peninsula and the looming mountains of Hakone, stood Odawara's one and only tourist attraction, its castle.

To a European, the word 'castle' carries very particular connotations – of mediaeval military power, thick stone walls with castellated battlements, stern cylindrical turrets and menacing portcullises, all adding up to the constipated geometry of Authority Imposed By Force. Architecturally, Japanese castles are nothing like that. They're normally white, for a start, with storeys separated from each other by long curving eaves roofed with heavy terracotta tiles ('stronger and lovelier than any we use in Europe,' noted the 16th century Jesuit Luis Frois). From a distance, they look like exotic wedding cakes, or magic birds poised to fly up into the air.

Architecture notwithstanding, the history of Odawara Castle reads like a grim catalogue of oppression visited on the local populace in the lulls between regularly-occurring attack, siege, resistance and capitulation. Some idea of its strength and importance can be gained from the fact that in 1590, when Hideyoshi Toyotomi sought to wrest it from Ujimasa, 4th lord of the Hojo clan, it took a three-month blockade by 150,000 sea and ground troops to do the job. Not that those three months were all spent in fighting. Japanese battles at the time normally took place in the open, using cavalry and infantry, with siege techniques surprisingly neglected. Hideyoshi's main weapon was patience, as he demonstrated by supplying his soldiers with an additional army of entertainers, courtesans, shops and foodstall operators. His troops, whose familiarity with their leader's tactics convinced them they were in for a long wait, marked out some plots of land and started growing vegetables. The officers had the same idea and set about building a number of landscaped gardens.

Inside the castle, the atmosphere was much the same: between indecisive skirmishes, the well-supplied defenders are said to have passed much of the time drinking, dancing and playing games.

The approach to the castle took us up a driveway lined on both sides with cherry trees and through a courtyard where, we supposed, Ujimasa mustered his men in times of peace before sending them out to smite encroachers on his fief or crucify a few peasants who were late with the rice tax. In fact, some imagination was needed even to suppose that much, because the yard had been converted in modern times into a wretched, shabby zoo. There were grey cranes from India, orange flamingoes from Chile, dejected foxes surrounded by lumps of raw chicken and Japanese macaques swinging miserably on car tyres suspended from rusty chains, all penned up in wire-mesh cages that still showed traces of institutional green paint. There were also a few grey and gloomy concrete enclosures to house an Asian elephant, a tiger and two black bears.

In contrast to the zoo, the castle itself looked impressive. Its foundations were massive walls of stone designed to lean inwards and thus survive earthquake damage, and there was a pair of bronze dolphins set head downwards at each end of the roof, a traditional measure for securing divine protection from natural disasters. The main building had four storeys, all open to the public and all organised as one of those rather desperate museums found in small towns all over the world, whose fine period items are mixed up with whatever pre-World-War-I items of bric-à-brac could be salvaged from local barns and attics when the collection was being assembled. Among the relics, we discovered wooden panels decorated with paintings of golden and scarlet carp, peacocks' tails or puffy white chrysanthemums, and several beautiful and inaccurate maps on crinkly Japanese parchment. One beautiful object which caught my eye was a delicate boxwood lute decorated with two slivers of ivory turned towards each other like symmetrical moons. Cold and formal portraits of unsmiling aristocrats frowned down from the walls as we slowly filed along with the crowd past glass cabinets full of cedar chests inlaid with complex marquetry or mother-of-pearl, colorful old prints, fine ceramics, musty paper lanterns in light wooden frames bound with polished strips of hammered copper, combs and other *articles de toilette*, including a collection of what looked like wands of amber tipped with carvings of flying birds . . . and weapons. Lots and lots of weapons: pikes, halberds, spear heads, arrow heads, long swords, medium-length swords, short swords, sharp swords, straight swords, curved swords and swords with the handles missing, longbows, arrows with ornamented heads, helmets decorated with horsehair plumes or those extravagant wings of beaten bronze which give the wearer the manic, other-world appearance made famous by Kurosawa's movies, thick cloth armour reinforced with brass plates sewn on in overlapping layers, and bridles and harnesses in red and gold, marked with the castle insignia of three leaves set in a triangle and enclosed by a circle of black.

But the real surprise came when we finished the tour and then took a look at the brochure which we had received with our tickets: the castle, it cheerfully admitted, was not the authentic relic of Japanese history we had taken it for but a ferro-concrete copy, built in 1960. The same is true of many other castles in Japan, because at the time of the Meiji Restoration, a century and a half ago, the government ordered most of the originals demolished, to break the power of the clans. Not that destruction and rebuilding were unknown to Japanese castles before that. Constantly exposed to the twin dangers of fire and earthquake, to say nothing of attack by enemies, any castle that stayed upright for 200 years was doing well. The solid permanence of Warwick or Caernarvon was unknown.

Yet whatever its age, Odawara Castle had an odd charm that transcended its obvious function as a tourist trap. Before leaving for home we would go up to the top floor, where visitors could stroll around the outside on a narrow walkway and peer at the unfocused distance through 30-yen-in-the-slot telescopes. There we would lean on the rail and eat an ice-cream while looking down at the town of Odawara spread out below, ninth of the 53 stations of the old Tokaido Road, where passing travellers once had to stop at the nearby Hakone Barrier and pay their compulsory toll to the castle lord.

11 | Fashion Parade

IF I HAD been surprised when Mrs Kawaguchi, the manager of StarTalent, had urged me to register with her agency as a model, I was dumbfounded when she actually began to find jobs for me. The first was a small part in a feature film called *Harimao*. The title character was part Robin Hood, part multi-purpose spy and part guerrilla fighter, and the film dealt with his efforts to carry out acts of sabotage, conduct complicated intrigues, recruit disaffected locals and otherwise undermine British rule in Malaya and Singapore in the months and weeks immediately before the Japanese invasion in World War II. One scene towards the end of the film featured the cream of colonial society – mainly British officers and their wives, played by a motley crew of Tokyo-based foreigners – attending a ball at the famous Raffles Hotel, where they were shown swilling champagne and dancing with what was supposed to be characteristic British indifference to the impending danger. But the spell was suddenly broken when the hotel manager, played by me, strode across the ballroom, mounted the stage, gestured for the band to stop playing and then delivered a short speech to the effect that the enemy was at the gates, chaps, and it was time to stop partying and leave the country immediately. Despite the urgency of the situation, the manager allowed himself time to make a few elegantly-phrased remarks about the hotel's long and distinguished history and to indulge in some affectionate reminiscences about luminaries who had stayed there in the past, including Noel Coward and Herman Hesse. This scene was shot at a splendid country hotel in the Hakone mountains, a couple of hours' drive from Tokyo, where all the extras were issued with appropriate ballroom outfits and spent a long day waltzing around a panelled banqueting hall while the same piece of music was played over and over again. For me, it represented the fulfilment of a long-held fantasy, with pretty little make-up girls hovering around like butterflies and repeatedly dabbing the sweat from my hard-working brow, cameras going up and down on miniature mobile cranes, production staff with clipboards striding about looking harassed, and a famous director making periodic appearances on the set and yelling 'CUT!' through a megaphone. But when the film came out a few months later, the truth came with it: the manager had been played by a ham. My only consolation was that the rest of the film was awful as well, so much so that it was abruptly withdrawn only two weeks after being released.

But as far as Mrs Kawaguchi was concerned, everything had gone just fine and she could now pass off my experience in the movies as a qualification for other jobs. Soon I was getting frequent requests to attend auditions. All the competing models would assemble at a subway station exit or some other Tokyo landmark, where they would be met by a representative of their agency and would then troop off in a body to the offices of the production company or ad agency responsible for casting the job. Here we would take turns strutting our stuff in front of a video camera for later assessment. This involved introducing ourselves (name, age and nationality), briefly describing our recent experience (without too much regard for accuracy) and then standing up and turning slowly round to show off our profiles. If the job required some special ability, such as tap-dancing, shouting angrily, acting coy or whatever, we would be asked to demonstrate what we could do. A few days later, Mrs Kawaguchi would phone up to tell me if I had been chosen or not.

Mathematically, my chance of winning any given audition depended on the number of competing models, and as there was no shortage of equally unremarkable-looking males in my age-group, I had trouble visualising myself on the threshold of an exciting new career. On the other hand, I had the advantage of being new in town, and the production companies often preferred to use someone whose face had not been seen before. But the majority of auditions remained frustrating because it was so difficult to guess what the producer was looking for: often he didn't know himself, and was just having a look at as many possible candidates as the model agencies could provide in the hope that one would 'click.' This made winning jobs into an almost completely hit-and-miss affair, although just turning up at a sufficient number of auditions meant that anyone and everyone would eventually get chosen for something. Mrs Kawaguchi's next success on my behalf, as unexpected as the first, was to get me chosen by a bank that had commissioned a series of magazine ads featuring fathers as seen by members of their families. She assured me that I was picked for this job because I really was a father, although I couldn't see that I looked any more fatherly than any other model of the same age. But things became clearer the following week, when the ad agency concerned called up and invited me to dinner at a hotel in Yokohama to discuss the project. They also insisted that I should bring my youngest daughter along.

In due course we turned up as directed and put away a large and expensive meal in the company of the creative director, the account executive, the copywriter, the photographer and the photographer's assistant. The illustration for each ad in the series was to be a photo of the father doing something deemed to be typical of fathers, and the text was to consist of a comment by one of his children, pointing up some fatherly aspect of his character. The connection with banking seemed tenuous to say the least, but the general idea was to associate happy families with the friendly bank.

The purpose of the dinner was to extract some useful comment or reflection from Flora. For a long time she gave no help at all, offering monosyllabic and completely uninformative answers to our hosts' endless questions. But they remained admirably patient and good-humoured, and a second helping of ice cream drowned in strawberry sludge did the trick. In response to a question about what, if anything, she found objectionable about her father, she admitted that she was embarrassed if I broke into song in public, for instance when walking through a park or along a street, because it made people stare. This hardly seemed like red hot copy material to me, but the agency people loved it. It was genuine and it had the human touch. All that now remained was to shoot the photos. For this they took me to a small, quiet yacht marina in a beautiful wooded inlet south of Tokyo, dressed me in a camouflage-green anorak and beige cord trousers, slung an old-fashioned Jeremy-Fisher-style basket across my shoulders and thrust an ancient bamboo fishing pole into my hands. Several hundred photos later they decided that the job was done and shortly afterwards I made a full-page colour appearance in several magazines as a broadly-grinning amateur fisherman whose children disliked him singing in public. I just hoped the bank got something out of it too.

Typecasting me as a father appealed much more to Mrs Kawaguchi than trying to pass me off as a budding movie actor, and the third job she came up with was clearly spun off from the fisherman ad. This time it was a TV commercial for a company introducing a new brand of ice cream. The scene showed a family at the dinner table: granny, mother, father and 14-year-old son. Suddenly the front door was heard to burst open and 18-year-old daughter, just returned from another day at college, was seen hurrying into the kitchen, opening the fridge and searching for the ice cream she had been saving. Finding that it had disappeared, she burst in on the rest of the family, demanding to know who had eaten it. Amid protestations of innocence from everyone else, Father shot a quick, guilt-filled look towards the camera and then ducked down behind his newspaper. Cut to the product, play the jingle and then fade.

*

After the ice cream ad came a string of failures. Mrs Kawaguchi continued to send me along to auditions, but whatever
the magic touch had been, it seemed to have vanished. I tried
out as Sherlock Holmes in a TV drama, as the mad inventor
of a new kind of cockroach trap, as a doctor giving a lecture
on tooth decay and the need to switch to a higher-fluoride
brand of toothpaste, and as a villain in another TV drama
who attacked a young woman and got beaten up by the hero.
Once I was selected as the violinist in a fake string quartet
being used in a poster to advertise some upcoming concert,
but the concert was cancelled and the poster along with it.
And when Mrs Kawaguchi proposed putting me forward as
a clothes horse in a men's fashion show, I thought that even
she was starting to lose confidence in me.

'You don't mean real fashion modelling, do you?' I asked
her incredulously. 'Strutting up and down a catwalk in those
weird magazine clothes that nobody ever wears? You must be
joking.'

But she wasn't joking. 'You keep saying you can't do this,
or you wouldn't be suitable for that,' she reproved me. 'I'm
telling you, just take my word. You are no good at judging
whether you are suitable or not. And for this job, please do
me this favour and go to the audition. The client has seen
your photo already – he asked to see you.'

So I did what she said and went along to the offices of
CHAMPION FIT, the clothing company staging the show.
There I was quickly and unceremoniously rigged out in a
succession of oddly-coloured outfits under the supervision of
half a dozen of the scruffiest and worst-dressed young men I
had ever seen. Each time I put on a new set of clothes, they
stood me up against a white wall and took snapshots with an
instant camera. When the image emerged, they would go into
a huddle and examine it carefully, but without making any
comment to me. After an hour or so of this, they announced
with cheerful smiles that I had been selected to appear on the
show. A youth with a red handkerchief round his neck and
no shoes gave me a small piece of card with a badly-drawn

map on it, indicating when and where I was to turn up.

Punctually at 10 o'clock on the appointed day, I arrived at the address I had been given, which turned out to be a derelict brewery. Several of the buildings were still standing, but empty and cold, like ships gone for scrap, their windows smashed, their masonry crumbling, their doors closed by iron chains and rusted padlocks. Patiently awaiting demolition, skeletons of ancient machinery tottered against the skyline, still and abandoned, their conveyor systems stiff with a filthy sludge of dirt and oil, their iron ladders streaked with rust, their rails bent and mangled. Underfoot, the ground had once been concrete and tarmac, but was now cracked by repeated frosts and long winters of neglect, with tough, cheerfully tousled weeds pushing cheekily up through the fissures, all amidst a chaotic litter of rusty cans, tangled lengths of wire, abandoned tools, broken fridges, slimy old tyres and moss-covered chunks of brick.

This latter-day bombsite was located beside some equally disused railway tracks, and the appointed meeting place was a large room which had once served, I guessed, as a ticket office. It was empty and cold, and the heaters weren't working. The only other person there was Max Walsh, a model I had met a couple of times before at auditions. We sat on the floor for half an hour, smoking cigarettes and waiting for something to happen. Eventually other models, young men in their early twenties, started to drift in. Among them was a group of Frenchmen dressed as 1920s' American gangsters – cream-coloured shoes, wide-brimmed hats pulled down low and double-breasted suits. We assumed that these were their outfits for the show, but it turned out that they had just arrived from Paris dressed like that.

All of a sudden, some young employees of Champion Fit turned up and pushed their way through the door with several enormous boxes. One contained a large quantity of fresh fruit, while another was full of cans of beer. A girl with short, bobbed hair who looked like Madame Mao was wandering around with a clipboard, ticking off the names of the models who had arrived. She had large glasses with red plastic frames and hooped gold ear-rings with three small white fish dangling from each one. I asked her when the show was supposed to start, but she didn't know. Please help yourself to the fruit. Max Walsh and I amused ourselves by eating bananas and trying to shy the skins into a garbage bin on the other side of the hall. Obviously we were still waiting for something, and a few minutes later, it arrived: a group of about a dozen black teenagers from New York. All of them had the sides and backs of their heads shaved to a grey stubble, leaving only a crest of thick black curls, like a topping of chocolate sauce. They looked like a set of mechanical dolls for a child to play with, fresh out of the box. Sizzling with energy, they immediately began to leap and pirouette around the room to the sound of inaudible music played through the earphones of their Walkmans.

As if cued by their arrival, the Champion Fit employees now ripped open two more of their huge cardboard boxes and produced quantities of identical blue bomber jackets decorated with rectangular badges carrying the slogan 'Do The Right Thing' and embroidered on the back with the following words in all the colours of the rainbow:

THE CHAMPION FIT
SHOW. April 18. wed
AUTUMN & WIN-
TER Collection
by KENJI KAWANISHI

There was a free jacket for everybody, and since it was still cold, we all put them on right away on top of whatever else we were wearing. By way of a bonus, the jackets turned out to be reversible, with an insanely garish red silk motif as the alternative look, copiously printed with Disney-style cartoon characters. Max chose this side for display: it made him look as if he had been cut out of a sheet of wallpaper from a child's nursery. The New York mob donned their jackets with shouts of glee and then went back to cavorting about like maniacs, slapping each other's palms, leaping on and off the table and shouting:

'Hey, man, what the fuck's going down, man?'

'I dunno, man, but can ya dig it, man?'
'No shit, man, this is fuckin weird, baby!'
'Ain't it the truth, brother, I fuckin . . .' etc etc.

Just as I was beginning to wonder if this strange party, at which, incidentally, Madame Mao was the only woman, was some sort of rehearsal for the fashion show itself, we were summoned to leave the hall and follow a boy with inch-thick soles to his shoes and a black plastic cap worn back to front on his somewhat oversized head. We wandered for a few minutes through the derelict compound and then reached a building which turned out to contain several huge, empty cavernous halls, once used for storing barrels of beer. One hall was the dressing room and make-up area, while the one next door was where the show was to be held. Both were in an unholy mess, but the first glimmer of reason shone down on the proceedings when we saw that the dressing room contained about 40 clothes racks with three different outfits on each and the relevant model's name on a large piece of paper pinned to the top.

Apart from Angase, which I correctly identified as myself, the names included Rafael, Randelle, Bibby, Hugo, Frederick, Yoyo, Daniel, Jean-Jean and Martyn. Dozens of people were milling around looking busy, dragging more cardboard boxes from one place to another or darting silently between the halls. By this time it was about 11.30. Madame Mao drifted past, murmuring that the show would start at 4 o'clock. Plenty of time. No-one seemed to require the models just yet, so Max and I sat down and opened up some cans of beer. We were joined by Martyn, a young American with curly shoulder-length hair and a thick moustache drooping at the corners. He was wearing an extraordinarily self-satisfied expression, whose cause, he admitted, was that he had found a box somewhere with a lot of brand new shirts in it and had thought it the right moment to add to his personal wardrobe. He had picked out a dozen or so that he liked the look of and left them in a bundle in the yard outside, stuffed behind a large, badly-dented barrel, from where they could easily be retrieved later on.

On the dot of 12, we were summoned into the adjoining

hall to hear the show's director explain what was going to
happen. The theme of the designer's new collection, he told
us, was derived from the movie 'Do The Right Thing' by
the American movie director Spike Lee. That explained the
badges. The black boys were professional dancers and had
been imported from New York to generate an exciting, energy-
charged atmosphere. They would be dancing, the director told
us, but no-one else, he added sternly, had his permission to
dance. The other models would please just walk. You come
in from over there, walk up to here, turn around and walk
back again. That's all. While he was talking, two young men
with a TV camera were being raised and lowered on the arm
of a small crane, trying out the different angles they would use
when filming the show. Music was blaring from two enormous
speakers the size of upended cars. All the models were talking
at once, like geese, while the New Yorkers, or 'spikeleys', as
Max Walsh dubbed them, continued to limber up by turning
somersaults, wriggling on the floor and gyrating extravagantly, as if they were under the spotlight in a discotheque. The
Frenchmen, hunched beneath their sinister Al Capone hats,
and with their hands thrust deep in their pockets, were looking completely bewildered. They obviously didn't understand
a word of what was being said. One of them, I noticed, was
a good deal older than his companions. He had a thick white
beard which made him look exactly like Karl Marx.

The director now called for a rehearsal, so all the models
except the spikeleys (who had separate instructions) trooped
back into the dressing area and stood in silence waiting for
the signal. The music became louder than ever. Nothing happened. Then the director suddenly came into view, gesturing
impatiently with his clipboard. We all moved forward in a
pack, wheeled to the left and headed up the main aisle of the
hall. At the same time, a pair of double doors opened at the
far end and the spikeleys appeared, also bunched together,
leaping and whirling and screeching. The two groups collided
in the middle of the hall, broke and mingled, greeting each
other like long-lost buddies who hadn't met since the great
old days of way back when. The Champion Fit boys and
girls looked on approvingly. The director beamed. To me,

it seemed pure chaos. I couldn't imagine what an audience would make of it. Come to that, where were they going to be accommodated? The hall was full of wires and equipment and other paraphernalia, but there were no seats anywhere to be seen.

At that point, lunch was announced. Packed meals in little plastic cartons were hauled out of yet more cardboard boxes, and everyone sat down wherever they could find a spot and got stuck into the rice balls and the sandwiches. Beer continued to flow, although the Champion Fit gang abstained, as Japanese people seldom consume any alcohol until the day's work is finished. I found myself in a dark corner with Karl Marx, who now had a rather striking girlfriend in tow. It turned out that he was a theatre director from Paris who had come over to visit Japan with one of the actresses in his company. Some Champion Fit talent scout had spotted that beard on the street and recruited it to take part in the show, which its owner found 'amusant.' The actress, whose name was Marcelle, was gazing round in a stupor, half-nervous and half-thrilled to be closeted in this strange place with a truckload of men and no other women. By this time, tongues had started to loosen and the air was thick with assorted languages. The Argentinian could speak German and Arabic. There was a tall Spaniard with gold teeth who knew some French. One of the Frenchmen had a little English, enough to handle basic interpretation for his companions. An American called Frederick, who told us he lived in Milan, was even more at home in Italian than in English. Several other people present had at least a basic knowledge of Japanese.

This did not include the spikeleys, but they had a separate language of their own. At first they were too shy to speak it, but eventually a small group of them warmed up enough to introduce themselves. Their names were Leroy, Stretch, Catman, Peter-Paul and, inevitably, Spike. The one topic of conversation which really got them going was Nightclubs of the World. Hard times had struck New York, they explained, because some Honduran immigrant, angry at having his advances spurned by a hatcheck girl, had recently set fire to a private club in the Bronx and burned 80 or so of his compatriots to death. The case had been reported in newspapers around the world, and now the New York police were mercilessly closing down every club in the city which failed to comply with the official fire regulations. According to Peter-Paul, this meant virtually every club that was any good. It didn't matter in the case of 'The Castle,' because that was a dump anyway, but he particularly regretted the loss of 'Fruitola,' an establishment which stayed open all night and served 16 kinds of fruit juice. However, all was not lost. A place called 'The Blockhouse' was due to open shortly and would definitely be the new spot to go. And 'Nails,' the all-time ultimate best nightclub anywhere in the world, was still in business.

The tour then switched abruptly to Europe, which the spikeleys had recently visited to accompany a band called 'Fine Young Cannibals.' They had appeared on Peter's Pop Show in Germany and then Top of The Pops in London, after which they set out to enjoy themselves in a club called The Fridge. They liked the music, but not the clientele, who were roused to jealousy by the spikeleys' skill at dancing and ability to attract girls, and expressed their feelings by throwing lighted matches at them. On balance, London came out all right, much better than Paris, where the spikeleys found the people to be too serious, too intellectual, too talkative, lacking in spontaneity and exuberance. 'All they ever do is sit on the fuckin wall, man,' said Leroy sadly. Stretch, a small fellow with large round eyes, who was dressed in a suit of what appeared to be carpet material and a matching bowler hat, asked if anyone could suggest a good place in Tokyo. The Spaniard quickly recommended The Diamond Club, which had five floors open for drinking and dancing and a private sixth floor where, he assured us, members unable to wait until bedtime could take their girlfriends and obtain immediate relief without being disturbed.

In wholly unsuitable counterpoint to this interesting and informative conversation, one of the Parisians now produced a ukelele and began to play some of those chittery-chattery French folk songs which go down well in St Germain des Pres and nowhere else. It was a relief when he was interrupted by

Madame Mao, who appeared from behind a concrete pillar and called out 'Make-up!' Rows of chairs, we then noticed, had been set up on both sides of some long tables, and beside each one stood a make-up man with a box containing the necessary powders, gels, unguents and instruments of application. Taking their places in turn, all the models received a generous smudge of tan-tone foundation about the face, to hide the pallor of winter, and meticulous attention to their hair. Mine was smeared with a sort of jellified foam and then carefully worked into the style of a Fifties spiv. When I checked in the mirror, I found that I had acquired a nasty, weaselly look, like a crooked riverboat gambler.

As it turned out, this was well suited to the clothes that Champion Fit had selected for me to wear. It was now time to put on the first of our outfits, and when I reached my clothes rack I found that I had been provided with two young girls to act as my 'dressers.' One of them went straight for my fly, which she unzipped with cool, professional fingers, while the other started unbuttoning my shirt. Working with speed and efficiency, they soon had me stripped to my underpants, like a plucked duck, and then went through the process in reverse, decking me out in a brown silk shirt speckled with yellow lozenges, a red and beige cravat and a green check three-piece suit. Brown and white shoes, ideal for creeping through the corridors of a paddle steamer on the Mississippi, completed the ensemble. At the next rack was Max Walsh, whose dressers were a pair of sad-faced boys with delicate features and long straight hair. His outfit made him look like a head waiter who had inexplicably lost all sense of his position. The cut of the clothes was more or less right but the colours had run amok, assaulting the senses with weird blocks of baboon-bum red, custard yellow, apopleptic purple and hospital staircase green. Throughout the hall, clothes were being changed at a frantic pace. Some of the Frenchmen were togged up like South American pimps, in pink, mauve and vermilion felt hats, embroidered bolero jackets, narrow green trousers and white loafers. The most bizarre outfits of all had been reserved for the spikeleys: they found themselves enclosed in skin-tight spandex body costumes decorated with harlequin patterns that made them look like a pack of jokers on the loose in a playing card factory.

Once we were all dressed, Champion Fit marshals began to organise us into a rough queue, consulting lists on their clipboards to make sure that everyone was in the right order. The designer, clearly nervous, darted here and there among the throng, picking off a stray thread from this shoulder, a speck of lint from that jacket and calling the make-up people to effect last-minute adjustments to faces and hairstyles. At last the music became louder than ever and one by one, the models began to be fed through the gap between the halls. When it came to my turn, I stepped out with as much cheerfulness and confidence as I could muster but could barely conceal my amazement at the sight of the auditorium, which had now been completely transformed. The walls were draped with coloured material, rows of seats had been installed and there was an audience of several hundred buyers, journalists and fashion experts from all over the world watching intently with pens poised over their leather-bound notebooks. Flashbulbs popped close to my face in rapid succession and a man with a TV camera on his shoulder, trailing a long thick cable, followed me up to the end of the catwalk, filmed me wheeling round at the far end and then panned back to catch me returning to where I had started. I didn't know whether to laugh or break into a run: I could feel my face beginning to twitch with nervousness. Instead, I forced myself to slow down, and gazed directly into the crowd with what I hoped was the confident, self-possessed air of the well-heeled modern boulevardier. But there were so many models and so many outfits that it didn't seem to matter.

Back in the dressing room, my 'dressers' fell on me like crows on a sandwich, unceremoniously stripping off my finery and stuffing me into the next outfit. This was concocted along semi-military lines and included camouflage trousers, heavy boots and a khaki beret with a German army cap badge, worn with a ghastly collarless cardigan in the sort of camp, ducky-wucky colours that would come over well in a magazine photo, and a waist-length brown cape affair that I could already visualize abandoned, unloved and unworn at the bottom of a chest in some theatre's wardrobe room. The marshals quickly hustled us back into a queue, this time in a different order, and we were propelled out again, one by one, under the glare of the lights. The show finished according to plan, with the carefully-rehearsed collision between the main body of the models and the squawking, gesticulating spikeleys. Somehow the designer found himself in the middle of the melee; seized by exuberant hands, he was tossed into the air as if he had just won us all a gold medal. The audience applauded rapturously, possibly because they were infected by the atmosphere of lunacy, or maybe because they really enjoyed what they had seen. The designer kept his head down from shyness, but you could see he was beaming to himself, clutching a huge bouquet of flowers, bowing and shaking hands with everyone and being extravagantly congratulated on all sides. A party was obviously in the offing, but I had had enough. Quickly getting back into my own clothes, I headed for the door. Outside, darkness was falling and everything was quiet. Everything, that is, except for a soft scuffling sound coming from behind a rusty old oil drum. In the fading light, I saw that it was Martyn, quietly retrieving his stash of stolen shirts.

12 | Hot Spring

ALL STARTALENT'S jobs paid a respectable fee, but the
ice cream ad was handsome. We decided to treat ourselves to
a weekend away somewhere, and after studying the map for a
while, picked out a hot-spring resort called Shuzenji, down the
coast to the southwest and then into the heart of the rugged and
mountainous Izu Peninsula.

A slow, four-hour journey by train and bus brought us to
the edge of the town, where we stepped out onto the road,
shouldered our luggage and set off to look for our hotel. It at
once became apparent that Shuzenji was not a single town but
a cluster of hamlets grown together, strung out along each side
of a narrow, steep-sided valley in which a river swollen with
snowmelt rushed and gurgled over huge, smooth boulders.
Some of the back roads were hardly more than footpaths, while
the main street, in which buses and cars could only pass each
other with difficulty, was lined with inns and souvenir shops.

The hotel stood right on the river and had large private
grounds sloping up a steep hill at the back. In front, domi-
nated by two immense cedar trees, was a small yard where

taxis could deposit newly-arriving guests or collect them when they were ready to leave. The foyer had a gloomy and lugubrious atmosphere: the only illumination came from the receptionist's cubbyhole and cast barely enough light for us to be able to make out a heavy wooden coffee table and a couple of battered sofas. On one side a few rocks were decoratively grouped together and we could hear the sound of water gurgling somewhere.

A maid led us to our room along a network of passageways whose twists and turns revealed that the hotel consisted not of one building but several, linked together by cedarwood walkways that crossed and recrossed a complex network of streams and ponds in the garden. The walkways were roofed but had no walls, so that while moving from one part of the hotel to another one was neither exactly indoors nor exactly outdoors. Here and there were some handily-sited benches made of bamboo and covered with thin cushions, where guests could relax and look over the railing at big, brightly-coloured carp rolling about in the water among the rocks and shrubs.

Our room was large – in fact there were two adjoining rooms – and was painted a foul mustard yellow which made it as gloomy as the rest of the hotel. But when we opened the paper screens covering the windows, we found a little alcove behind them containing two comfortable old bamboo chairs and a view that might have been designed for a movie set. Right below the window ran the river, its foaming white caps racing and tumbling over the rocks, while on the opposite bank stood a venerable temple half-hidden in a copse of trees. Thrusting into this picture from the left hand side was a branch of an ancient cherry tree, gnarled and moss-covered but still hung with a few clusters of delicate, pinky-white blossoms.

The hotel had several different baths, some indoors and some in the grounds, which were available to male and female guests at different hours. The best one out of doors was approached by a stone-flagged passage that climbed up through the hotel garden past tall camellia bushes and thick stands of bamboo with a few moss-covered stone lanterns visible here and there through the foliage. The bath was surrounded by large boulders and had a floor of small glazed pebbles. From some source underground came a constant flow of hot water which trickled into the bath along a groove cut into one of the boulders. An electric lantern was set on top of another boulder to provide a little light for guests who chose to take their baths at night, under the stars.

We spent the afternoon wandering around the town, crossing the river on bridges with vermilion-painted handrails and following little flower-bordered lanes past elderly wooden houses, dingy noodle shops and silent shrines. Everywhere there hung the slightly sour, sulphurous smell of the volcanic stew simmering beneath our feet: in one small municipal park we sampled hot water gushing from a spigot set in a rock – it tasted pure, if not exactly delicious – while watching a pair of municipal gardeners carefully working their way across an open patch of gravel from which they were removing tiny weeds one at a time with sharp-bladed penknives.

The temple after which the town was named was dedicated to Kobo Daishi, a famous wandering monk of the 8th century who went to China and returned to introduce Shingon or esoteric Buddhism to Japan. He is one of the great legendary heroes of his country, credited with miraculous accomplishments the length of the land – boring through miles of mountains to create networks of caves, altering landscapes with his bare hands to force the passage of roads where none could go before, diverting rivers with inspired avalanches, building great bridges, reshaping and blessing wherever he went. As if that wasn't enough, he was also credited with inventing the syllabic form of writing called *hiragana*.

The statue that stood beside the temple showed that these deeds were not performed by some delicate aesthete but by a stocky, chunky man with strong legs, broad shoulders and features like a retired commando. He was dressed in a simple robe, leggings and sandals, and had a moon-shaped hat slung on his back. In his right hand he carried a staff as tall as himself, and in his left a round begging bowl.

The town's souvenir shops were all alike, but their crowded aisles showed that duplication wasn't hurting business. As well as shelves crammed with vases, teacups and other items of pottery, they were big on wooden carvings: the walls were festooned with masks of gods, demons and familiar characters from Noh plays. There were also some life-size eagles with outstretched wings, glaring from their mahogany perches, loping bears and some of the long, flat wooden fish that are still sometimes hung in temples to symbolise simultaneous wakefulness and immobility, and are also struck with small wooden mallets in the same way, and for the same purpose, as a gong.

Right in the middle of town, where the crowds were busiest, there was a large rocky islet in the river with an irregularly-shaped basin scooped out of the top of it and fed by hot water piped up from some source deep below the riverbed. This public bath supposedly came into existence when Kobo Daishi struck the rock with his staff and water gushed out in response. The islet was linked to the shore by a wooden footbridge, while the bath on top of it was screened by a flimsy wattle fence with a dilapidated roof of thatch. The degree of privacy thus afforded was vague – the presence or absence of bathers could be perceived, but passers-by would have had to do some serious neck-craning if they wanted to see anything specific. Beside the footbridge was a sign announcing that the bath could be used free of charge by anyone at any time. Oblivious of the milling crowds, a young couple touring the area had stopped to enjoy a soak together, leaving their jackets slung across the seats of two gleaming red bicycles parked against a nearby wall.

*

A further indulgence paid for by the fee from the ice cream ad was my acquisition of another motorcycle. The search for a replacement clutch cable for the Honda had led me to a little shop run by a man called Fujimoto, who had a passion for Harley Davidsons. When he wasn't stripping and rebuilding one or other of the two he owned, he was performing the same service for a small army of friends, who used to crowd into his workshop, sit around looking at American bike magazines, borrowing tools, drinking cans of beer and generally getting in the way of their unfailingly genial and good-humoured host. At the back of the workshop was a 250cc Yamaha which had been left with Fujimoto in part payment for some service and was now doing nothing but taking up space. When I declared an interest, Fujimoto could hardly wait to get it off his hands.

The great advantage of the Yamaha was that it allowed me to use the motorway network (no bike smaller than 250cc is allowed). I could now go to Tokyo more quickly and for less money than by train, and also went on several exploratory rides along the coast and over to Mt Fuji, where there was a scenic road called the Skyline, which crossed the southern flank of the mountain at a high enough altitude to give a clear view over the forests on the lower slopes and down to the wide arc of Sagami Bay.

Throughout Japan, I quickly learned, solidarity among bikers is strong. On country roads at least they nearly always acknowledge each other with a raised hand and at rest stops on the motorways they all park in the same section and sit around with coffee or cans of fruit juice, admiring each others' machines, studying maps, talking about where they've been and giving each other tips on good places to stay. Most of them make a point of dressing the part when they go out, choosing colourful, close-fitting leathers, repel-everything boots and expensive, full-face helmets. They also tend to be very serious and responsible in their attitude to motorcycling, an attitude partly inculcated by the problems of getting a licence. This is invariably both demanding and expensive: with lessons (all conducted on specially laid-out courses inside a driving school) plus the test, the cost can easily reach the equivalent of a month's pay, and very few people pass the first time around. A car licence covers anything up to 50cc, but after that, there are separate tests for each size-category of bike, in ascending order of difficulty. For 400cc or over, the test begins with the applicant laying the bike carefully on its side on the ground and then picking it up again. In addition there is a carefully choreographed sequence of actions for the proper way of getting seated and checking traffic conditions before setting off, followed by a complex slalom section, a tricky ride along a narrow, raised beam (not too fast and not too slow), various stopping and signalling manoeuvres and finally a written test with separate sections for mechanical knowledge and highway code. To make even one mistake in this test is to invite certain failure.

Another awkward moment in the Japanese biker's life comes when the *shaken* falls due. This is a combination of vehicle safety check, mandatory government insurance and tax. The *shaken* must be renewed every two years, but bikes of 250cc or less, I was relieved to learn, are exempt. But the cost is always high, especially if any repairs are needed, so one of its effects is to make owners think very seriously about whether they really want to pay that much to keep their bike on the road. Many decide that they don't (or can't), but of course a bike with only a couple of months of valid *shaken*, or none at all, is tough to sell. Second-hand dealers therefore have plenty of relatively cheap machines for sale, often with very low mileage.

Carrying a passenger is allowed on ordinary roads but not on motorways, so if the girlfriend wants to come along she's got to ride a bike of her own. Many do just that, with the result that the proportion of females among the nation's bikers would surprise anyone who still thinks that Japanese girls are all delicate flowers who spend their time kneeling on the floor in kimonos, pouring out tea. Accidents are a grey area in terms of legal responsibility: the police have a rough rule of thumb which assigns the fault to the larger/heavier vehicle. The car will usually be blamed before the motorcycle, the motorcycle before the bicycle and the bicycle before the pedestrian. The system is flexible but Japanese policeman usually aren't, which can obviously lead to miscarriages of justice: hit-and-run is therefore a lot more common than it should be.

Young people mostly prefer low-slung, domestic-made racing machines with high-pitched whining engines and brightly-coloured fairings, but there is also a strong prestige market for foreign bikes – especially Harley Davidsons. There are two types of Japanese Harley rider: the first is middle-aged and respectable and travels the highways with his friends in solemn, well-disciplined processions of fifteen, twenty or even thirty machines together, sometimes preceded by a white Mercedes. The other, to which Fujimoto and his friends belonged, is the textbook version: long hair, bandanna, ear-rings, studded jeans jacket and oily boots. This rare species mostly keeps a low profile but is sometimes coaxed into the open by camping and beer-drinking weekends organized by the Rising Sons Club, a group of Harley devotees drawn from the many American military bases around Japan.

Fujimoto took me along to spend a day at one of these blow-outs, which was held in a remote spot among the Tama Hills, west of Tokyo. By the time we arrived there were already about a hundred machines parked in a long, curving line, their chrome gleaming, their handlebars jutting upwards like metallic antlers and their polished paintwork blazoned with decals and badges. They were ranged like a guard of honour around a grubby delivery van whose back doors were open, like arms flung wide, to acclaim an elaborately restored 1950s' vintage Harley which was the club's totem.

Several other vans had been used to bring supplies, since the fixed-price tickets to attend the event covered all food, drink and entertainment. There were stacks of cases of American beer from the base and several barrels from which people were taking turns to refill their paper cups, using a pistol-like dispenser on the end of a hose. In one corner of the site, under some trees, someone had set up a barbecue the size of a barn door and placed two large plastic garbage cans beside it, each filled to the brim with enormous steaks. These were for general consumption: anyone who felt hungry at any time just helped themselves. The atmosphere was loud, cheerful and boisterous: every few minutes more new arrivals turned up, each performing a triumphant and deafeningly loud circuit of the site before adding their bikes to the line.

Fujimoto attended all the club's get-togethers on a regular basis, partly because he simply enjoyed them and partly for motives of business. He quickly set up a small stall on which he laid out a variety of badges, T-shirts and baseball caps marked with Harley Davidson insignia, several small parts and tools, and a sign offering on-the-spot repair or painting services. While he busied himself with his customers, I got into conversation with some of the Americans, who were reminiscing about their experiences in the Gulf War. One tall young man with spiky red hair and freckles described how he had spent 18 hours a day in the bowels of some ship assembling 'ordnance' for the Navy's air arm to drop on the Iraqis. He willingly admitted having spent all the waking hours in constant fear that the ship would take a direct hit, which would certainly have been very final.

This went some way to explaining the black humour with which he described a special bomb which had been devised for use on the Republican Guard. It was carried by a C-130 transport aircraft and delivered by simply opening the cargo bay doors and pushing it out. Detonation took place about 50 feet from the ground, and the effect was to completely obliterate everything in an area the size of a football field. After it had been dropped, the C-130 would make a long, slow turn and then come round and drop another. This time, however, the bomb contained leaflets instead of explosives. The message was simple: 'Either you surrender, or we'll do it again.' The laughter which greeted this story was loud and happy, but evidently without any malice. It simply reflected the listeners' shared sense of relief and satisfaction at having been on the side with the most effective technology. They had no hatred for the Iraqis – in fact some of them expressed sympathy. But from the moment they arrived in the Gulf, all any of them wanted to do was finish the job quickly and efficiently and then get out alive. If the technology of destruction was the most effective means to that end, they embraced it. They were all technology-mad, from the gunners to the weather forecasters. That was why they loved Harleys, too.

*

Fujimoto had a few stories of his own, which he liked to tell whenever an audience of cronies had gathered to watch him fixing some bike in his workshop. One I remember particularly was about an old school friend and neighbour of his called

Ikeda. Ikeda was a painter by trade and a collector of antique motorcycles. He also had a little three-year-old daughter called Doremi, named after the first three notes of the musical scale. Anyway, Fujimoto explained, Ikeda and his wife had been going through a bit of a bad patch. Lack of money, no real prospects, getting a bit tired of each other, that sort of thing. So along the way, the wife had found a new boyfriend to liven up her life – a biker, all leather, chrome studs and chain grease. Not to be outdone, Ikeda took up with a cute little doll of a girlfriend who worked as a waitress in a coffeeshop just up the road from Fujimoto's workshop. So far, nothing much out of the ordinary. But then Ikeda's wife got pregnant. That was right out of order. A clear breach of the rules. Ikeda didn't like it. In fact he was furious. But before anyone made up their mind what to do about it, the biker-boyfriend got crunched by a truck on the Chuo Expressway. Floods of tears and clouds of grief. And then the waitress-girlfriend, who Fujimoto said had been secretly cultivating a better prospect elsewhere, developed a real or pretended guilt crisis about the fact that Ikeda was married. After a few tantrums she disappeared, leaving an acutely tense, frustrated atmosphere behind her.

At this point, fate introduced a new ingredient. He was a Buddhist monk, middle-aged, completely bald, softly spoken and given to wearing those round, wire-rimmed glasses that stand for wisdom and serenity. He also turned out to be an affable, kindly fellow. Took an interest in the Ikedas' affairs. Tried to be helpful. Acted the adviser, the counsellor, even the referee. And then, as it seemed with a little absence therapy in mind, he invited Ikeda to come and stay for an indefinite period at his own house in the mountains, in the north of Japan. The pair of them set off. No further contact. After a while, wondering when or if Ikeda was ever coming back, the wife called up the monk on the phone. His reply was that Ikeda had indeed stayed there for a few weeks but had then gone away. 'I assumed he had gone home,' declared the holy man.

But he hadn't. So where was he? He must have been somewhere, because he was still making withdrawals from the family account. But he never got in touch with the wife, which was odd. Nor his daughter, which was inexplicable. So after a bit more fretting and fruitless telephoning here and there, the wife decided to put matters in the hands of the police. They launched an investigation. And by displaying an admirably stoic determination to consider all the possibilities, however unlikely, they eventually dug up the missing Ikeda. Dug him up from under the monk's kitchen floor, where he had been buried and neatly cemented over. Apparently the monk had stabbed him to death with a view to getting his hands on Ikeda's paltry savings – because in Japan, you don't need a signature to get into someone else's account. The personal seal that everyone carries, plus the bankbook, are enough.

The abrupt transition in this story from the mundane to the macabre, seemed to me to have an almost medieval flavour. It was a tale that belonged to the dirty alleyways and scruffy noodle shops of old Edo. Other people evidently thought so too. 'Yes, naturally it made the papers,' Fujimoto said, as he reached under the bike he was working on and began to loosen a retaining bolt on the exhaust pipe. 'Next thing we knew, there was a TV company snooping around here, asking questions. They wanted to make the story into a drama. Rewritten, of course, in a feudal-era setting.'

Another reminder of the ways of old Japan which I came across as a result of knowing Fujimoto was the subject of *kanpo*, Chinese herbal medicine. His old widowed mother, with whom he lived in a small flat above the workshop, had originally come from Toyama, an area on the coast of the Japan Sea that was famous as a source of folk remedies. In days gone by, medicine sellers from Toyama were a common sight in towns and villages all over Japan, walking from place to place with large boxes on their backs from which they dispensed the pills, herbs, decoctions and infusions which ordinary people relied on before the advent of modern medicine. The old lady still had a small practice and her patients were always calling round for roots, teas and other specifics, or just to replenish the family medicine chest and chat.

Among her books and papers, Fujimoto's mother had a yellowed newspaper cutting which mentioned a book, available in Japanese, English and several other languages, called

'Kotei Daikei.' The article described it as 'an all-encompassing reference book at the center of *kanpo* knowledge.' This sounded worth having, so I set out to try and get hold of it. My first stop was a well-known *kanpo* shop in central Tokyo, where the owner assured me that the book did exist and was available in English, although he didn't have a copy. Next I went the rounds of the main foreign-language bookshops but none of them was able to help. A call to the publishers brought a denial that any translation had ever been made.

Puzzled, I returned to the *kanpo* shop, where the owner insisted that he himself had seen the book in English and gave me the names of two specialist medical bookshops to try. On the phone, one said they didn't have it, but they could offer me another Chinese book in English on a similar subject. The other said that although they didn't actually have the 'Kotei Daikei' in stock, it was published in Hong Kong, from where they would soon be getting a new consignment. But when I went round to place an order, I found that the kindly and helpful gentleman of the phone call was the subordinate of a dragon-faced manageress who belonged to the that-book-doesn't-exist school of thought. So instead I tried the shop which claimed to have another famous Chinese medical text-book. This turned out to be the 'Shang Han Lun,' described in a subhead as 'The Great Classic of Chinese Medicine,' which immediately persuaded me to buy it. But it turned out to be disappointingly obscure, classifying physical malfunctions into such mysterious categories as Lesser/Greater Yin Disease, Lesser/Greater Yang Disease, Sunlight Yang Disease, Absolute Yin Disease and so on. The commentary repeatedly declared that the book was the greatest medical work ever written, but failed to explain what the categories meant, or whether, say, gallstones were a lesser *yin* condition or a sunlit *yang* condition or what. The text consisted mostly of such statements as:

> If the patient of the sunlight yang confirmation suffers from a loss of memory and has signs of stagnant blood and hard stools but no difficulty in moving the bowels, he should be treated by the purgation method with ti-tang-tang (Rhubarb and Leech Combination).

Applying this kind of advice in practice promised to be a tough job. On the other hand, the edition contained a fascinating appendix which listed the source books from which it had been compiled. The books themselves had all been lost, but the list of their titles, which itself dated from around 200 AD, drew back the curtain on an astonishing panorama of medical – and by implication, general intellectual – writing and knowledge. They included 'Medical Classics' (seven schools of thought in 216 volumes); 'Classics and Formulas' (eleven systems in 274 volumes); 'Divinity' (ten creeds in 205 volumes) and 'Bedroom Arts' (eight documents composed of 186 essays). The last-named group contained, among other things, 20 books of the 'Yellow Emperor's and Three Kings' Aphrodisiac Formulas' and 17 books under the general title 'Bedroom Formulas For Fertility.' A note at the end of the appendix stated sniffily that the 'Bedroom Arts represent a science that is concerned with temperament and ways to control the desires and suppress inner sensuality by following the way of the sages: restraint.' But with all the books lost, it was hard to believe that this was the whole story.

13 | In the Saddle

A FEW weeks after I acquired the Yamaha, it developed an annoying fault: if it was left standing for more than half an hour, it began to stink of petrol. When I examined it, I found two barely visible cracks in the paintwork at the bottom of its stylishly angular tank, from which tiny tears of fuel were very slowly welling up and weeping onto the engine. Diligent probing with the blade of a screwdriver disclosed a couple of badly corroded patches with several small but substantial holes. My own attempts to solve the problem with a metal-based filler kept ending up back at the beginning, with the holes apparently plugged but a few drops of petrol still defiantly escaping. So one night over a beer I mentioned it to Kimura, and he volunteered to fix it for me.

Kimura's welding business stood on a bare patch of land among some fields about 30 minutes' drive away. His employees were half a dozen young Thais who had come to Japan ostensibly as tourists and quickly melted out of sight in search of jobs. They lived right there in the yard, in two large steel shipping containers which had evidently been filched from some Yokohama dock. These they had done their best to fix up as a tolerable two-room home: there were some wooden bunk beds, a table, some tatty armchairs, a TV and an enormous fridge for the beer. In winter they could get up a good fug with a paraffin stove, but the temperature in summer had been almost unbearable until one of them had found an old air conditioner abandoned beside the road and managed to repair and install it.

On the face of it, their conditions were wretched – a classic instance of ruthlessly exploited immigrant labour – but the Thais themselves were well pleased with the arrangements. They made about 50 dollars a day and reckoned it would take them two or three years to save up enough to go home and start a business of their own: perhaps a taxi or two, or a fleet of pedalos beside some beach, or a sailboat in which to take tourists to offshore islets, or a couple of apartments to rent out. Their families back home were goggle-eyed by the size of their remittances and would write them anxious letters asking if they had given up work and turned to bank robbery, which filled them with delight and pride.

They all had unpronounceable names except one, who called himself 'Boy'. When Boy arrived in Japan, he spent his first few days squatting silently in a corner on the floor at Kimura's house and looking completely bewildered by his new surroundings. He neither spoke nor understood any Japanese, but he had a few words of English, which he would occasionally try out in a soft whisper, and the appealing Thai habit of expressing thanks by putting his palms vertically together, raising them to his forehead and bowing. Now, only three months later, he looked quite different. The studious young aesthete had been replaced by a tough-looking young man who stamped about the site in a wrinkled leather jacket and filthy jeans, laughing heartily and handling an oxy-acetylene blow torch as casually as a pair of chopsticks. A thin moustache had sprouted from his upper lip, and on the few occasions when we went out drinking, he liked to demonstrate his newly acquired habit of running a playful hand up the waitress's skirt. But he and his companions were disinclined to waste money in bars, so they passed most of their free time in the steel containers, drinking beer, watching television, flicking through pornographic magazines and playing cards for small change. And about once a month, usually after the completion of some especially difficult or lucrative job, Kimura would bundle them all into a van late at night and drive them to a place in Yokohama where they could have an hour or two with a girl for the equivalent of a day's pay.

They were fortunate to be employed by Kimura, as he was genuinely fond of them and treated them like children of his own, with kindness and patience tempered now and again by a gruff bark when the need arose. He had friends in Thailand himself, including the police chief of some small town whom he would visit for brief but intensive golfing holidays, and it was from this man that he had first got the idea of employing young Thais in his business. He was amused and even charmed by their gentle manners, although he became exasperated when these characteristics translated into incompetent work habits. He frequently mentioned their apparent inability to remember simple instructions, however often they were repeated: again and again he would explain that the hammer belonged *here*, the wrenches *here* and the cutter blades *there* . . . but they seemed congenitally incapable of retaining what they were told and would quickly lose their awareness of the tool itself, somewhere during the process of using it, and just cast it anywhere when they were finished with it. Kimura attributed the backward condition of Third World countries precisely to their lack of discipline in such simple matters, not at all to the Big Issues, the inadequacy of the education, the rampant official corruption or the stubborn survival of anachronistic social customs which jettisoned able-bodied young men for obscure faults of caste or birth and compelled young women to spend their youth whoring in bars. The days when poor families in Japan were forced to sell their own daughters into similar slavery to buy food or pay debts are still remembered by older people today, and Kimura was one of many who considered it a clear sign of social progress that the same fate was now reserved for people in poorer countries.

In accordance with Kimura's suggestion, I took the tank

over to the yard the next day and we all sat in one of the containers and drank a few beers and looked at the holes and talked about how fixing them would be just a five minute job, which unfortunately they were too busy to do right now, but if I wouldn't mind waiting for a couple of days . . . ? Of course not, any time will be just fine. Have another beer. During the course of the next fortnight, I would ring up the yard from time to time and ask how they were getting on, but Kimura was always out, or occupied with a customer or away for a few days. One time he picked up the phone himself without realising who was calling and was so embarrassed by his own procrastination that he assured me he was fixing the tank at that very moment and would be dropping it off at my house on his way home that evening. To begin with I didn't want to make too much of a fuss, but as time went on I became more and more impatient and one day went round to the site, walked into the container, picked up the tank, which had acquired a coating of oily filth while lying untouched on the same shelf where I had left it originally, said a quick hullo and goodbye and walked right out again.

On the way home, I got off the main road, which was jammed with traffic, and took a quieter route through the fields. This took me past a little hamlet where there was a restaurant which I had visited a few times before. Since I had plenty of time, I decided to stop in and have a drink.

The restaurant was run by an old friend of Hasegawa's called Yamada. Its name was *Kura*, which means 'saddle', and had been chosen to commemorate a time gone by when Yamada had lived in California and supported his young family by selling riding accessories to the local ranchers. Yamada came outside to have a look at the offending petrol tank, and while I was explaining the problem and he was assuring me that he could fix it in five minutes, a large crow on the telegraph wire above us had two rapid bowel movements, one on the tank and the other on my head. My obligation to provide some entertainment having thus been satisfactorily discharged, we went inside, leant the tank up against the leg of a table and sat down while Yamada's son went off to get a bottle and a couple of glasses.

Yamada was a squat, chunky man of about 60, with the look and build of an ex-middleweight. He had small hands with short, blunt fingers, a craggy face that still had something boyish about it, and a shock of silver hair that grew in one collective tuft out of the top of his head. His moody, volatile temperament was a local legend. When something annoyed him his eyes would flash and his finger would stab accusingly at the air between himself and his opponent, but he could easily snap out of it and switch to a sunny cheerfulness that expressed itself in rich, deep chuckles and a huge smile that made his mouth turn up joyfully at the corners like a slice of melon. He and Hasegawa were old friends and took a wicked delight in needling each other. Yamada never missed an opportunity to mock Hasegawa's political pretensions, declaring that the local wheeling and dealing was as dirty as the national variety, while Hasegawa countered by declaring that public service was at least a more worthwhile occupation than working as a 'part-time waiter' – a sly dig at Yamada's propensity to leave the running of the restaurant to his wife while he himself sat around and chatted to his friends.

Yamada had been born in Yokohama in 1928, thirteen years before Japan's attack on Pearl Harbor. His father had run a confectionary business, employing a dozen or so people to make sweets and cakes which he then sold to retail shops in Yokohama and other nearby towns. But the war brought disaster, first by cutting off the supplies of raw materials, which were diverted to meet military requirements, and then by destroying the factory, which was obliterated in a bombing raid. The family then went through a bad period in which father got drunk and everyone went hungry.

By the time the war came to an end, Yamada was 16 years old, fed up with being hungry and determined to try to resurrect the family business. His first move was to make the rounds of their former suppliers in Chinatown, which the Japanese police were barred from entering under Occupation rules and which was therefore enjoying even more prosperity than usual as a centre of the booming black market. The Chinese were pleased to see him back and quickly offered to restore his supplies of sugar, flour and anything else he might need. They even found him new premises.

In a few months Yamada had the business up and running again, in fact doing better than ever, since the end products were not only small and tasty but also cheap enough for even the war-ruined inhabitants of Yokohama to afford. Over the next few years, the sales area spread north through Tokyo to the rural prefectures beyond and south to the Izu peninsula, from where itinerant pedlars would travel up on ancient motorcycles hitched to small, flat-bed trailers, load up on confectionary and then travel back to sell their wares in the towns and villages they passed through. The irregular nature of black market commerce meant that there were frequent opportunities to trade in other restricted commodities as well, so that Yamada's network was bringing him an average daily profit, as he confided to me in a whisper one day when we were alone and drunk, 'equivalent to the wages that ordinary people had to work six months to earn.' As a dutiful son, he never kept any of this money for himself, but handed it all over to his father, from whom, as he confidently expected, he would one day inherit the business. But it didn't turn out that way. There were arguments at home about the direction the business should be taking – mild bickering at first, later developing into full-scale stand-up rows – and finally Yamada had had enough. 'You can have the money, the stock, the contacts, everything,' he told his father during their last dramatic confrontation. 'What belongs to me is my time. From now on, I go my own way.' With which he stormed out of the house to start a new life. It wasn't until many years later, he admitted, that he came to realise how his own youthful energy and success had undermined the remnants of his father's self-confidence.

Yamada's principal memory from his early teenage years was of constantly being hungry. Many of his conversations would eventually lead back to the enduring theme of how tough it was to get food when the war was on. Sometimes there was nothing to be had but beans, for days or even weeks on end. Sometimes a neighbour would give him a tomato or a green pepper and he would carry it conscientiously home to be divided up among his family. Sometimes he would make long sorties on foot to the mountains to search for wild plants, but plenty of other people were doing the same thing and there wasn't a lot to be had. Occasionally he had a stroke of luck, as for instance when a horse that was pulling a cartload of sweet potatoes fell down dead one day, upsetting the cart and scattering the potatoes all over the road. Frequent recall and repetition had conferred legendary status on this period of want, and now that it was over, Yamada liked nothing better than to sit and watch his customers filling their faces with huge meals. One of the house specialities was raw horsemeat, served in rolled-up, paper-thin slices on a bed of lettuce and onion and dipped before eating in a fierce mixture of soy sauce and mustard. Another popular choice was 'Country Sausage,' which consisted of slabs of sausage meat burrowed inside a bed of hash brown potatoes with an egg dropped on top. And then there were the steaks, which arrived sizzling from the grill accompanied by juicy, lightly-fried onion rings and hot corn on horseshoe-shaped steel plates that Yamada had designed and made himself. Quality was an obsession: *Kura*'s cold store contained several massive chunks of beef from which each steak was sliced to order, in accordance with the customer's preferences in cut and thickness. Yamada had an all-consuming contempt for restaurants that served inferior meat. If anyone mentioned one of his competitors, he would most likely say 'Shit! That sonofabitch don't know nothin'!'

'Shit' and 'sonofabitch' were two more of Yamada's treasured souvenirs from America, as were his six pairs of highly polished cowboy boots, his collection of Western shirts with popper buttons and a walnut-wood piano which he had had shipped all the way from Chicago. He had loved living in California and would certainly have settled there permanently if his young daughter had not been diagnosed as suffering from some deformity of the hip bone. Yamada could not afford the treatment in America and anyway doubted that his grasp of English was sufficient to track a reliable path through the jungle of medical terminology. So the family moved back to Japan and lived in a cheap apartment while the operation was performed. The daughter's recovery required two or three years of intensive physiotherapy, which Yamada undertook himself. I never found out exactly where the money came from to escape from the dreary apartment, but by the time the kids were all of an age to go to school, Yamada had restored his fortunes, acquired a sizeable piece of land and set about building the house and the restaurant with his own hands. The outside had a rough, whitewashed cement finish while the interior was timber, log-cabin style, the walls hung with horseshoes, some coloured prints of rodeos in wooden frames, a cowboy hat, a guitar and other Western paraphernalia.

In these surroundings, Yamada had grown into a cantankerous but much-beloved paterfamilias, supervising his family's various activities and also seeing to the customers, who were welcome at *Kura* to the extent that they didn't irritate the boss. That he had no actual need of them was clearly shown by the presence of a brand new Jaguar in the car port, one of the many fruits of his judicious investments, but they were welcome if they were interesting characters, or if they had something to contribute. If not, he would get rid of them in short order. 'Shit!' he would sometimes say of a recent reject, 'I told that sonofabitch not to come back here any more.' Once he was audited by the local tax office, whose supervisor declared that Yamada wasn't running the restaurant properly: he was curtly advised to raise his prices in order to make more profit. A few months later, the same supervisor telephoned to order a table for himself and some of his minions, who were having a party. 'Sure, you can come if you want to,' Yamada told him. 'But I warn you, I haven't raised my prices. Instead, I'll be cutting the steaks especially thin – just for you!'

Fools and time-wasters were not tolerated either, although exceptions would sometimes be made, for instance for Hasegawa, who had the unfortunate habit of taking ten minutes to say what anyone else could say in thirty seconds. When Hasegawa launched into one of his long, tedious speeches about the universal brotherhood of man and the desirability of friendship among all people throughout the globe, regardless of race or creed, Yamada would wink at the listeners, reach behind the counter for his old, stem-wound pocket watch

and flourish it in the air, saying 'I'll give you three minutes –
if you haven't got to the point by then, I'm not listening any
longer!' It was a dangerous atmosphere for anyone who was
excessively timid, or who took offence easily. Even families
who dropped in for a quiet meal were quickly dragged into
the conversational circle and if Fielding or I were there, the
school age children were sternly ordered to seize this opportunity to practise their English. 'Come on, come on,' Yamada
would tell them impatiently. 'Private English teachers cost a
lot of money, you know. If your father had to pay that, he
couldn't afford to bring you to eat here in this restaurant.
So hurry up and grab your chance. Say something! Say your
name, or what class you're in, or what you like doing. Don't
worry about these two' – jerking a thumb at me and Fielding
– 'I know they look strange, but they're kind at heart. What's
more, they're off duty. You don't have to pay them a thing.'
At which the parents would look acutely embarrassed and
lean across the table with a bottle outstretched to fill our
glasses.

Unlike Hasegawa, for whom political discussion was about
securing a consensus and who therefore preferred mild gen-
eralities to serious debate, Yamada held strong views on
everything and was always ready for a good argument. One
issue that always got him fired up was the notion that the
guilt for the Pacific War had all been on Japan's side and
that the Allies had been knights in white armour by comparison. To give me the correct picture, he would carefully
describe how the stage had been set by the racist economic
policies of Europe and America. Look how they had tried
to prevent Japan from building her own empire in east Asia
while clinging greedily to their own! No wonder this had
worn Japan's patience down. The end result – the attack
on Pearl Harbor – had been inevitable. Treacherous? Bah!
Somewhere in his voluminous reading, Yamada had come
across a report from the London *Times* that had character-
ised the similarly sudden and unannounced attack by Japan
on Port Arthur, which launched the Russo-Japanese War in
1904, as 'an act of daring', and was coldly contemptuous
of Western historians who took a different view of such

tactics when their own countries were on the receiving end.

That atrocities had been committed he was quite willing to concede, but the only ones of which he had first-hand knowledge had been inflicted on Japan. Once he had been on a beach near Yokohama when an American plane swooped down out of the sky and emptied its guns at the civilians, including many women and children, who were spending a quiet afternoon lying in the sun. Yamada particularly remembered the cries of the injured as they lay and waited for medical attention, which was slow in coming. Among them was a little girl whose jaw had been shot off by a tracer bullet. She died within minutes in the arms of her mother, her bright red blood soaking quickly into the yellow sand.

Sometimes one or other of his older customers would join these conversations and add their own reminiscences. One was an old woman who had been born and brought up in the far north of Japan, on the island of Hokkaido. Her childhood memories painted a picture of a world barely imaginable from modern Yokohama, a world of bears glimpsed on berry-picking trips to the mountains with her family, of salmon in such quantities that she and her friends could wade into the rivers in the spawning season and catch them by hand, and of winter journeys to visit relatives, carried along in a horse-drawn sleigh whose bells tinkled as it crunched over the frozen snow. But by the time the war came she had married and moved south, to the city of Fukuoka. One spring day, she recalled, a squadron of American planes had flown over the town, which was built entirely of wood, and then all of a sudden it had begun to rain, even though there were no clouds in the sky. Almost at once, the inhabitants realised that it was not rain that was falling but gasoline; and when the planes turned back to drop their incendiary bombs, the town was so thoroughly consumed that not merely individual houses and streets were burnt out but entire areas were rendered completely unrecognisable. Others had their own tales, often centred on terrifying air raids that left knots of dazed survivors camping out in the open amid the charred wreckage of their former homes until some alternative shelter could be found. But most returned obsessively to the subject of food, how they and their families had subsisted for months or even years on handfuls of beans, or gruel made from roughly-ground millet, or normally inedible vegetable matter such as the stalks of pumpkins.

Food, food, food. It was like a refrain. What about England, Yamada wanted to know. Sure, people there had suffered during the war – deprivation, bombs, menfolk killed or missing or captured. But they hadn't starved like the Japanese, had they? Did I think I could imagine what it was like? Once, Yamada drew my attention to one of his regular customers, a man whom the experience of hunger had left with a peculiar neurosis: he always ordered far more dishes than he could possibly eat, apparently for the pleasure of being surrounded by sheer quantity.

It was also through these conversations that I learned of the hatred and disgust felt by many older Japanese towards Russia. Russia had seized Japanese territory, the controversial four islands off Hokkaido, and had also taken some 650,000 Japanese troops prisoner on the Asian mainland and put them to work in labour camps in Siberia, where several thousand had died. These, according to Yamada, were not acts of war: they had taken place after Japan's surrender and were therefore shots below the belt. But the rest of the world was indifferent. Very well. That was quite enough reason for Yamada and his associates to avoid facing the facts about Japan's own misdeeds, particularly its alleged cruelty towards prisoners of war. If Japan had indeed done any wrong, they felt, it had been paid for by the villainy of the Russians.

The most that Yamada would concede was that there was a balance of karma at work. He had little time for what he called the Christian way of thinking, the idea that two wrongs are both wrong. No, they cancelled each other out – couldn't I see that? And as for the problems faced by Russia after the fall of communism, he regarded them as simple poetic justice. Probably greatly exaggerated too. Shortages of food? But look how fat the Russian people all seemed to be! What kind of starvation was that? Anyway, hungry or not, let them dig their way out of economic chaos the same way the Japanese had, by hard work. And let them learn the same

lesson too, the lesson of the futility of war. Let them follow
Japan's example and commit themselves to peace. At this,
everyone around the table would nod in agreement. Peace,
that's right. You said it, peace. Peace was the national obsession, repeated up and down the country like a mantra, a magic
charm whose invocation excused Japan now and forever from
involvement in potentially dangerous international problems.
Fielding, to stir things up, affected not to believe in it. 'What
do you mean, peace?' he would say in mock-scornful tones.
'Japan has the greatest martial history of any country in Asia.
You people have a taste for war – a talent for it. Look at your
history! And look at your TV! There are samurai dramas on
there every day, all swords and fighting and people getting
killed. No, this talk of peace nowadays – it's just a fashion.
The Japanese are a warlike people, maybe among the most
warlike in the world. Just wait. One day Japan will re-arm,
and then it will all begin all over again.' This line always set
off another round of furious argument.

Naturally, Yamada's peppery character made sure that he
found plenty of contemporary targets for his wrath as well.
Soon after I first met him, he was diagnosed as having a stone in
his kidney and had to go to the hospital for a few days to have it
broken up by bombardment from some kind of laser. While he
was away, his wife and son went out for a drive in the Jaguar
and had the misfortune to be sideswiped by a bus. The car was
only two weeks old, but the bus driver admitted that he was
at fault and his insurance company would pay to repair the
damage. That evening, however, a stranger came alone to the
restaurant to eat. He had his meal, made some conversation,
including asking a few innocent-sounding questions, and then
paid up and left. But instead of going away, he hung around in
the road outside, walking up and down, staring at the house
and jotting things down in a small notebook.

Shortly afterwards, the insurance company abandoned its
initially cooperative stance and began trying to shift the blame
by alleging a different version of events from what had actually
happened. Just about the same time, Yamada came out of the
hospital. When he learned what had been happening, his rage
was pretty to see. 'Those sons of bitches think they are just

dealing with a woman and a boy,' he told me on the phone. 'I'm going to fix them tonight. If you want to help me, come around and watch. It'll be even more embarrassing for them if a foreigner is there too.' That evening, in response to a summons that did not allow for the possibility of refusal, two employees of the bus company showed up at the restaurant along with three people from the insurance company, including the mysterious diner from the night of the accident. Much of what was said was too difficult for me to understand, but the best bit was when Yamada affected to lose his temper, angrily accusing the insurance company of sending someone to spy on his family and business while he himself was confined to a hospital bed. Since they were guilty, they could do nothing but squirm. 'You shit!' Yamada roared at the offender, using the English word. 'You're nothing but a SONOFABITCH!' The sleuth said nothing but went red in the face and bowed his head, so low that it touched the table. 'That's no good!' snapped Yamada, piling it on for all he was worth. 'Do you imagine that I will accept your apology for trying to strongarm my family? You're not fit to associate with human beings. Go and stand with your face in the corner, now, until we've finished talking.' And sure enough, the wretched man got up from his seat and walked over to the corner, standing there against the wall like a schoolboy in disgrace. This was so desperately humiliating to the insurance company representatives that they were ready to agree to anything at all to put matters right. 'Getting my Jaguar fixed will take a long time,' Yamada told them sternly. 'New parts will have to be ordered from England, plus the paint of course, as it will have to be completely resprayed. So the question now is what car you'll be supplying me with to drive around in until mine is ready.' They offered him a top-of-the-line model from Nissan, but Yamada wasn't in the mood to make anything easy for them. 'I don't drive Japanese cars,' he said scornfully. Eventually they settled on a Mercedes. 'Make it a red one,' Yamada told them. 'Silver's too common. And make sure there's a telephone inside it too – I might want to make some calls.'

Yamada's idea for fixing my leaking motorcycle tank was

characteristically direct. Kimura, the consummate professional, had spoken of some kind of delicate brazing process, something careful and painstaking and artistically finished, which would not merely seal the holes but also leave the surface of the tank completely smooth, concealing the fact that any repair had ever taken place. Why waste time with all that stuff, Yamada felt, considering that the bike was old and only worth a paltry sum anyway.

'The point is, to get it so that you can ride it, right?' he said. 'I knew all along that what your welder friend was suggesting would never work. Brazing is fine, but not for this job. The steel is too thin – if you heat it, it will just buckle and bend. Those cheap people at Yamaha, they don't use any good steel when they make bikes now. Shit! That friend of yours doesn't sound like a proper welder to me. He probably doesn't even have a licence. Listen, I have some special solder that I got from a plumber I know. They use it for joining waterpipes with. It has silver in it, so it won't corrode. Come on, let's go in the back. I'm telling you, it won't take five minutes.'

In the event, it took a bit longer than that, because we took another couple of beers along with us and we also had to take time out to look at a planing tool that Yamada had just finished making and wanted to show me. He was always making and building things. Apart from the house itself and its huge brick fireplace, of which he was especially proud, he had designed and constructed most of his furniture and many other objects besides: a low table with beautifully carved legs, a long chest with several drawers made of highly polished walnut and a complicated contraption on which a fishtank was suspended in the air. Outside in the garden was a combination kennel and wire enclosure for his two Scotch terriers and a large greenhouse for an orchid collection he was planning to start.

Mostly, though, he preferred working on smaller projects. One was a beautiful miniature bow and arrow which he was going to present to a widow whose recently deceased husband had been keen on hunting. Another, inspired by the unwelcome intrusion into his garden of a couple of neighbourhood cats, was a full-size crossbow with lethal-looking steel shafts which mysteriously disappeared shortly before completion (vetoed by Yamada's wife, according to Fielding). Now it was the plane he had just finished, which was designed for shaving flakes from a chunk of dried fish called *katsuo*, or bonito. The flakes were used for flavouring, either mixed with soup or sprinkled on rice, and the commercial version could be bought from any supermarket. But Yamada insisted on the genuine article. 'I know a man who still dries them by the old method,' he explained. 'It's a long job, but it's the only way to get the proper taste. First he cuts the bonito up into three pieces and then boils it. You have to use soft water, he says, otherwise the flesh gets cracks in it. After that he picks out all the bones and removes the skin, and then bakes the fish over a pinewood fire. There's more to the process than that, but this is what you end up with.' He handed me an object that looked and felt like a wooden shuttle for an old-fashioned loom. 'This is really fish?' I asked. It was rock-hard, like petrified wood. 'That's right,' said Yamada, taking it out of my hands. 'That's what I buy from my friend. And this is how you turn it into flakes.' He reached behind him and laid his plane on the table. It was made of two smooth pieces of cedar which slotted neatly together to make a box about the size of a child's pencil box, with a blade set at an angle across the top. He rubbed the hard, dry piece of bonito lightly over the blade a few times and then opened the box to show me the pale pink, curled-up shavings which had collected inside.

After we had finished examining the plane and drinking the beer, Yamada turned his attention to the tank. The first job was to clear off the rust with a wire brush, which proved more difficult than expected because the head of the brush was not properly fixed to the handle and kept flying off. Then the soldering iron took a long time to heat up, as it was a rather ancient model. Some of the holes in the tank were quite big, and I was curious to know how Yamada would prevent the solder falling through them into the tank. 'You don't know anything, do you,' he said amiably in response to my enquiry. 'Best if you just shut up and watch.' Then he bent his head closely over the tank and started to build fat banks of shiny wet solder around the edges of the holes, joining them together afterwards with a single deft pass of the iron.

By the time I left Yamada's place, it was dark. Fixing the tank had indeed taken only a few minutes, but getting ready to start had taken nearly three hours. That was the pattern at *Kura*. So on the way home I stopped in at another bar, and this time found myself on the next stool to a foreigner I had never seen before, a young Peruvian with sharp, intelligent features called Juan Sato Dextre. Juan had only recently arrived in Japan. We got talking, in a mixture of my feeble Spanish and his equally limited English, and the next day I took him round to be introduced to another Peruvian family we had recently come to know when their daughter had joined ours at Pine Hill Primary School. That led to a party which eventually ended up in Juan's one-room apartment over the machine shop where he worked every day stamping out parts of car parts on a huge press. And while we were sitting there drinking beer and admiring the erotic pin-ups on the wall over Juan's bed, he suddenly announced that we should all come upstairs to meet his Pakistani friends, who could speak English. So we all climbed up the iron staircase fixed to the outside of the building, and arrived at the door of another small apartment, this one containing Mr Shah, a middle-aged and much-travelled native of Karachi who was living like Donald Duck with his two young nephews, Mr Ali and Mr Imran. They worked for the same employer as Juan and spent their days stamping out machine parts and packing them into boxes and loading the boxes onto the backs of trucks.

The Pakistanis were gentle and hospitable, with beautiful dignified manners: they took each new arrival's outstretched hand in both of theirs, then stepped back and made a sweeping gesture with one arm, bidding him welcome. Their apartment consisted of a single large room with a kitchen in one corner where they cooked themselves elaborate meals every night, serving them on plain china dishes spread out on newspaper on the floor, all of them sitting round together and scooping the food into their mouths with chunks of home-made chapatis. They spoke very little Japanese, didn't care for Japanese food and didn't drink alcohol, which was the social kiss of death, although they didn't mind because all they wanted to do in Japan, like the Thais who worked for Kimura, was to save as much money as possible as quickly as possible and then leave. Consequently they were in the habit of spending all their free time in their little apartment with four televisions, which they had collected from garbage dumps, all on at the same time, with a tangled confusion of wires and cables trailing all over the floor. In one corner lay an unused multiplex receiver, which they had also brought home from a garbage dump without understanding its function, so I showed them how to wire it up and receive certain TV programmes, old American movies and the like, in English. This pleased them so much that in return they promised to lend me some videotapes of cricket matches which they said they could get from their pal Mr Rafiq, who lived in Tokyo and was employed by a Moslem-food-and-video business.

By chance, Mr Rafiq was visiting them at the time: he had been asleep behind a partition, but when he heard his name mentioned, he woke up and came out to join the party. He was a solemn young man with beady eyes, a short-clipped moustache and artistic hands with long, delicate fingers. In a few months' time, he told us, he would be making a short visit to Pakistan to marry some young lady picked out for him by the senior members of his family. While waiting for the great day, he had decided to remain faithful to his prospective bride, in fact completely celibate, although strangely enough he seemed also to have gained an extraordinarily intimate knowledge of the different varieties of foreign *mizu-shobai* (water business) girls, not only around where he lived but also in the neighbouring prefectures of Gumma, Saitama and Ibaraki, where the food-and-video empire had additional outposts which his duties required him to visit.

This knowledge had only come into his possession, he wanted us to understand, because when he went out with his friends they always insisted on visiting the sort of bars where people got drunk and sang karaoke songs and associated with morally dubious women . . . which was why Mr Rafiq was able to explain to me in detail and with an almost too passionate conviction that Filipino girls were no-good girls, fucking girls, at least 95% of them, and not only that but CLEVER (he tapped the side of his head) meaning that they were expert at saying I love you, please come to this bar again soon, I want to meet you outside, I like you better than all the others and so on but they didn't actually give much for the money – a few quick thrusts was the best you could expect – in contrast to Chinese and Korean girls, who were not always so easy to get into the sack but were at least more kind, more to be trusted, and Thai girls, who were quite simply dumb, pushovers for an hour in a love hotel, relatively cheap and willing to act as if they enjoyed it.

Mr Ali and Mr Imran, who were both in their early twenties, were visibly embarrassed by this conversation. They were always glad of the chance to see a bit of tit if it appeared on late-night TV, but they wouldn't actually have wanted to go to the store, as it were – not actually buy anything. They screwed up their faces and turned their heads aside and giggled and punched each other on the arms when Juan innocently offered to take them to a bar he had found where there was a delightful Filipino girl called Shirley who would just love to take care of their needs. I kept my mouth shut, although I knew the bar Juan was talking about – it was where he and I had met the night before. I also knew, as Juan did, that Shirley would never see 50 again. But that was no disqualification. According to Shirley, she had plenty of customers.

14 | When Temperatures Rise

SOMETIME IN June, the rainy season began. The sky was dull and gloomy for days on end, with frequent bouts of long, steady rain interrupted by occasional breaks of sharp, bright sunshine. When it was falling, the rain was heavy and intense: it drummed continuously on the tin roof and wooden walls of the house and quickly formed rivulets that ran down the street outside and gurgled in the deep gutters. After it passed, the sodden ground would steam slightly and heavy drops of water fell from the trees and bushes or lay where they had collected in little pools in their upturned leaves. The temperature that had made May such a warm and pleasant month, like the best of an English summer, now began to rise, and the air thickened with humidity that made sweat trickle down our faces even when we were indoors sitting still. We took up the habit of wearing short towels around our necks, handy for mopping wet brows, and also kept a supply in the freezer. It was a voluptuous pleasure to strip to the waist and rub ourselves down with these ice-crusted pads of damp cloth, although the effect was short-lived and we would soon find ourselves feeling as hot as before.

The nights were especially close and sultry, worse when the air was weighted down with the threat of rain than when it was actually falling. Sometimes we would be woken in the small hours by the hum of a mosquito passing close to our ears and would then have to turn the light on and kill the offender before any further sleep was possible. This was quite an easy job, as the mosquitoes were not very fast movers at the best of times, and lumbered about like old-fashioned biplanes when their stomachs were full. They flew and settled, took off again and settled elsewhere, then flew some more, so they could be both seen and heard: one well-timed clap of the hands left a black, long-legged body flattened on the palm in an alarmingly large smear of blood. To keep them out, all the windows were fitted with mosquito netting, but this was old and torn in several places so they could find a way in without much difficulty if they wanted to. Inside the house we burnt incense sticks, which were reasonably effective, or else 'green coils' sold for anti-mosquito purposes, which smouldered for hours and produced an acrid smoke that killed the intruders off. The smoke was a little uncomfortable to live with, but better than the smell of the modern alternative, the electric mosquito killer. This was a little square of plastic with a tiny hotplate on which you laid a blue tablet that gave off a mosquito-lethal gas as it was consumed. It was highly effective, but the smell was faintly nauseating, sweetish and sickly, like a lump of plastic slowly vapourising in an invisible soup of gaseous electricity.

Another insect that began to make an appearance as the weather warmed up was the cockroach. Few buildings of any kind in Japan are without a resident colony of *gokiburi*, and old houses invariably have plenty. Most of the time they did their best to stay out of sight, but they were enervated by hot temperatures and sometimes emerged from their private network of cracks and crevices and scuttled disgustingly along the bottom of the wall to disappear under the furniture before we could make a move to catch them.

The main weapon in the war against them was a device called a *gokiburi hoi hoi*, which we obtained at the supermarket.

This was a kit consisting of a tube of some thick, clear, viscous substance and a little cardboard house, open at both ends, which the householder assembled like a child's toy, from a flat sheet of cardboard with perforated lines showing where the bends and folds should be made. When it was finished, it looked just like a brightly-coloured little cottage, with a red-tiled roof and flower-bordered windows from which smiling cartoon cockroaches with bulging eyes were depicted waving their antennae in cheerful greeting. But the real cockroaches which ran along the floor by the walls and hurried into the welcome darkness of the little house, thinking it a safe haven, soon found they had nothing to be cheerful about. The viscous stuff in the tube was a kind of glue which never dried: this was squeezed out all over the floor of the *gokiburi hoi hoi*, with the result that those who entered stuck fast and never emerged. After a week or two, the trap was wrapped in newspaper and thrown away, complete with victims, and replaced by a new one. We never had any trouble with mice, but there was a mouse version available as well, rather larger and with a lot more glue.

As well as having to carry an umbrella every time I went to Tokyo, I bought a plastic rain suit to wear while riding the Honda to the station. It was made of a light vinyl that was completely waterproof, although wearing it for even five minutes was enough to become soaked with sweat inside. I kept the bike under some trees in one corner of a nearby vacant lot, whose owner was planning to clear away the vegetation and build a house there at some undecided time in the future. In the meantime, the trees and shrubs sheltered what little remained of the local wildlife: a large colony of fierce mosquitoes, of course, a few brown lizards that darted here and there among the leaves and coarse grass on the ground, and some yellow and black spiders half as large as my hand, which had long, thin, armour-plated legs and spun enormous webs from overhanging branches to some convenient anchor point below, such as the Honda's headlight or handlebars. There were no wasps, but sometimes we would see a species of hornet, about an inch and a half long, fat and hairy and reddish-brown, which looked capable of giving a nasty sting.

But they were too big even to get through the holes in the mosquito netting covering our windows, and flew too slowly to pose much danger.

Far more numerous were the cicadas, which clung to hidden places in the trees and passed the days calling out to each other, or perhaps just to the world at large, over and over again. The sound they made was like one of those cheap, friction-driven toy cars which you push repeatedly along the floor to build up momentum and then release, a repetitive series of identical cadences climaxing in a final extended cry, a long, slow descent of the register that seemed to contain a note of derision, as if they were saying 'Yar boo sucks, yar boo sucks, yar boo sucks to yoooooooooooooooooooooou!' And finally, only heard at night when everything was still, the soft and beautiful ringing noise, like tiny bells, made by a harmless little stick-like insect called *suzumushi*. Some people even kept these creatures as pets, simply to enjoy the noise they made, which – according to Sumiko from next door – 'makes people feel cool when the weather is hot.' *Suzumushi* were sold in tiny cages with bamboo bars, and fed on wet foods like pieces of cucumber or watermelon.

At the weekends, if the rain held off for a few hours, we would often get together at Fielding's house for a barbecue or else go and do the same thing on some beach, stuffing all the bits and pieces into whichever luxurious car he was driving at the time. Fielding had a wealthy friend called Hideo, who lived down the coast in a large, cliffside villa where he padded around barefoot all day in designer jeans, his hair in a long ponytail, entertaining a small army of friends who seemed to have nothing better to do than hang around and sponge on him. Where Hideo's money came from was a bit of a mystery, as he had no regular job, but one of his many sidelines was a part ownership of a business that imported second-hand luxury cars from Europe and America, which were then resprayed and reconditioned before being sold. The turnover was rapid, and since Hideo's property had plenty of space, there were always two or three cars parked outside his house – Ford Mustangs and Cadillacs from California, BMWs from Germany, Range Rovers and Jaguars from England. Hideo had known Fielding from the prosperous days when he was first in Japan, and was always willing to lend him a car for a week or two until a probable buyer was found and it had to be taken away to be sold.

Loading both families and all the paraphernalia into one car was a considerable challenge which not only meant cramming the boot beyond its capacity and tying the lid down with string but also wrapping additional objects in an old blanket and lashing them onto the roof. But we found some good beaches along the Shonan Coast, well south of the overpopulated tourist centres, where we could swim and sunbathe or clamber up onto the concrete breakwater and watch the local fishermen sitting patiently around in a circle mending their huge nets. Instead of a complete barbecue, we took only the grill, which we would lay on stones around a shallow pit scooped out of the sand for the charcoal. The beer came in a cooler box which had been rescued from the *gomi*, along with the rest of Fielding's beach equipment – a guitar or two, a gaudily-coloured sunshade, an inflatable boat with several puncture patches and two different-sized oars, and an assortment of balls, baseball bats and tennis rackets with broken strings. The children clambered around on the rocks with plastic buckets searching for crabs, shellfish and other marine life: there was plenty to catch including, on one occasion, a medium-sized octopus which they managed to scoop up in a net. One of the local fishermen spotted them struggling to keep the writhing creature captive and took them to the fishing cooperative building across the road to show them how to prepare it. First he rubbed it all over with coarse salt, then rinsed it and quickly plunged it into a saucepan of boiling water. After a few minutes he took it out again, laid it on a wooden board and cut the tentacles into bite-sized chunks which we shared out on the flat top of the harbour wall.

Other times, when we didn't feel like battling our way through the traffic to the coast, or if there was a threat of rain, we would stay close to home and set up the barbecue in Fielding's front yard. Various local friends would be summoned to join in, some like Hasegawa arriving alone with gifts of beer and snacks, others bringing children and grannies and coolboxes of their own filled with extra food and drink.

In order to add a more local flavour to our menu, Fielding and I decided to acquire a yakidai, the shallow, rectangular barbecue used for cooking yakitori, Japan's popular little chicken kebabs. For this we had to go to Kappabashi, a street in northeast Tokyo where every shop specialises in something to do with the restaurant trade. Some are wholesale suppliers of food, stacked to the ceiling with huge cans of coffee, peach halves and hamburger sauce, their shelves crammed with plastic sacks of processed ingredients and catering-sized plastic bottles of everything from salad dressing to disinfectant. Some are devoted to glassware and crockery laid out for inspection on wooden racks or tied up in enormous bundles with coloured plastic string ready for delivery. Some offer uniforms – white jackets with brass buttons, bow ties, striped waistcoats, tall chefs' hats and bunny-type outfits for nightclub waitresses. Some provide everything for the prospective coffee shop owner: tables and chairs, cups and saucers with colour-coordinated sugar bowls and milk jugs, coffee grinders and percolators, signboards saying 'Open' and 'Closed', menu cards and cash registers and assorted decorative accessories such as framed paintings, statuettes of Pinocchio, varnished wooden barrels, glass fishing floats wrapped up with knotted rope, plastic pine branches and plum blossoms, china dogs, cats and dragons and scarlet butterfly-shaped ashtrays edged with gold.

But the best and most interesting shops were huge treasure-caverns stuffed with every imaginable item of cookware: woks and frying pans, saucepans and casseroles, copper kettles and iron cauldrons, long knives and heavy cleavers, whisks, funnels, strainers, scoops and tongs, nests of lacquer boxes, pastry cutters shaped like hearts, like stars, like fish, like maple leaves, industrial-sized gas-rings and rice cookers, counters, racks and display cabinets, sieves as big as tennis racquets, wooden spoons as big as canoe paddles, ladle bowls as big as soldiers' helmets. And, of course, plenty of yakidai, fuelled by either gas, for commercial use, or charcoal. We picked out a modest one about two feet long and threw in a couple of packs of thin bamboo skewers.

One of these barbecues took place a few days after Fielding had obtained a carload of turf squares and laid a handsome new lawn around his children's sandpit. Whether the turf had originally been intended for a golf course or whether it was simply a general prophylactic measure I never found out, but the stuff had been generously treated with a heavy dose of dia-tetra-poly-ethyl-acety-poisono-toxicide before being sold. We didn't know this at the time, but having sprawled on the grass for most of the afternoon, I found out all about it the next day, when I woke up to find my back covered with a savage rash that felt like being eaten alive by red ants and looked even worse than that.

After the obligatory 24-hour period in which Tough Guys sneer at such a womanly notion as running to the doctor at the first sign of discomfort, I went to the doctor. The local dermatologist operated a clinic at which students from Yokohama Medical College often turned up for a little front-line training, so he was nothing if not interventionist in his methods. First he took a Polaroid picture of my back, presumably to give the lads a laugh in the karaoke bar later, and then prescribed an assortment of pills – four different kinds – and, in honour of Japanese doctors' well-known propensity for chemical overkill, five tubes of some unlabelled cream. Then, to make assurance doubly sure, I was laid out on a couch and treated to 'light therapy', which turned out to be dermatologist jargon for a brief toasting under four immensely complicated-looking lamps with red bulbs, each one containing a little heating element. The procedure was to grease down the patient, lay him out flat and then grill him lightly with these lamps, for about five minutes per side. It must have been quite effective, as the rash subsided within a few days. Or did I have the pills to thank? Or the cream? Whichever it was, I was left feeling slightly ashamed of the contrast between my theoretical preference for slow, sensible Chinese herbal remedies that take account of the Whole Person and my instinct to escape from discomfort as fast as possible by taking the interventionist route.

In general, visits to the doctor were like a lottery. Instead of the general-practitioner-family-doctor system we were used to in England, we found that all the local medicine men had their own clinics and worked their own areas of specialisation. Naturally, there was a good deal of competition. This was known to be responsible for the absence of clinics offering preventative health advice: attempts to set up such clinics were vigorously opposed by the Japan Doctors' Association, which objected to the idea because it would cut into neighbouring doctors' patient lists. But on the face of it, there was a wide choice of experts in different disciplines – ear, nose and throat men, paediatricians, osteopaths, obstetricians and dermatologists as well as a generous sprinkling of chiropractors, acupuncturists, masseurs, herbalists like Fujimoto's mother and even faith healers. None of them gave the impression of being much more reliable than any of the others, and the conventional ones relied mainly on an air of confidence and lots of antibiotics. Restricted as they were to their own fields, they seemed less like doctors concerned with all-round health than simply repair and maintenance technicians whose job was to identify and correct malfunctions in the nation's workforce. Because of this, we tried to keep the children away from them as much as possible. Whatever the complaint might be, the only certainty was that they would walk out with orders to follow yet another course of antibiotics. Sometimes it was unavoidable, but what we were after was the diagnosis, not the cure: as often as not, the antibiotics went straight into the garbage.

From reports in the press we learned that Japan's blind faith in antibiotics had begun to take its inevitable toll. A growing number of patients in hospitals and nursing homes, long exposed to excessive dosing, were now found to be afflicted by a powerful new bacteria called MRSA, against which conventional antibiotics had little or no effect. Reluctantly suspecting that this was the result of pharmaceutical companies' greed combined with doctors' incompetence, the Ministry of Health had embarked on a characteristically toothless 'crackdown' to prevent the problem from spreading. Plans were under way to revise the 'guidelines' on the use of antibiotics. (Didn't doctors learn about this in medical college?) Manufacturers were to be asked to 'provide information' on the proper use of their products. (Didn't they already do so?) Hospital employees were to receive 'special training' to help them combat MRSA outbreaks. Not for the first time in Japan, the sound of the stable door being slammed was not loud enough to drown out the hoofbeats of the disappearing horse.

We also found doctors reluctant to talk about the treatment they prescribed. A specific question would get a vague, generalised answer, as if they had been deliberately taught to defend their treatments by revealing as little about them as possible. Friends and neighbours confirmed that patients were seldom told any details about their illnesses, still less about the drugs they were ordered to take. Even personal medical records were deemed to be the doctors' private property: individuals had no right to see what was written about them. One of the main problems is that medicine is potentially such a lucrative profession in Japan that it attracts the interest of the rich as well as the able: virtually every medical college is said to contain students who have bought their places by bribery alongside those who have won them by examination. As a result, many doctors are frankly incompetent, prescribing by the book instead of in response to their own diagnostic skills. Even the reliability of 'the book' was in doubt, since doctors have the right to sell medicines as well as prescribe them and are therefore easily lured into mutually profitable arrangements by pharmaceutical companies which supply large volumes of heavily-discounted drugs to be passed on to patients who have no real need of them. The doctor then claims reimbursement from the government, which pays him at the officially-set maximum price, not the discount price at which he bought the drugs in the first place. At the same time, even with the obligation to purchase unidentified drugs of dubious value, visits to the doctor are relatively inexpensive at the point of purchase. Like most employed people in Japan we subscribed to the national health insurance scheme, which levies a fee related to the individual's income and covers about 70 per cent of the cost of treatment.

If the professionalism of doctors was open to doubt, that of dentists was even more suspect. When one of our daughters complained of discomfort, Reiko took her to a children's dental clinic where the problem was traced to a simple cavity. Fixing it required five separate visits to the clinic and not only left the cavity filled but the whole of the offending tooth artistically encased in some shiny, silver-coloured metal. The fact that it was a baby tooth which was certain to come out by itself within a year or two made it plain that the sole motive for all this elaborate work was money.

Still, whatever the motive may have been, there was no doubt that dental methods in Japan were different from those of England. One of my own fillings came out one day and when I went to a local dentist to have it replaced, he was so intrigued by what he found that he summoned both his partners and five nurses, who all gathered round to peer into my open mouth and exclaim in amazement at what they considered the primitive way of doing things in foreign countries. Replacing my filling only took two visits: one to clean the cavity and put in a temporary filling, and the second, a week later, to remove the temporary filling and put in a permanent one. Why they couldn't have done the job properly the first time I didn't ask.

One reason I was in a hurry to recover from the rash acquired from Fielding's toxic lawn was that I had just joined a health club in Tokyo and members with 'skin problems' – an expression whose meaning was not clearly defined but which probably referred to any condition that looked unpleasant – were asked to stay away until they had recovered. Jesse had introduced me to the club, which was called 'Fit City'; it was a chain operation, with six separate premises in different parts of Tokyo. Since I was going into the city at unpredictable times, for meetings at ad agencies, modelling auditions and narration jobs, I thought that membership would give me something positive to do while killing time between appointments. The way I visualised it, I would be pumping a little iron in the gym for a while and maybe running a few hundred yards on one of those conveyor-belt things, then enjoying a quick swim in the pool and finishing up having a beer or two at the club bar with a couple of the other members, all of whom would of course be older and fatter than me.

In the event, it didn't work out quite like that. To begin with, I turned out to be one of the oldest members in the place. Most of the others looked somewhere between 19 and 23. They were all remarkably beautiful – it was a toss-up whether the girls or the boys were more desirable – and didn't seem to have the slightest need to go to a keep-fit establishment of any kind. Even worse, the club didn't have a bar but just a little counter in the reception area where my fellow-members were in the habit of winding up their aerobics sessions with a smug bowl of natural yoghurt or a self-righteous glass of freshly-squeezed orange juice. Still, I got into the habit of dropping by a couple of times a week when there weren't too many other people around, swimming up and down the tiny pool until I ran out of breath, sitting for a while in the jacuzzi with the club Fixture, an enormously fat young man whose nose was permanently buried in a comic book, or spending time in the steam room, which was like resting in the shade on a warm day in Saudi Arabia.

One of the curiosities of Fit City was that the patrons seldom spoke to each other, even if they were crowded together. In that way, it was a bit like being on the subway. One exception was a Japanese law student called Sugai who got the idea firmly fixed in his head that I was both able and willing to find him a job with an American company. Every time he saw me, he asked how I was getting on, making it clear that his career was more or less on hold until I came up with the goods. But most of the members pursued their goal of bodily health and fitness in sepulchral silence. The women were even reticent with each other, preferring to float around with blank expressions, their eyes focused on nothing in particular, as if they were barely conscious of the presence of anyone else. Many of them were effectively models for a new fashion I had never seen before, which was apparently designed to conceal what their skimpy and presumably carefully-chosen swimsuits were trying equally hard to reveal. Beneath their costumes they wore 'swim-panties' as large and shapeless as gym bloomers, whose elastic edges traced forbidding lines here and there around their hips, while the cups of their brassieres were stuffed with special pads marketed under the name 'Nipless', which had the effect of displaying a neat geometric square where a nipple would normally be expected to be. It was extraordinary to see how completely these simple accessories robbed them of their femininity. They looked like shop window dummies that had been inexpertly repaired after an accident.

The male patrons were equally image conscious. They had a passion for cosmetics and would conclude their fitness sessions in the men's changing rooms by setting out little pads of cotton wool and bottles of creams and lotions and then leaning forward into the mirror and applying a careful beauty treatment. The swimming pool was primarily a place for ritualised posing: they would stand at one end in the waist-deep water, glowing with self-admiration, and roll their heads slowly around their shoulders or flex the rippling muscles in their well-tanned arms. Sometimes they would turn around to face the overflow drain that ran around the edge of the pool and spit into it. After about ten minutes of this preparation, they would suddenly throw themselves forward into the water and swim as fast as they could to the other end of the pool and back again. Then they would resume their former position and start flexing their muscles again. When I described this to Jesse's wife, she said, 'Yes, that's exactly what they're like in bed, too.'

15 | Return to the River

ANOTHER IDEA for helping the family budget along was to write travel articles for the newspapers. To this end I had already written to introduce myself to some of the main city and prefectural tourist boards. Perhaps they would care to invite me along if they had some upcoming event or newly-opened facility they wanted to promote? For a long time nothing happened, but just when I had begun to forget all about it, the mailman brought me an engraved invitation to attend the inaugural voyage of a ship called the 'Vingt et Un', sailing one July evening from Takeshiba Pier in central Tokyo.

Any hope that this might turn out to be a luxury voyage to some exotic group of islands was quickly dispelled. The 'Vingt et Un', named in honour of the impending 21st century, was built for short cruises of an hour or a couple of hours' duration around the murky waters of Tokyo Bay. There were two public restaurants on board, a handful of private dining rooms, various lounges, a snack bar, a cocktail bar called 'Petit Pearl', which served 27 different imported beers, a souvenir shop and a 200-seat theatre, presumably for business presentations. The idea was that patrons could take a short lunchtime or evening cruise and entertain themselves or their clients to a meal along the way.

Every effort had been made to give this inaugural cruise a high-class atmosphere which, to judge by the modest prices listed in the company's brochure, wouldn't be available when normal operations began. Glittering chandeliers hung from the ceiling, and the walls were hung with freshly commissioned Raoul Dufy-lookalike pastels. Drinks were served by a team of waitresses wearing thick make-up and uniforms tailored in what was supposed to be a European, *fin-de-siècle* style. A young woman in a beautiful black evening dress sat on a stool and quietly plucked away at a large golden harp. Several long tables had been set up, covered in heavy white damask cloths and decorated with bowls of delicate pink orchids whose slim, speckled petals curved demurely outwards like the tongues of rare birds. There were large platters of luxurious food, served buffet-style – tiny vol-au-vents, medallions of beef, thin slices of roast duck, grapes, cubes of melon and pyramids of straw-berries. In the middle of the table was a life-size swan that had been artistically sculpted from a large block of ice.

Apart from the company's own executives and their female assistants, who had been press-ganged in to show the corpo-rate flag, the mouths engaged in nibbling these delicacies from short golden forks belonged to a mixture of journalists, tour operators and young, low-ranking diplomats from foreign embassies. For an hour and a half the ship chugged slowly across Tokyo Bay while everyone asked everyone else how long they had been in Japan and what they were doing there. Struggling for ideas to turn this frankly boring occasion into an interesting magazine feature, I jotted down a note about a photographer who was taking a lot of pictures and then looked up just in time to see him shooting one of me. This seemed not only a sign of mutual desperation but incestuous as well. I cobbled together a piece and submitted it here and there, but wasn't surprised when no-one wanted to print it.

This failure inclined me to think that I wouldn't be getting any more such invitations, but towards the end of July another letter arrived, this time offering me the chance to join a group of foreign writers who were being invited to cover a big festival in Kitakami, a town in Iwate Prefecture, a few hundred kilometers north of Tokyo. By coincidence, Reiko and I had already planned an August visit to the family HQ in Niigata and the dates fitted in conveniently. Reiko could go on ahead with the children by train, and I would take the motorcycle up to Kitakami and then ride across country to join them after the festival was over.

The only problem was that the writers were booked to travel to Kitakami together by train, so how could I get the bike up there without riding it? In Japan, simple. One of the parcel delivery companies, whose nationwide network can carry any package to any destination in 24 or 48 hours, would be happy to oblige. I rode over to the nearest depot, filled out the form and was even given a map of how to get to the equivalent depot at the other end to collect the bike on arrival.

On the morning of departure, the writers met up at Ueno Station, Tokyo's terminus for trains to northern Japan. Apart from myself there was a girl staffer from a press agency in Singapore, a freelancer from Korea, an Australian who worked for an in-flight magazine, and three Americans who were full-time newspaper correspondents in Tokyo. On board the train, the atmosphere of our little group was cheerful and friendly, although tinged with a slight element of caution as everyone sized up everyone else's experience of Japan and tried to work out where they all stood in the professional pecking order. It soon became apparent that the others all had magazines or newspapers which had already commissioned or agreed to print their stories, so I pretended that I had too. On the spur of the moment, I picked on the *Sunday Express* Colour Magazine. No-one had actually heard of it, but the name had a good, national-circulation ring. I was quite impressed myself. Maybe I would go ahead and give them a try.

At Kitakami Station, a reception committee of town officials was waiting to greet us and take us to lunch. First there was a photo-op for the local paper, which called for a group pose alongside three individuals dressed in old-fashioned straw overcoats, leggings and thong sandals, with scarlet demon masks hiding their faces. Then we crossed the station plaza and checked into a modern, 10-storey hotel where lunch was awaiting us in a private room. Before we started eating it, seven town officials each made a speech of welcome, expressing their hope that we would have an interesting time and then be able to write reports which would inspire our readers to come and visit the Kitakami area. One by one, the writers then rose in turn to reply, saying how pleased and honoured they were to have been invited and that they would certainly write reports which . . . Halfway through the delivery I lost my way and began to stutter and stumble, groping for the right words to bring it to an end. But a burst of polite applause let me know the audience had heard enough. As with karaoke, a speech didn't have to say anything intelligible. Being willing to stand up and make it was what mattered.

Iwate prefecture is an area which, like Durham in Britain or Kentucky in the USA, normally ranks low on the list of tourist priorities. But Kitakami's Summer Folk Arts Festival is the exception, a major annual event that attracts visitors from all over the country and performers from towns and villages as much as 150 kilometers away. Instead of all conducting separate festivals of their own, as they did in the past, each community now sends a representative troupe to join in the single, large-scale bash which takes over Kitakami's checkerboard streets for three consecutive days and closes them to traffic around the clock. There are between 50 and 100 official groups of dancers, all of which have one chance to compete for prizes in a formal performance. The rest of the time they repeat parts of their routines informally here and there around town, so that from midday until well after midnight there's always something for spectators to watch. These shows go on in the streets, in little parks and in the grounds of temples – any place that offers the troupe enough open space to manoeuvre. The unifying theme of the festival is harvest celebration, although it's always held in early August, before the rice is ready to cut, so that local farmers can spare the time to attend. The atmosphere all over town is rowdy but good-natured, a riot of colour and costume, music and masks, traditional incantations and propitiatory dances designed to celebrate the season of plenty and ward off any evil spirits which might endanger the coming crop.

Businesses naturally close down for the duration, so everyone has time on their hands. Smiling old ladies, as small and wizened as raisins, stop to chat in the middle of the road, stooping over gnarled wooden sticks and exclaiming to each other in impenetrable dialect. Teenage couples dawdle hand in hand along the local lovers' lane, a tunnel of leafy cherry trees beside the river. The patrolling policeman pauses in a quiet street to catch the latest baseball scores on his pocket radio, and roaming groups of children, gloriously unsupervised, trundle homemade carts along dusty alleys and skip flat stones across the surfaces of streams. After nightfall, the streets fill up with crowds of people wandering randomly from place to place: young toughs with cockscomb hairstyles and flashing silver buckles, mothers clutching youngsters by the hand, fathers with toddlers astride their shoulders, and bands of schoolgirls in blue and white cotton *yukata* tied with gaily coloured sashes, squealing softly to each other as they clop along in their wooden sandals and flap the air in front of their faces with festival-giveaway plastic fans.

Every few yards along the main streets are rickety little stalls lit by strings of electric bulbs and doing a roaring trade in cheap toys, plastic monster masks, flexible rubber dinosaurs with bloodstained jaws, T-shirts, souvenirs, goldfish, lucky dips. Foodsellers shout for attention through clouds of smoke that billow from beneath grubby canvas awnings: their customers queue to be served, then walk slowly away gnawing at rubbery grilled squid, charcoal-blackened cobs of yellow corn or fatty morsels of chicken on sticks. Others sit down to eat on the edge of the pavement or the low wall of some dingy car park, and gobble savoury fried noodles with pickled ginger on the side from glinting foil trays. Cans of beer and soft drinks are dispensed from plastic garbage pails filled with ice water, and for the children there are weirdly-coloured ice lollies shaped like space rockets, fluffy cocoons of candy floss and pyramids of shaved ice in plastic trays, flavoured with a couple of squirts of raspberry or melon cordial.

Wherever a display or performance is taking place, the

crowd stops drifting and bunches together to watch. One popular attraction was a duel between two straw boats, each the size of a small truck, borne along by yelling young men in loincloths, short jackets and headbands. Gathering pace with each step, the boats rushed headlong towards each other and collided violently, lurching half over and even tipping a few of their occupants out onto the ground. To cheers and applause from the watchers on either side, their crews hauled them apart, withdrew back down the street, inspected the damage, gathered their breath and then did it again.

Other main events included the demon sword dancers, 150 strong, and a popular local favourite called the Deer Dance. Even in the warm, comforting glow shed by the hundreds of pink and yellow paper lanterns strung high above the street, there was something inescapably sinister about this performance. A band of 40 faceless figures, dressed in dark costumes and home-woven straw sandals, with branching antlers attached to their head-shrouding masks, stomped back and forth in vigorous unison to the deep, insistent thump of heavy drums. Even the children in the crowd fell silent as the dancers executed their studiedly ferocious routine of short, stabbing footsteps and sweeping arm gestures, leaping acrobatically and emitting sudden piercing yells. I sat on the ground to watch, with one of the festival organisers beside me, but he couldn't tell me what the dance was originally meant to signify. Something to do with hunting wild deer in the nearby mountains, he thought. In days gone by, the dancers would make the rounds of local homes, where they would frighten off any lurking evil spirits (and terrify the children) by snarling ferociously and brandishing wands hung with coloured paper streamers and dried seedpods that rattled mysteriously. Then they would be given a cup of *sake* and something to eat in exchange for the protection and good fortune their visit had brought to the house.

During the daytime, with the aim of ensuring that the visiting writers had plenty of material for their reports, our hosts had laid on a few trips to places of interest out of town. The first involved an hour's bus ride to Geto Onsen, where a few dilapidated wooden buildings were clustered together around some natural hot springs at a trailhead high in the mountains. The waters, according to the brochure, were rich in radium: their curative power had been discovered by a wandering woodcutter, who chanced on the place one day and observed a white monkey treating its injured leg in one of the bubbling springs. Many rural hot springs in Japan publicise themselves with variations of the wandering woodcutter story. From November to May the snowbound roads cut Geto Onsen off from the world, but during the warm months of the year it offered unpretentious accommodation and endless baths to guests seeking relief from asthma, rheumatism and similar conditions. Some came for the day, or stayed at the inn for a weekend, while more dedicated sufferers booked themselves in for weeks at a time, taking up residence in simple self-catering apartments and spending their days immersed in one or other of the ferociously hot pools along the edge of a shallow, fast-flowing mountain river. Our guides were keen to show us all the facilities, including one pool inside a deep cave, where naked elderly bodies of both sexes lolled motionless in the steaming water, or rose and waded slowly from one vantage point to another, looking more like ghosts than humans in the dim yellow light emitted by lamps fixed to the wall. For a movie about necrophagous witches boiling old corpses to make soup, it would have made an excellent set. Naturally, the writers were invited to sample the waters, but no-one felt up to the cave. Instead we took our foreign sensibilities down to the river bank, divided up by sex and spent a few dutiful seconds scalding ourselves in the open air.

After lunch, the bus took us back down the mountain to Kitakami and then out to a wooded hillside overlooking a river, where the local authorities had put together a tour-ist attraction called the Michinoku Folklore Village. Several ancient buildings originally constructed in different parts of northern Japan had been taken apart on site, transported here and then reassembled to make a theme park illustrating Daily Life In Days Gone By. It's an unpromising formula in any coun-try, suggesting not only a fake version of the past but also, in all probability, the lurking presence of tea shoppes and stalls selling shoddy souvenirs. But in this case the intrinsic architectural interest went some way to overcoming the unreality of the setting. We wandered slowly around among the pine trees snapping photos of the Farmhouse, the Charcoal-Burner's Hut, the Storage Barn and the Stone Age Pit House. To our surprise, we were also encouraged to go inside these structures, sit anywhere, touch anything, open the creaking lids of old chests, pick up kettles and ornaments, finger the dusty wheels of ancient looms and generally poke about as much as we liked. This was a lot better than listening to some tedious lecture while standing on the wrong side of a velveteen rope. Because of Japan's wet climate, with its extremes of heat and cold, houses made of traditional materials like wood, clay and paper rarely lasted much more than a century before having to be torn down and rebuilt. But here, many of the main timbers at least were hundreds of years old, cut from huge old nardwoods in the days before the country's original forest cover was all logged out. Artificial though it was, the assembly of thickly-thatched roofs, age-blackened mahogany floors, rusting farm implements and termite-gnawed antique furniture offered as authentic a view of pre-modern rural living conditions as any modern visitor was likely to find.

As soon as we returned to town I went over to the delivery depot, collected the Yamaha and rode it back to the hotel, leaving it in a small car park out at the back ready for an early getaway the next morning. The festival was moving towards its climax, and with evening coming on, the streets were filling up once more. Altogether, the visiting performers, tourists and spectators add something like 100,000 outsiders to the town's resident population of around 60,000, and it seemed that all of them were on the move together. On the last evening, the focus shifts to the wide eastern bank of the Kitakami River, where everyone finds a place to sit and watch the finale.

This is a lavish, two-hour firework display conducted from the opposite bank. The costs are considerable and are met by local commercial sponsors, whose names are announced over a PA system before their contribution is lit. 'And now, A Hundred Golden Stars, brought to you by the Kitakami District Bus Company!' or 'Once again this year, by established tradition,

Hanamura Plastics is pleased to present the unforgettable Red Rocket Extravaganza!' Sipping cans of beer or fruit juice and fanning themselves briskly to stir a little breeze out of the sultry, motionless air, the watchers stare up in fascination as the fireworks soar one after another into the sky with a whoosh! and detonate at around 150 feet with a bang that shakes the ground beneath them. And all throughout the display, hundreds and hundreds of paper lantern-boats, each one lit by a single candle to symbolise the soul of someone's departed friend or relative, are launched from a bridge upstream and drift past the crowd in silent farewell, floating down the wide, slow-flowing river and disappearing in the distant, whispering rapids.

*

When my bedside radio alarm woke me up at 5 o'clock the next morning, rain was pitchforking down out of a charcoal-coloured sky. It hardly seemed the right time to set out on a journey by motorcycle, but the forecast promised an early improvement and with the festival over, there was nothing to keep me in Kitakami. Swathed from head to foot in vinyl I loaded my things onto the back of the bike and then rode out of the hotel car park into the deserted streets.

Soon the rain eased off and the clouds began to lift, exposing the tops of the mountains that stood on each side of the road. They were steep and forbidding, with outcrops of wet black rock visible here and there among the greens and browns of the vegetation. The road wound its way along the bottoms of the valleys which narrowed in places to become deep, sunless gorges, with a foam-flecked river on one side and a sheer wall of rock on the other. It was as though the mountains opposed any attempt to penetrate them and had only been defeated by slow, patient construction along the lines of least resistance. Many remote parts of rural Japan have this air of impenetrability, of seeming to imprison their inhabitants inside small, precisely-defined territories bounded by walls of mountains. This is certainly one reason for the widespread national belief, contradicted by the atlas, that Japan is a small country.

But the broad valleys of Japan's great rivers and the plains and lowlands that lie between the mountain ranges give quite a different impression. Here the countryside is wide and open, often with much the same cheerfully ramshackle air as rural America. For every traditional house I passed, there were fifty more built without the influence of architects or the interference of planning authorities: cheaply-built shacks with tin-clad walls, corrugated iron roofs and rambling, untidy yards with space and to spare for the pick-up truck, the piles of logs and the mud-spattered items of farm machinery. Commercial premises too seemed to flaunt their empty space like a badge of wealth – sprawling, half-used junkyards and improbably large roadside restaurants with almost-empty car parks.

Along the main highways, commerce wore its tackiest face. A multitude of corporate identities revolved slowly on the tops of tall poles, plastic effigies of famous cartoon characters waved mechanically at the passing traffic, and great round gasometers painted with 'Mr Smile' faces smiled their vacuous smiles at nothing in particular. Yet the winking lights, neon glitter and garish modern colours had not entirely eclipsed the past. One roadside eating house, in an admirably successful attempt to attract the attention of passing customers, had set up on display an object that brought me skidding to a halt in surprise. It was the huge figure of a man, made entirely of straw, 20 feet tall, with a grinning face, outstretched arms and an enormous erect penis (the watermelon-sized glans delineated by carefully-tied cross thongs) jutting proudly from his loins. Now reduced to the status of an advertising gimmick, it had evidently been adapted from some old local fertility symbol, left over from the days before furtiveness became a sign of sophistication.

What with stops on the way it was early evening by the time I arrived at my in-laws' home. The men – Grandfather and his two sons – saw me come through the door and called me over to join them. They were sitting together around a low table, drinking beer and eating grilled fish with salted beans.

The talk was of a monkey hunt that had taken place the day before. Such hunts were no longer conducted for their own sake, as in the past, but sometimes during the summer wild monkeys would still come down from the mountains in packs to scavenge in the fields. This time, they had made several successful raids on a nearby watermelon patch, and its owner had made up his mind to hit back. Most of the locals owned shotguns, and a group of them had got together and lain in wait through the night for the monkeys to come back. Around dawn, they arrived. Seven were shot dead, while the rest escaped. 'You can't blame them for coming down and looking for food,' said Grandfather. 'You can't stop them, either. The best you can do is frighten them off for a while. But in a week or two, they'll be back.' In the old days, he recalled, the monkeys were hunted for their skins, and also for their heads. A local medical recipe called for the head of a monkey, the head of a badger and the head of a rabbit to be burnt together and then pounded up to form the base of a concoction used for treating diseases of the blood.

Here, as in Kitakami, it was the season of Obon, the festival of the dead. The spirits of departed relatives are deemed to return to their native place, where they are welcomed and regaled with three days of feasting and dancing. Their presence carries no suggestion of fear or dread – quite the opposite. One of the first jobs for each family is to build a small fire in front of the family grave in the local cemetery, or outside the front door of the house; the rising smoke provides a route, or a physical vehicle, by which the spirits can descend to earth. At the end of the festival they are sent back the same way, or by river-lantern if the right sort of river is nearby, or by some other vehicle provided for them, usually of a long, vertical character. Long poles, for instance, can do the job as well. Meanwhile the home is made clean, tidy, cheerful, welcoming. A table may be laid with some of the dead person's favourite things – a special dish of food, a pipe, a book, a musical instrument. A pail of water is placed by the door, so that they can wash their feet on arrival. Priests go from house to house to recite prayers or read texts, and some families summon a medium to come in late at night and try to make direct verbal communication.

Each village holds its own parade and night-time sessions of dancing, usually in the open space in front of the local temple. After dinner, we pushed Grandfather in his wheel-chair along to watch. A small wooden structure about 12 feet high had been built for the occasion. On top there was a small stage decorated with fresh branches of bamboo and brightly coloured paper streamers. This was occupied by the musicians: a drummer, who squatted in front of a pair of barrel-like drums and beat them rhythmically with thick, short, stubby sticks; three or four people keeping the melody going on short bamboo flutes; and a vocalist with a microphone, who did the singing and chanting. The drum-ming was evidently tiring work, as the musicians changed places every 20 minutes or so, skilfully effecting the switch with no break in the music. They were all ages, too: I was surprised to look up at the stage after one particularly robust burst from the drums and see that the performer was a girl of about 13, concentrating intently with her tongue protruding slightly from between her lips.

Drifting in and out during the course of the evening, the villagers and their children stood around the temple precincts watching, chatting to friends and joining in the dancing for stretches of anything from ten minutes to an hour. The music was not tuneful, but insistent, intense, repetitive. The dancers moved in a circle around the stage, following a simple sequence of movements which varies slightly from one region, or even village, to another: here it was two swaying steps to the left, one to the right, one to the left, one forwards, three more to the right and then CLAP (everyone together). Repeating this sequence kept the circle constantly moving slowly to the right. The dancing was not fast, but in the sultry night air the dancers quickly became hot and tired, so festival attendants moved constantly among the throng with a cup in one hand and a large kettle full of *sake* in the other, keeping everyone properly lubricated.

*

The local river, called the Arakawa, rises somewhere deep in the mountains to the north. As it descends, it cuts an erratic, fast-flowing course through deep green gorges and tangled woodlands, emerging at last into an irregularly-shaped tongue of lowland on the northern edge of the rice-rich Echigo Plain. Right at the spot where it comes out of the mountains into the first flat fields and embarks on the last sinuous stage of its journey to the sea, was Grandfather's village, one of a group of hamlets known collectively as Sugikawamura.

Even if there were no other evidence, the geography of the place – a flat, fertile, western-facing valley irrigated by the meandering river and bounded by steep, thickly wooded mountains – suggests that it has long been a site of human settlement. This is confirmed by archaeologists, who have excavated several 'shell mounds' along the valley – rough heaps of burnt stones and discarded molluscs preserved in layers of hard-packed earth – and also by the many fragments of ancient tools and arrowheads in grey or yellow flint and black obsidian unearthed by local people working the land.

For the inhabitants of Sugikawamura, the Arakawa is a lifeline that brings more than just water. Its flow carries intelligence of conditions in the mountains – the progress of the spring snowmelt, the volume of the heavy summer rains, or the sudden spectacular strike of an autumn typhoon. At such times it lives up to its name (the character *ara* signifies 'rough' or 'wild') by quickly being transformed into a seething torrent of mud and mountain debris that uproots trees and bushes, casts their stripped and broken limbs along its pebbly shore and rolls rocks in its bed to new positions further downstream. Before the 1960's, when a massive civil engineering project tamed the river with a high bank of reinforced concrete, prolonged rains would periodically swell its waters until they overflowed into the fields, washed out the roads, destroyed vegetable gardens and flooded the villagers' houses. At other times the river's ferocity subsides completely – late summer, for instance, when it flows clear and clean, slow through the deeper pools and chattering softly in the shallows, and the level drops to uncover long islands of banked-up shingle tufted with coarse weeds.

Early in the morning and at dusk, when few people are about, elegant grey herons glide down from their nests and step delicately along the water's edge, methodically scanning the surface for signs of unwary fish. Their easiest catch is the *kajika*, an ugly little creature two or three inches long that looks like a fat, blunt-headed tadpole and rests in the water by facing upstream and slowly flicking its tail to counteract the force of the current. People catch them pretty much the same way that herons do, wading slowly along bent over at the waist, their faces peering into glass-bottomed wooden boxes which they use like divers' masks, and then scooping them up one at a time in a teacup-sized net on the end of a slim bamboo pole.

More serious anglers come to the river for the seasonal catch of *ayu*, or sweetfish. Parking their four-wheel drive RVs along the shingle banks, they set up elaborate camps and spend whole days in the water in thigh-length waders, patiently casting and re-casting their 15-foot rods wherever the current is strongest. The *ayu* are small – even the adults are only six or eight inches long – and have silvery undersides and yellow or green streaks along their back and flanks. Like salmon, their lives are partly spent in the river and partly in the sea. In the autumn they spawn near the mouths of rivers and the fry then swim out to the sea, where they spend the winter. In spring they return to their river of origin and swim upstream, where they grow rapidly. Then from the middle of August until early November they head back downstream again to lay their own eggs. The species is fiercely territorial: both males and females stake out their own areas and then stay within those limits, feeding on lichen-like weeds which they nibble from the rocks. If a rival strays into their territory, whether prospecting or marauding, a fight breaks out at once: anglers therefore use one live *ayu* as bait to catch another, and often land individuals with one or several scars from such encounters. Some people take them away to eat at home, but the best place to enjoy them is right there beside the river, sprinkled with salt, impaled on wands of willow scrub, arranged around a brushwood fire, grilled and eaten whole, head, bones and all.

16 | Open and Shut

THE HOT, sultry weather dragged on into September. I was grateful not to have to go to Tokyo every day, as it was already hard enough to summon the energy to climb the stairs every morning and plough on with the steady stream of writing jobs that continued to come in on the fax. Heat exhaustion seemed to be affecting everyone else, too: our social life was going through a quiet spell, with Kimura only just back from a trip somewhere and Hasegawa mercifully too preoccupied with business affairs to propose any more sessions at the local karaoke joints. But we still exchanged frequent visits with Fielding and his family. Fielding had collected a new assortment of part-time teaching jobs, including one at some music college for women only, where he was the object of keen interest – not to say naked passion – inspired by his latest car, a large, shiny gunmetal blue Pontiac on temporary loan from his ever-obliging friend Hideo. Most of the time, unknown to his admirers, he found it too expensive to drive, but every week or so he would call round for me in the evening and we would take it for a spin on the freeway or drive over to *Kura* to have a few beers with

Yamada. Yamada affected to be unimpressed by it. 'It's too big for the roads round here,' he said. 'And shit, it makes too much noise.' But as his wife admitted, he liked to have it parked outside. It was the sort of car that people passing by were bound to notice.

On one of these occasions, soon after we arrived, the door opened and a well-dressed couple in their sixties peered in with anxious expressions on their faces. Thinking that they were customers, Yamada bade them a cheery welcome and gestured to a table by the window. But they hadn't come to eat: this was a personal visit with some formal purpose. The couple bowed deeply and launched into a ritual recitation of long, complex phrases of gratitude. Apparently Yamada had done these people some service, and they had come round to thank him. Fielding and I took our beers and moved to another table, out of earshot, while they got on with it.

Naturally I watched the proceedings out of the corner of my eye. First the couple did some thanking. Yamada replied with protestations. They waved his modesty aside and did some more thanking. Both sides bowed repeatedly. Yamada began to look a little uneasy, as if he thought they were overdoing it. He pushed his chair back, said something and then laughed loudly. The couple laughed too. Then they produced a long box carefully wrapped in white paper, evidently a gift. Yamada protested some more. The couple smilingly insisted. Yamada called for his wife, who emerged from the kitchen and started exclaiming her surprise and appreciation. The couple started to go through the thanking routine again. The Yamadas mimed their grateful acceptance of the gift and bowed some more. At this, the couple bowed even deeper. It was like some kind of animal mating ritual.

After they had gone, Yamada joined us at the table and explained what it was all about. 'It was because of their son,' he said. 'Shit! What an idiot he is! Well, no, that's unfair. He's not an idiot – just weak. But I fixed him up. Now he's going to get married. His parents think it's because of me.'

'Why?' I asked. 'What did you do?'

This couple, Yamada explained, had only one son and they had been trying for some time to get him married. He wasn't unwilling, but he was a dull, indecisive fellow who had never had any success with girls. The parents kept arranging introductions, but none of them ever came to anything. Eventually they came across a girl who seemed an ideal prospect, and they urged their son to make a special effort. The son lived in an apartment of his own, down the street from Yamada's restaurant, and used to eat there sometimes, so he explained the situation to Yamada and asked for his advice.

Characteristically, Yamada proposed that he should take the bull by the horns and invite the girl to come and stay at his apartment. There was a public holiday coming up, so they could make a three-day weekend out of it. Excited and nervous at the same time, the young man took Yamada's advice, issued the invitation and was accepted. The girl came to the apartment on a Friday and on the following evening, the pair of them came to dinner at the restaurant.

'She was a nice girl,' Yamada said. 'She had a direct, sensible way of talking – no simpering or giggling behind her fingers. I went and sat at the table with them and asked how they were getting on. Something was wrong, I could see. It took a while before I could tell what it was, but eventually it came out. The girl was saying she wasn't sure about getting married, perhaps they were too young, perhaps they needed more time to get to know each other . . . all that stuff. The boy said he wanted to get married, but he didn't want to put her under any pressure. He thought she should take all the time she needed to think it over. She shouldn't be rushed. Finally, he went to the toilet and while he was away from the table, the girl told me what they had done the day before, adding in a matter-of-fact kind of way that she had ended up sleeping alone in the young man's bed, while he slept on the kitchen floor. The poor girl – naturally she felt rejected. He didn't mean to reject her, of course. He was just shy. But what was she supposed to do? "If it's like that again tonight," she said, "I shall give him up. He says he wants to marry me, but he doesn't show it." '

'So when the boy came back to the table, I let him have it. "You sonofabitch," I told him. "You're no good. You can't go through life like this, only thinking about your own feelings. Love is like business, like any kind of dealing with other people

– you've got to consider what the other person wants too. Like this girl you've got here with you. You invited her to stay with you for the weekend, fine. But if you want her to marry you, you've got to do more than talk about it. You've got to show her you love her. Tonight, don't you sleep on the kitchen floor. Tonight, you fuck her! Or else you'll lose her!" '

I gaped stupidly. 'You told him that? In front of her?'

'Shit! Of course in front of her! So he couldn't get out of it.'

'She wasn't offended? Or embarrassed?'

'Maybe. So what? I don't care about that. Anyway, no – I think she was grateful.'

'So then what happened?'

'He did what I said! It all worked out fine. Now they are living happily together, getting married next month. Everything is okay. He's all right, that boy. He just needed a push, that's all.'

'And those were his parents who just came in and thanked you?'

'That's right. He told them the whole story. The girl told her parents too. The funny thing is, about a week ago, they came round here to say thank you as well. Can you imagine it? "Thank you for helping to get my daughter fucked"!' He brayed with laughter and slapped his knee. 'They didn't say it like that, of course. But that's what they meant.'

Yamada, in fact, often got involved in his customers' personal problems. He was well known as an efficient fixer. I had always thought of the Japanese as a reticent people, excessively anxious to preserve a facade of equanimity, unwilling to air any dirty laundry where others might get a glimpse of it. Perhaps it was for that very reason that Yamada's outspokenness was in demand: it was a catalyst that could solve intractable difficulties by breaking the logjam or just by creating an atmosphere in which people felt able to speak their minds. These little dramas invariably provided good entertainment, although naturally Yamada's robust style of intervention didn't always guarantee a successful outcome.

*

The next day I had a job in Tokyo in the morning, and late that afternoon, soon after I arrived back, Fielding's wife Kiko showed up on the doorstep with bad news. Fielding had been arrested. The police, she said, had turned up out of the blue at lunchtime (Fielding was out), impounded the car and set about searching the house. They also told Kiko that they had arrested Hideo. Apparently the grounds of Hideo's spacious private home had been one of several storage points used by a gang of car thieves from Tokyo. Their method was to steal luxury cars, keep them out of sight for a few weeks, respray them, forge a new set of import documents and then resell them somewhere else in Japan. The police had had Hideo under observation for some time, but had only stumbled on Fielding when a passing patrolman happened to notice the Pontiac, which was on the stolen list, parked outside his house. Anyway, Kiko went on, when they had finished their search of the house, and failed to find anything illegal, they sat down to wait. And when Fielding returned, they slung him in the wagon and took him away. Now what was she supposed to do?

When this happens in England, the pieces usually fall into place quite quickly. After all, the police have 24 hours in which to either charge the suspect or release him. He has more or less prompt access to legal advice and doesn't have to answer any questions if he chooses not to. One way or another, what with the bail laws, the minor offender is very likely to be back in the pub within a couple of days, telling his pals all about it. Not in Japan. For a start, the police can detain the suspect for up to 23 days without making any charge. He can have a lawyer if someone sends him one, but the police won't provide one until the case comes before a judge, at which time the court will appoint one. What happens in the meantime depends on the nature of the charge and, even more important, on the demeanour and attitude of the prisoner.

What the police are looking for in every case is repentance, cooperation and A Confession. They know how to get it too –

something like 98 per cent of all people convicted of criminal offences in Japan confess while in police custody. People who cooperate from the beginning can expect to be treated tolerably well. The conditions of detention will be spartan, but they probably won't be subjected to any unnecessary cruelty. But those who resist come under immediate pressure. Physical violence may be involved (there are plenty of well-documented cases), although mostly it seems to be reserved for low-level Japanese criminals and Asian foreigners, and is as likely to be handed out as a punishment for insubordination as to obtain information.

The main method of applying pressure is the verbal interrogation, in which the accused has to tell the same story and answer the same questions over and over again. This may go on for weeks in sessions of several hours' duration, started and stopped at unpredictable times and interrupted by breaks too short for proper recuperation. Recalcitrant suspects may also be kept in windowless cells with the light on all the time, so they quickly lose track of what day it is. Simple disorientation techniques like this are backed up by such standard procedures as saying 'We've arrested so-and-so, and he says that you did such-and-such' or 'If you tell us where you got the stuff, we'll reduce the charge' or 'If you don't tell us the name of the guy, we'll add another charge – whereas if you do tell us, we'll let you out on bail.' These offers are not always false: what charge finally comes to court, what evidence is presented and what sentence is demanded by the prosecution are matters that depend on how the interrogators choose to present the individual's case. If he is difficult, they set out to throw the book at him. But if he changes his mind after a few weeks and decides to cooperate, they may revise their original intention and go lighter on him.

For this reason, no-one facing a criminal charge in Japan wastes time on hoping for a fair trial: the expectation is that the trial will be a stitch-up, a proceeding designed to paint a coat of legality over decisions already taken elsewhere. Nor is it worth spending much mental energy on the thought-train that goes 'I'm innocent, so soon they'll find out and let me go.' There are plenty of people in Japanese jails for offences they did not commit, as the authorities know perfectly well. But it does not follow that the individuals concerned are always the victims of a miscarriage of justice. In many cases, they are inside with their own tacit consent. They have agreed to take the rap for someone higher up – a senior gangster, for instance. In other countries, buck-passing is more often an upward process: the accused denies responsibility by blaming a superior, by saying, in effect, 'I was only following orders.' In Japan, it's the other way around: the suspect is more likely to blame an inferior. 'I knew nothing about it,' he says. 'My assistant handles those matters.' For politicians and business leaders, this defence is routine. It's a lie, of course, and everyone knows it's a lie, but it has the happy effect of providing a culprit who can be found guilty and punished. Behind the scenes, the fall guy will be compensated and his dependents cared for. But up front, he's the guilty party. Case solved, conviction rates maintained.

But whatever the final result of an investigation or a trial may be, the fact of having been arrested in Japan, on even a minor charge, immediately brings the person concerned to the brink of disaster. If the police do not get the confession they want, they can ruin not only the suspect but anyone else who has any kind of connection with him. They may conduct a search of his office, or call up his clients and ask them to make a statement describing what they know of his character. This means goodbye job and maybe goodbye career as well. They may talk things over with his landlord – goodbye home. They may harass members of his family, even those who live in some faraway part of the country, so that the same problems fall on them too. Because if word comes out that a close relative of theirs, a brother or a cousin, has been arrested for theft, or assault, or drug trafficking, the prospects for that next promotion or even that forthcoming marriage are liable to fade away like mist. If this seems unfair and unjust, well, so it is. It's the price of effectiveness.

For relatives and associates who have no knowledge of or connection with the crime, the best defence of their own interests is to renounce the criminal – to say 'Well, I always knew he was no good' or else 'I had no idea he was such a dishonest person, and certainly won't be having anything to do with him in the future.' For this reason, it is common for Japanese criminals to be completely abandoned by everyone who knows them as soon as they are arrested – friends, acquaintances, colleagues, even family. After their sentence has been served, things can go back to normal. They will be accepted back into their families or, in the case of professional criminals, regarded by their associates as a hero. But in the meantime, they frequently expect and receive no overt support of any kind.

The jails are bad too, run according to a harshly disciplined regimen spiced with what used to be known as brainwashing techniques. Once I cut a picture from a Japanese newspaper, which showed convicts filing along past a life-size cardboard cutout of a little girl holding a placard on which was written an inspiring message to the effect that 'I hope you are repenting of your crime, Daddy, and won't do anything bad ever again.' Everything possible is done to maximise the prisoner's sense of guilt. This was illustrated by another newspaper story, this time about a man who filed suit against the government for violating his constitutionally guaranteed freedom of thought and conscience by forcing him and other prisoners to recite 'ethical' slogans. According to the prisoner, inmates at Tokyo's Fuchu prison had to repeat the following five statements out loud every day: 'Be obedient and say "yes" all the time'; 'Do soul-searching'; 'Be ready to say "sorry" at any moment'; 'Be modest'; and 'Say "thankyou" during morning meetings before work.'

As well as having to recite the same slogans in English, foreign prisoners face other, equally daunting conditions. Talking is permitted infrequently, certainly not every day. One bath a week in winter, two in summer. Exercise twice a week. No exercising in the cell, no walking up and down, no lying down and no standing 'without good reason.' The inmate is basically supposed to sit cross-legged in silence, stare at the wall and meditate on the damage he has done to society, his family and himself. No visits are permitted except from a lawyer, Embassy representative or immediate family member. A limited selection of books may be made available. The study of Japanese is allowed, as is keeping a diary, although this may or may not be confiscated when the sentence is completed. Work, of course, is prescribed for everyone. Letters are a privilege, to be granted or withdrawn at the discretion of the authorities. A prisoner becomes eligible for parole when 60–70 per cent of his sentence has been served: whether it is granted or not depends once more on behaviour and demeanour. One additional refinement is that the courts rarely sentence foreigners to be deported: instead, they are met on their release by the immigration police, who immediately arrest them for overstaying their visa and deport them as an administrative measure.

To find out what had happened to Fielding, we gave Kimura a call. True to form, he dropped everything and took Kiko off to make enquiries. Fortunately he wasn't being held in prison but in pre-trial police custody where conditions were a good deal better. He was in a cell with four others and there were no restrictions on talking or moving around. At night, the inmates were issued with a thin mattress, two blankets and a hard pillow. In the morning, the first job was to fold these up carefully in the prescribed manner and then clean the cell, washing the floor with a wet cloth just as schoolchildren did and making everything perfectly tidy for the morning inspection. Food arrived in individual plastic boxes and the menu was the same for every meal: a bowl of tepid, watery *miso* soup, a small piece of smelly fish and a bowl of rice that had gone crusty from long exposure to the air. Visits were allowed once every three days, for 30 minutes, with all conversation to be conducted in Japanese.

Fielding's detention threatened to be a lengthy one, since he was not a member of the car thieves' gang and would be disinclined, I felt sure, to confess otherwise. Hideo, of course, had admitted everything and been released after ten days on payment of a substantial bond. I wondered how long Fielding would last. In their conversations with Kiko, the police made it clear that they didn't believe he was telling them the whole truth. He had admitted being in possession of a stolen car – that much was fact. But he denied knowing anything whatever about where Hideo's cars came from, about the gang or how it was organised, or even the names of any other people who might be involved. The police felt that if they were patient, they would end up doing better than this. Eventually, Fielding would cooperate. It was just a matter of time.

The affair was widely reported in the newspapers and I was very curious to find out how our friends and neighbours would react. For the first couple of weeks there was a funereal silence from every direction, but eventually I got a call from Yamada's wife, who twittered away like a bird about Fielding's poor wife and those poor, poor children. She was so worried – wasn't there anything that could be done? Actually yes, there was plenty that could be done because Kiko had no money to speak of and, if Fielding were to be convicted, which seemed highly likely, would now need to find a cheaper place to live, a kindergarten or nursery to park the children, and a job. So off I went to The Saddle to see if I could drum up a little action.

When I arrived, Yamada was slugging whisky and regaling a couple of customers I had never seen before with the details of The Fielding Affair. He had known for some time, he was explaining, that something fishy was going on. First a Mercedes, then a BMW, then that black thing – what was it? a Ford Camarro? – then that Pontiac; naturally, it stood to reason that no-one would lend all those cars to Fielding just out of friendship. When I reminded Yamada that he had never said anything about it before, he said that it had been 'none of my damn business.' But he had had his suspicions, oh yes. That Fielding. When he was around, a man of the world who put two and two together couldn't help eventually coming up with a very smelly five. This went on until the other customers departed. Then Yamada's wife came in and the three of us got down to a proper tête-à-tête.

The first thing Yamada wanted to know about Kiko was – what was she living on? How much money did she have? I didn't know the answer to this question precisely, and even if I had I certainly wouldn't have told Yamada. I mumbled something about not knowing, but being aware that things were pretty difficult. Those poor children, exclaimed Mrs Yamada, what can be done to help them? Well, I said, for a start they're going to need a new place to live, because the present house is larger than they need and much more expensive than they can afford. It then turned out that the Yamadas knew someone who was negotiating at that very moment to rent a shop, above which there was an empty apartment which they didn't need. Yamada wasn't sure of the rent, but he guessed a figure which was about half what Fielding's current place cost. It sounded ideal. And I was so glad to see them offering some practical help that I made a big deal out of the idea and assured them that it was just what was needed. The Yamadas were pleased and flattered to find that I thought so highly of their generosity, and they began to make a few disparaging remarks about other long-standing friends of Fielding's in the area, Japanese friends, who were conspicuously not doing or saying anything at all. In particular, Hasegawa came under the hammer. After all, Yamada pointed out, Hasegawa was the one who was always making speeches about international friendship and Japan's urgent need to forge close links with people from other countries so as to promote a deeper relationship of trust in the context of the global development of society . . . and all that stuff. Apparently he had turned up at the restaurant a few days before with one of his sidekicks, and Yamada recounted with glee how he had laid into both of them. 'You're always talking about international friendship, you two,' he barked. 'Well? Now's the time to show that you really mean it!'

This was just the way I wanted the conversation to go, so I did my best to help dig the pit that Yamada was already digging for himself. If I could get him to disparage a few other people for not helping out, he would be obliged to do something himself. After all, all these people had plenty of money – they could cough up some cash, for a start, if they were so worried about Kiko and the children. But I didn't bring that up right away. Instead I got them to say that they would find out the facts about the famous cheap apartment, and I would get Kiko to come round and see them to talk about it. By the time I left, we were all positively glowing with self-congratulation. Look at us! We're doing something!

The next thing was to go round and have another little morale-boosting chat with Kiko. She was feeling thoroughly ashamed and depressed about the whole affair and didn't really want to see anybody, but I persuaded her that she should talk to the Yamadas about the apartment. Then I went off to see the man who ran the local secondhand shop. There was also a lot of clearing up to do in the house if they were going to move out and someone would have to go through Fielding's things and sort out what was worth keeping and what wasn't. (Poor Fielding hadn't even come up for trial yet, and here we were starting to act as if he was already tried and sentenced.) But sympathy aside – dammit, Fielding was an absolute magpie. The house was stuffed with junk he had obtained from various *gomi* tips, and most of it was going to have to go right back there. But there was a small mountain of videos and stereo equipment, plus a couple of cameras, so I sent the secondhand shop man round to the house and he took away a generous carload and gave Kiko a wad of money in exchange. At last it felt as if we were getting somewhere.

Kiko said that she felt she could talk things over with Yamada's wife, who was basically the kind, fussy, mother-hen type, but she didn't feel up to a deep discussion with Yamada himself. I knew what she meant. 'Abrasive' was Yamada's middle name. So to set the meeting up, I asked Reiko to phone Mrs Yamada and make this point. She'd understand, being a woman herself. Sometimes women like to talk about these things together, without any men around. Nothing wrong with that, I thought. What difference does it make who helps her, male or female, as long as someone does? But this turned out to be a serious tactical mistake. At 10 o'clock that evening, Yamada rang me up, drunk and roaring, and demanded to know what all this women-only shit was about. So round I went once more to the restaurant, this time for a damage limitation exercise. Yamada was furious that Kiko had the nerve to not want to talk to him, the Great Fixer, who was at that very moment moving heaven and earth to help her. I calmed him down, but I started drinking as well, and soon we were both red in the face and the conversation was taking on a dangerously dramatic tone.

The whole thing was beginning to irritate me, all the manoeuvering, the smoothing of ruffled feathers, the way it seemed necessary to wriggle like a snake to get any kind of help or support at all. At one point, Yamada said that anyway, it certainly wouldn't be a good thing to actually give Kiko any money, any cash, and that set me off. WHY NOT? I demanded angrily. Of course it was a good idea to give her money. What she needed was money, precisely money, cash, banknotes – not advice and head-shaking and stupid pontificating. Yamada was a bit taken aback by this, but he wasn't giving in so easily. In fact it now occurred to him that the whole situation was probably Kiko's fault anyway. She must have known what Fielding was up to. Even if she did know, I retorted, what could she have done about it? Fielding wasn't the type to listen to other people's advice. He would have told his wife to shut her mouth or he would shut it for her. Well then, said Yamada, she should have divorced him. Walked out on him and taken the kids with her.

Momentarily stunned by the cold-bloodedness of this suggestion, I said nothing. And before I could recover Mrs Yamada chimed in and said that Kiko was going to have to divorce Fielding anyway. Why? I asked. Because for a woman in this situation to get welfare, Mrs Yamada said, her chances are enormously increased if she divorces the husband. Yes, that's the way it is in Japan, she added. Lots of women divorced their husbands when they got sent to jail. Afterwards, they could remarry if they want to. But while the husband was in prison, divorce was the best thing. Divorce was what made those hard-hearted welfare people in the ward office loosen the civic purse strings. In fact, she went on, she herself was acquainted with a couple of women in just that very situation. In spite of myself, my interest was aroused. Maybe one of those women could tell Kiko what she needed to do to get some welfare money. Of course they could, said Mrs Yamada – I'll introduce her to them and they'll tell her all about it.

The following morning, Kiko had an appointment with the Yamadas. Before she went I had a little chat with her and primed her about what to say and what not to say. Don't say you ever suspected anything about the car! Say you have never even met Hideo! Don't say that things are 'all right' at the moment! Say you need a cheaper place to live! Don't say your parents might help you! Say they are too straightlaced and too old for you to tell them anything! Don't say they're retired schoolteachers with savings! Say they're too poor to help you! Say you don't have any other relatives! Say you intend to get a job and work hard to look after the children until Fielding comes out of jail! Say you pawned your engagement ring to buy the children's shoes! (No, don't say that – that's going too far.)

Kiko listened to me patiently, then left the children with us and set off. The kids played about for a while and then got tired, so they fell asleep on the floor. It was just as well they did, because when Kiko returned after a couple of hours, her eyes were red with weeping and it was quite apparent that the encounter was unsuccessful. Throughout the interview, apparently, Mrs Yamada had sat there in silence while her husband gave it the full finger-wagging bit. Certainly he would introduce her to the cheap apartment, but of course she would have to have the deposit money and the advance rent, plus a secure source of income to keep up the payments, plus a guarantor who would back her up. Plus promise not to let the children draw on the walls with crayons or otherwise wreck the place, or make a noise that might disturb the neighbours.

When I heard Kiko tell what happened, I felt disappointed, but realised right away that I shouldn't have been. Introductions are a sensitive matter in Japan, and hedged about with all sorts of dangers. If person A introduces his friend B to person C, with a view to C giving B a job, or helping B out in any way, and C accedes to the request, A has incurred a deep and lasting obligation. And if B subsequently does something wrong, or misbehaves in some way, even years later, the problem will rebound on A's head. An introduction is more than an introduction – it's a personal recommenda- tion. So that if Yamada were to introduce Kiko to the famous apartment (whose existence was now beginning to take on a sort of mythical character) and if there was any kind of trouble, Yamada's reputation would be on the line.

We had had an illustration of the problem a few months before, when one of Yamada's pals decided to sell his old camper van for a knockdown price and Yamada called me to ask if I wanted it. I went to take a look, but it was a dinosaur – enormous, a gas guzzler and also old and battered. So I politely declined. But of course Fielding the magpie wanted it instead. So Yamada introduced Fielding, Fielding bought it and everything was fine. Until one day when it broke down with some complaint that would have cost too much to fix and Fielding decided to get rid of it. He did so in a typical Fielding way, which was to drive it to some place 20 miles away, park it, remove the plates, throw the key in the bushes and come home by train. A few days later, the police found it. They checked the chassis number and found that the van was registered in the name of a foreigner. Hmm, a foreigner. Better find out what kind of foreigner. So they checked back further and discovered the name of the previous owner. They then called him up and asked him about it. Naturally he told them that he had sold the van and it was none of his business. That should have been the end of the story, but the idiot then called up Yamada and gave him an earful about having introduced such an unreliable buyer. That made Yamada angry, so he called Fielding and . . .

So anyway, the upshot was that Kiko didn't get introduced to the famous apartment, didn't get any practical assistance of any kind, and into the bargain got a bunch of earache from Yamada about her responsibilities as a wife and mother. The poor Kiko, poor children talk had evaporated: in the cold light of day, the Yamadas' idea of a solution was that she should apply to her parents for help. Better still, go back to their home in the depths of the countryside and live there. In other words, everybody's favourite idea for coping with an awkward problem – ignore it and hope it just disappears!

I guessed what was going to happen next, so I said to Reiko – when the phone rings, you take it. And if it's Yamada, tell him I'm not here. No sooner were the words out of my mouth than the phone started ringing. Reiko answered it. 'I'm so sorry,' she said, 'but he went to Tokyo this morning. I think he'll be back quite late tonight. What's that? Kiko? No, she just dropped in to pick up her children and then left. I think she had to go to the dentist.'

In the late afternoon, Yamada rang up again, this time from a nearby phone booth. Could Reiko direct him to our place because he had brought something for Kiko which he would like us to . . . er, to deliver for him. A few minutes later there he was on the doorstep with a casserole of hot food from the restaurant. Why didn't he deliver it himself? Because, unaccountably, he couldn't remember exactly where Kiko's house was. Perhaps one of your children would be kind enough to take it round for me? Why of course – right away! Kiko will be delighted! The silence that greeted this remark could have been sawn in half with a plank of wood. Yamada wanted to get away as soon as possible, so he quickly went through the standard bowing bit – please come around to my restaurant any time you like and please give my best regards to your esteemed husband – and then climbed into his car and drove off. He was obviously uncomfortable, considering his speeches about helping friends in trouble. I couldn't help feeling sorry for him. What he dreaded above all was that I might tell the story elsewhere, might badmouth him to other people. Other people like . . . like Hasegawa! God forbid. Still, I gave it a few days first, just to make him suffer. Then I turned up out of the blue at the restaurant, walking in cheerfully and blithely as if nothing had happened.

He went a bit green when he saw me, and almost fainted with relief when I told him that I had just looked in to thank him for being so kind as to have a fatherly chat with Kiko, which was of course just what she needed, and that I had no doubt that she benefited very much by getting the advice of a couple of mature people who had seen more of the world than she had. Yamada could hardly believe what he was hearing. Suddenly he remembered that he had a bottle of excellent Greek wine which he was sure I would like to try. He certainly got that right. So we sat and drank the Greek wine and talked about everything under the sun except The Problem. And after about half an hour he couldn't stand it any longer so he said – 'By the way – about Kiko . . .' and I let him go through his self-justification story, nodding sagely and agreeing with him at all the important points. By the time I left he had completely recovered, in fact he made it clear that he thought he had handled the whole thing with his usual consummate skill. And on the way home I dropped in on Kiko and she told me that she had just received a surprise visit from Hideo, who was burning with shame at the trouble he had brought on Fielding and his family, and by way of recompense . . . well, not recompense, because nothing could undo what had been done, but by way of lightening her load, as it were, he handed her enough money to pay the month's rent and bills, and announced that he would be back the following month to do the same thing again.

But by that time, much to everyone's surprise, the affair had petered out by itself. The police decided that Fielding was telling the truth after all, and the only charge he had to answer was being in possession of a stolen car. Not that this necessarily meant a light sentence, as we learned when the judge, peering down from his perch like a constipated crow and croaking out the words in his best ultra-formal Japanese legalese, announced a prison sentence of one year. Then, after giving that a few seconds to sink in, he suspended it for two years. Ten minutes later, Fielding was on the street again and heading for home.

17 | Way To Die

Y AMADA, OF COURSE, had expected things to turn out that way. 'You see?' he said. 'I told you. Japanese police have kind hearts. They don't like to make trouble for people. But that Fielding – he was lucky. It's because he has those two small kids. That's why they let him go. Anyway,' he went on, 'come over here and take a look at this.'

Slung over the back of a chair was a fluffy green jacket with a zip front. It looked brand new.

'I got it for my uncle. He just turned 77 last week. 77 is a special age in Japan, did you know that? Because when you write it, you see . . . here, let me show you.' Yamada reached across the table for a scrap of paper and a pencil. 'You see this?' I watched as he wrote '77' in Japanese and then added a *kanji* underneath. 'They look similar, don't they?' he said. 'The strokes that make up "77," are like the strokes of this *kanji* here. The way you read this is "*ki*." It means . . . how do you say . . . delight, rejoicing, something like that.'

'So why does that make 77 a special age?' I asked. 'Is it supposed to be some kind of a landmark year, when a person reaches some special level of wisdom, or experience?'

'No, nothing like that,' said Yamada with a touch of irritation. 'Like I just told you, it's because the number 77 looks like this *kanji*. And it's not just 77, either. There are plenty of other examples. Like 88, which is written like this.' He bent over the paper again. 'You see? It looks like *bei*, the *kanji* for "rice," doesn't it? So the year in which a person is 88 is called *beiju*. For instance, we might say "this year is my grandfather's *beiju*." '

'But what's the age of 88 got to do with rice?'

'Or take 80 – that's another one. When someone is 80, we call it *sanju*.'

'*San-ju*? But *san-ju* means 30.'

'Not that *san-ju*! Don't be so stupid! This *sanju* is quite different. Here, look. It means "umbrella".' He described the shape of an open umbrella with his hands. 'Kind of like covering . . . protecting everything.'

I felt like I was wading into deeper and deeper water.

'So anyway, what about the jacket?'

'Well, when I remembered that my uncle's 77th birthday was coming up, I thought it would be good to give him some little present. My wife said "What about a camera?" but I didn't like that idea. What's the point? He's too old to start learning about cameras. He probably wouldn't have any use for it. So I thought – why not call him up and ask him directly? "Hey," I said, "what d'you want for your birthday? You choose." So he did. "I want a jacket," he said. Well, that sounded easy. "OK," I said, "what kind of jacket?" "Something warm for winter," he said, "but in a light material, not heavy." "What colour d'you want?" I asked him. "I like green," he said. "OK," I told him, "leave it to me."

'So the next thing, I rang up a friend of mine called Koseki – he's the president of a company that imports clothes from Europe. I've known him for years. "Hey," I told him, "I need a jacket." Then I described it. "Have you got one like that?" I asked him. "Not you again, Yamada," he said, "you're a real nuisance. Why can't you do your shopping in the shops, like ordinary people? You are always making trouble for me." "Look," I told him, "all I'm trying to do is bring your company a little business." So he had it checked out on his company's computer and it turned out they did have such a jacket, but it was down in Osaka. So the Osaka warehouse sent it straight up to Koseki's office in Tokyo, and in the afternoon, he brought it around here personally. And after he had gone – I don't know what made me hurry, but I did – I put the jacket in the car and took it round to my uncle's place.'

'And did he like it?' I asked.

'He loved it,' said Yamada. 'It was just what he wanted. But he never wore it. Because that same night, just about half an hour after I left, he dropped dead of a heart attack.' He looked so disappointed after all the effort he had made that I couldn't help myself – I burst out laughing.

And then, quite unexpectedly, we got news from Niigata that Grandfather had gone, and suddenly death didn't seem like a laughing matter any more.

*

It was entirely characteristic of Grandfather, who had always been attentive to details, observances and shifts in human affairs, that he should have been the first to recognise his own approaching end. He didn't make any kind of fuss, but just quietly called his eldest son aside, told him that he felt his time was coming and instructed him to send for an ambulance.

By the time he reached the hospital, he was already drifting in and out of consciousness. They laid him on the bed in a small, shabby little room on the fourth floor and connected up the oxygen mask and the glucose drip. Even with the oxygen, his breathing was weak and irregular, and the skin on his face and hands turned sallow and slack. The doctor was a decent, straightforward type who didn't mumble or prevaricate or hold out false hopes. He declared straight out that anyone likely to want to see Grandfather before the end should be summoned at once. So over the next few hours they came, singly or in twos or threes, shuffling quietly into the room and standing for a few moments around the bed, then bowing in respect and shuffling quietly out again. During this time, Grandfather never stirred nor gave any sign of wakefulness. Deprived of both legs, weakened by years of living in a wheelchair, dependent on others for almost all of his physical needs, and further afflicted by slowly worsening respiration, he was clearly approaching the end of his time. And on the morning of the following day, with his sons sitting beside him, he drew his last breath and passed away.

Although it had all happened so quickly, preparations for the funeral were soon under way. By the time Reiko and I arrived with the children, later the same day, two huge wreaths of coloured paper, the size and shape of archery targets, had been set up on wooden legs outside the house. Inside, a large rented altar had been installed. This was made of the aromatic Japanese cedar called *hinoki*, and featured a complicated arrangement of decorative shelves and elaborately worked compartments on which many different objects were set. Among them was an image of Shaka-sama, the original Buddha, surrounded by thirteen small electric lamps shaped like candles; two real candles, tall and white, one on each side of a bowl in which incense was burning; offerings of fruit and small bowls of food; two five-foot high lotus plants, made of gold paper; and several enormous bunches of flowers, each one with a wooden tablet inscribed with the name of the giver. There was one from his children, one from his grandchildren, one from his four surviving sisters, all well into their eighties, and one from an old family friend of special importance.

To begin with, Grandfather was laid on the floor on a thin *futon*, with his head pointing to the north, and the family gathered round to perform the first part of the rites. Each person in turn took a soft white cloth, dampened it and then gently wiped his face and hands. When this was done, his sons lifted him into a large, deep rectangular coffin which was placed in front of the altar. Everyone helped to arrange around him the various things he would need for the 49-day journey to heaven on which he would shortly embark. Most of the items were standard equipment for Japanese Buddhist voyagers to the next world: a narrow white headband, similar to those worn by pilgrims, a shallow bowl-shaped straw hat to shield him from the weather, straw sandals, a wooden staff to lean on, little cakes to give to any ill-disposed spirits he might meet along the way, so that they would let him pass without interference, a satchel with a long strap, worn slung from the shoulder across the body, and a modest sum of money. This was not real money, but small squares of white paper on which his children wrote the value with brush and ink. Various personal items also went into the coffin, and one of the sons cut two life-size imitation 'legs' with scissors from the side of a cardboard box, since Grandfather no longer had his own. Then we all knelt round together and decorated the inside of the coffin with flowers before putting our hands together and praying for a few moments in silence. After all this had been done, the lid was placed on top of the coffin and covered with a large cloth of red and gold brocade.

The first stage was now complete, so a meal was served for all the relatives present and beer and *sake* were available to anyone who wanted them. The evening passed in quiet conversation: occasionally someone would get up and go over to the altar, kneel down in front of it on a cushion, take a stick of incense from a box, light the end in one of the candles, shake out the flame and then set the stick upright in a brass bowl three quarters full of soft ash provided for that purpose. Then they would put their hands together, bow their head, pray briefly and return to their place. This ritual was performed from time to time by everyone present and also by each new arrival – a relative or just a friend – who came to the house. As the hours went by, the relatives retired to bed one by one, although they kept going for as long as they could since custom requires that at least one person must remain awake and keep the body company all the time that it stays under the family roof. This responsibility fell to a cousin from a nearby village, who was now the oldest male in the family: when I finally fell asleep at about four in the morning, he was the only one left awake.

From early the next morning, crowds of relatives and friends began to arrive at the house to attend the cremation. The coffin was opened once more and the immediate relatives gathered round and took turns to touch a few drops of *sake* to Grandfather's mouth and gently lay their hands on him for the last farewell. Then the lid was replaced and nailed down: everyone, including the grandchildren, gave a few symbolic taps to one or other of the nails with a golden-coloured hammer before they were all driven home properly. The coffin was carried to a minibus and set off for the crematorium with Grandfather's eldest son and eldest grandson. The rest of us followed in procession in our own cars.

The crematorium was about twenty minutes' drive away, set among paddy-fields on the outskirts of the nearest sizeable town. Water lay in the paddies in dark, motionless pools, with sodden brown stalks from the previous harvest sticking up through the surface in short, scraggy clumps. In the parking lot stood a few stunted, leafless trees. The sky was overcast and dark. A bitter wind blew around us off the Echigo plain. Nobody felt inclined to speak.

Cremation being a secular affair, the person in charge of the proceedings was not a priest but an attendant from the crematorium – a short, grey-haired man dressed the same as everyone else, in black shoes, black tie and a black, double-breasted suit that hid almost all of his crisp white shirt. On top of this outfit, diagonally across his body from one shoulder, he wore a banner of purple silk, three inches wide and trimmed with braid. Giving instructions in a quiet, respectful voice, he directed the unloading of the coffin and its removal to a hallway with an altar set up in the middle. At the far side were two pairs of heavy doors, behind which were two cremation chambers. As everyone paused briefly to pray at the altar, the coffin was set on a trestle beside these chambers and two small hinged doors in the lid were opened so that those present could take a final look at Grandfather's mortal remains. This painful task was accomplished with great dignity by everyone except a distant aunt, unseen for so long that hardly anyone remembered who she was: holding a large handkerchief to her face, she stepped forward in a theatrical manner, laid her head against the side of the coffin and uttered a few declamatory sobs before being led aside. Then the door of the chamber was opened; a coffin-sized shelf made of firebrick was slowly wheeled out on a steel platform; the coffin was lifted up and placed on top of it; the platform was wheeled back into the chamber; the heavy door was swung shut; and the attendant pressed a button to start the cremation. A large red light came on over the door and there was a soft roar from inside as the gas jets were lit. The attendant turned to face us all, bowed deeply and announced that the cremation would take 'about two hours.' He indicated a waiting area where we could have tea or just sit around until it was over.

Those two hours passed interminably slowly. Emotions remained under tight control. Eyes were dabbed with large white handkerchiefs, faces stared fixedly out of the windows, hands were clasped behind backs. Wives and aunts tried to busy themselves with cups and teapots. Daughters and cousins bent their heads and spoke softly together. Uncles, brothers and husbands sat without speaking, chain-smoking cigarettes and staring at their shoes, or else sought solace outside, pacing up and down with their jaws clenched and their eyes lowered to the ground. In spite of the cold wind, a turn in the car park seemed less oppressive than the vigil in the waiting room. As I walked round and round, I passed others doing the same; we acknowledged each other's sadness with stiff little bows, but found no words of consolation to say. The children, unsure exactly what we were waiting for, how long we would stay in this gloomy place or what would happen next, chattered together in whispers or ran out to play on the bridge over a little river which trickled between the paddies. From time to time I glanced through the glass door that led to the hallway, where the red light maintained its steady glow above the furnace doors.

Finally the attendant reappeared and bade us all return to the hallway as the cremation was finished. We gathered around the furnace door, which was slowly opened. The platform was wheeled out. Although I had known what to expect, I was momentarily stunned. Some discernible remains of Grandfather could still be seen – no coffin, no flesh, no belongings, but a scattering of soft white ash on top of which lay a few thoroughly incinerated but still recognisable bones. There were three or four vertebrae, most of the pelvis, some ribs and the remains of the skull, which had sunk in the middle and looked like a large, half-collapsed egg. I heard the eldest son draw in his breath sharply: he stared open-mouthed at the platform as if at some spectacle beyond the range of human belief.

No-one moved except the attendant, who calmly took up a long pair of wooden chopsticks and began to sort through the ashes, speaking in a quiet but perfectly natural voice as he indicated which bit was which. Here, you see, was a fingernail which had not been entirely consumed. And here a . . . let's see . . . ah yes, a tooth. Very slowly, and with great care, he sifted through the ashes for anything that might be left; whatever he found, he gently picked up with the chopsticks and laid to one side. Then he set up a plain white ceramic urn beside the platform on which the remains lay and passed among us distributing a pair of the special chopsticks to each person. Taking turns, we drew near and selected a bone, which we picked up with the chopsticks – two people lifting each fragment of bone together – and placed in the urn. What was left of the skull went in last. It was too big to fit on top of the bones already in the urn, so they had to be pushed down a bit, which made a soft, powdery crunching sound.

This sorting of the bones sounds ghoulish in prospect, but when it actually happens there's something strangely comforting about it – seeing and touching the remains of someone you knew as a living person only days before helps to explain what happened and where they have gone. Rather than difficult or unpleasant, it seems gentle and solicitous. It also answers at least part of the question 'what happens to the body after we die?' In countries where burial is the custom, the dead disappear into the darkness of a box and the box into the darkness of the earth. The mystery of decay and dissolution, that slow process that haunts the imagination of the living, remains mysterious by being hidden from view. Or else the body is reduced by high-temperature cremation to nothing but a small quantity of fine, almost-white ash, with no clear evidence as to how the transformation took place. Here, it was different. This is what happens to the body! And this is where it happens – in front of family and friends, so that nothing is hidden, everyone sees, everyone takes part. Other Eastern cultures have even more explicit customs, as for instance when the body is buried for long enough to let the flesh decay and then dug up again so that the family can all take part in cleaning and polishing the bones, which they then keep as a memento and bring out to join the party on festive occasions. Except in the remotest areas, the Japanese way does not go that far, but it's frank and open and everyone shares it, and that helps. We watched the attendant as he added the last scraps, making sure that nothing was left behind and then replaced the lid of the urn and lifted it into a wooden box, which he covered with a sleeve of gold brocaded paper. Then he took the box reverently up in his hands and placed it carefully in a large sling made of white cloth which he hung around the neck of the eldest son. The eldest grandson then drove his father home, and the rest of us followed.

Back at the family home, all the guests had to perform a brief ceremony of purification outside the front door, so as not to carry the taint of death with them into the house. A small table had been set up and covered with a white cloth: on it lay two saucers, one piled with salt and the other with *miso* bean paste. Beside the table was an old-fashioned wooden bucket half full of water and two long-handled ladles made of bamboo. Each guest in turn took a pinch of salt and sprinkled it lightly over their chest and shoulders, and then put a further pinch of salt and *miso* together on the tip of their tongue. This was then rinsed out with a half ladleful of water: any water remaining was tipped onto the ground and the ladle returned to the bucket for the next person to use.

Comforting though it was to know that procedure had been correctly followed and ritual obligations fulfilled, the cremation had been deeply affecting. It was good to find that the women neighbours who had come in to help were now ready to serve a large and excellent meal. No matter how downcast 50 or 60 friends and relatives may be, they cheer up quickly enough when it's time to take their places at long, low trestle tables and get stuck into a good meal. Much is drunk, of course, and quickly; faces recover their cheerfulness and take on a pinkish flush, ties are discarded, people get up and move to a different place to press yet more drink on their fellow-guests and start conversations with them. Trays are carried briskly back and forth, the talk gets louder, there are stories, reminiscences, exchanges of news, interruptions, bursts of laughter. Each person has several different dishes before them at the same time, and dips into them in any order: there is no protocol beyond the obligation to join in, to help restore an atmosphere of conviviality. Should anyone be momentarily overcome by distress and feel the need to step over to the altar, light another stick of incense and say a few words of prayer, that's fine – no-one else will take any notice or say 'Cheer up', no-one will need to loosen any collars or run for restoring glasses of water or otherwise interfere. Artificial gaiety is quickly replaced by the real thing, the party continues for hours: and when the food is finished, the drinking continues because the drink never runs out.

Just as a family reunion provides a welcome opportunity for people who love each other but meet only rarely to catch up with news and enjoy each other's company once more, so it allows those who don't get along to savour the taste of long-held grudges and perhaps even discover new examples of loathsomeness in the particular object of their dislike. Thus Eldest Sister, already the focus of general contempt, managed to rekindle the fury of her brothers- and sisters-in-law by asking them when they would be leaving for home. Second Brother caused a scene by criticising the silly, affected way of talking that one of his sisters had acquired through years of living in Tokyo. A middle-aged cousin, whom alcohol often reduced to tears for no clear reason, rose to his feet and began to sob incoherently about Grandfather, a performance from which the rest of us were rescued by his wife, who took him by the collar and dragged him out of the room. And when still another relative became loud and garrulous, his wife crept forward and knelt on the floor behind him, out of his line of sight, and wagged her index finger in an urgent negative at anyone poised to refill his glass. But no-one took any notice, so she pursed her lips in disapproval and retired stiffly to the kitchen.

The following morning, shrugging off bad hangovers and overlooking any moments of awkwardness from the evening before, everyone donned their black clothes again and prepared for the funeral, which was to be held in the house in front of Grandfather's altar. First came several friends, acquaintances and neighbours from the village, to pay their respects and leave an envelope containing a gift of money. This custom serves the dual purpose of lightening the financial burden imposed by a funeral and ensuring that the donor's own family will benefit from the same community assistance when the equivalent need arises. In return, the giver receives an envelope containing a handkerchief or some other small present to signify the bereaved family's gratitude.

By 10 o'clock the room was filled with 50 or 60 black-clad guests – suits for the men, formal kimono for the women – kneeling close together in rows on thin, flat cushions. Splendidly robed, the village priest arrived with two shaven-headed assistants who unpacked their sutra-books, gongs, cymbals and other paraphernalia from the depths of a battered brown suitcase and laid them out in front of the altar. The service lasted about an hour and was heard in silence, without participation, by the assembled company. Mostly, it consisted of the three priests reciting passages from sutras in a steady, insistent chant. Each one chanted at a different pitch, which established a pacific if somewhat monotonous harmony: when they needed to pause to refill their lungs, they did so at different places in the chant, so that there was no break in the vocal continuum. From time to time a gong rang out, filling the room with a deep, clean resonance. There were also long passages of steady, rhythmic tapping on a wooden drum with a stick whose doorknob-sized head was wrapped in layers of cloth to muffle the tone. The chanting went on and on and relentlessly on, punctuated at brief and sudden moments by crashing brass cymbals that jolted the atmosphere like claps of metallic thunder. At the same time, a small double-chambered box was passed from hand to hand along the rows of guests: one compartment was filled with tiny scraps of sandalwood while in the other a pile of the same chips was smouldering on a bed of pea-sized chips of white quartz. Each person took a pinch of the sandalwood, raised it to his forehead, bowed and then added it to the smoking pile. By the time the box had been passed round twice among all of the sixty or seventy people present, the pile of burning incense had reached a considerable size and a haze of blue smoke hung thickly in the air.

This ceremony concluded, all that remained was to carry the ashes to the village cemetery for interment in the family grave. Several villagers in baseball caps and muddy rubber boots were already gathered outside the house to pay their respects, and some of them joined in as we all set off in procession. At the head went a group of men carrying long paper banners inscribed with writing and attached vertically to bamboo poles. Some of the banners were plain-coloured, while others were marked off in four sections of green, red, blue and gold, symbolising east, south, west and north, the four cardinal directions. Next came the eldest grandson carrying the box with Grandfather's ashes in a white sling around his neck, together with his father, mother, brother and sister, this group shod in nothing but flimsy straw sandals as a mark of their bereavement. Behind them walked the other brothers and sisters and their children, with the remaining relatives and friends bringing up the rear. Nearly everyone carried flowers.

Stretching for nearly a hundred yards, the procession moved up to the end of the street, crossed the main road and the single-gauge railway track and then followed a narrow lane past the village temple to the cemetery, which lay in a dark grove of tall cedars. Most of the graves were old, a century or more, and were marked by small piles of moss-covered boulders carried up from the bed of the nearby river in the days when no-one could afford anything more elaborate. Here and there, a few modern gravestones had been installed, including the one that Grandfather had set up for his own family. It consisted of a stone chamber, about four cubic feet in size, surmounted by a black marble plinth with another, smaller one on top of that, and finally a rectangular column of the same black marble engraved with the family name.

With the priest directing operations, we all gathered round

and watched while the eldest son shifted the front section of
one of the marble plinths to reveal the entrance to the stone
chamber where the bones of Grandfather's own parents were
already interred. Very carefully, and with a white cloth spread
out below the aperture to catch any scraps which might be
dropped, he took the lid off the ceramic jar and tipped the
ashes into the chamber. The fragments clattered softly as they
disappeared from view. Then he laid the jar down and heaved
the marble block back into position to close up the entrance
again. Everyone else formed a line and waited for their turn
to lay their flowers against the grave, add lighted sticks of
incense to those already smoking in the bowl and put their
hands together for a final brief prayer. The shelf formed by
the marble plinth quickly became crowded with offerings –
small bowls of rice and soup, fruit and other foods, tumblers
of *sake* and cans of beer, vases with more flowers. The ceramic
jar which had held the ashes was unceremoniously broken and
the pieces buried in a shallow hole dug to one side of the grave.
As if unsure what to do next, the onlookers stood in silent
groups or moved quietly here and there among the dripping
trees. Then the priest announced that the burial was over, so
we all turned away and squelched carefully home along the
muddy path.

As before, this formal chapter in the proceedings was followed by a large meal, this time laid out in colourful abun-
dance in the banqueting room of the local Rotary Club. The
three priests participated, seated at a top table by themselves.
A few short speeches were made and presents were distributed
to all the guests to thank them for attending. After we had
finished eating, those guests who were not family members
left for home. Before doing so they said their formal farewells
to the family, getting down on their knees and bowing again
and again so that their foreheads brushed the floor.

In the afternoon, twenty or so members of the family
walked round to the village temple and knelt in silence while
the priest recited an excerpt from the Lotus Sutra, accompa-
nying himself on a drum with another cloth-headed drumstick
and a huge brass bowl which rang out when he struck it like
a mighty gong. When he had finished, we wandered around

the temple, lit sticks of incense before the lacquered tablet commemorating Grandfather's own father and examined an ancient palanquin and various other local relics that were stored in the temple for safekeeping. Before leaving, we were all invited to take tea with the priest and his wife in a room with a high ceiling and dark, wood-panelled walls.

The sky remained overcast and gloomy for the rest of the day. Rain fell fiercely in brief showers, and a wild wind tugged at the trees, which swayed as if bowing and shook their leaves with a soft hissing sound. Before the light faded I went back to the cemetery with the brothers and the grandsons. We made a small bonfire and burned everything that had been used for the procession and the burial – the box that had held the urn, the brocaded paper sleeve, the paper banners, the straw sandals. Then we stood round talking and passing cans of beer and glasses of *sake* from hand to hand: when these were half-empty, they were added to the offerings on the grave. Already there were some signs of disturbance: a freshly-torn cellophane wrapper lay on the ground, with no sign of the rice cracker it had contained, and a large yellow apple had rolled slightly aside, its flesh deeply scored by the marks of a beak. The birds had been watching us. Now it was their turn.